POLITICAL ASPECTS OF THE ECONOMIC
AND MONETARY UNION

The International Political Economy of New Regionalisms Series

The International Political Economy of New Regionalisms Series presents innovative analyses of a range of novel regional relations and institutions. Going beyond established, formal, interstate economic organizations, this essential series provides informed interdisciplinary and international research and debate about myriad heterogeneous intermediate level interactions.

Reflective of its cosmopolitan and creative orientation, this series is developed by an international editorial team of established and emerging scholars in both the South and North. It reinforces ongoing networks of analysts in both academia and think-tanks as well as international agencies concerned with micro-, meso- and macro-level regionalisms.

Editorial Board

Timothy M. Shaw, University of London, London
Isidro Morales, Universidad de las Américas - Puebla, Mexico
Maria Nzomo, University of Nairobi, Kenya
Nicola Phillips, University of Warwick, UK
Johan Saravanamuttu, Munk Centre for International Studies, Canada
Fredrik Söderbaum, Göteborgs Universitet, Sweden

Other Titles in the Series

South Africa's Multilateral Diplomacy and Global Change
Edited by Philip Nel, Ian Taylor and Janis van der Westhuizen

European Union and New Regionalism
Edited by Mario Telò

Crises of Governance in Asia and Africa
Edited by Sandra J. MacLean, Fahimul Quadir and Timothy M. Shaw

The Politics of Economic Regionalism
David J. Francis

Reconstituting Sovereignty
Rory Keane

Political Aspects of the Economic and Monetary Union
The European challenge

Edited by

SØREN DOSENRODE
Institute for History, International and Social Studies
Aalborg University, Denmark

LONDON AND NEW YORK

First published 2002 by Ashgate Publishing

Reissued 2018 by Routledge
2 Park Square, Milton Park, Abingdon, Oxon OX14 4RN
711 Third Avenue, New York, NY 10017, USA

Routledge is an imprint of the Taylor & Francis Group, an informa business

Copyright © Søren Dosenrode 2002

The editor hereby asserts his moral right to be identified as the author of the Work in accordance with the Copyright, Designs and Patents Act, 1988.

All rights reserved. No part of this book may be reprinted or reproduced or utilised in any form or by any electronic, mechanical, or other means, now known or hereafter invented, including photocopying and recording, or in any information storage or retrieval system, without permission in writing from the publishers.

Notice:
Product or corporate names may be trademarks or registered trademarks, and are used only for identification and explanation without intent to infringe.

Publisher's Note
The publisher has gone to great lengths to ensure the quality of this reprint but points out that some imperfections in the original copies may be apparent.

Disclaimer
The publisher has made every effort to trace copyright holders and welcomes correspondence from those they have been unable to contact.

A Library of Congress record exists under LC control number: 2002100077

ISBN 13: 978-1-138-73018-2 (hbk)
ISBN 13: 978-1-138-73012-0 (pbk)
ISBN 13: 978-1-315-18951-2 (ebk)

Contents

List of Figures   *vii*
List of Tables   *viii*
List of Contributors   *ix*
List of Acronyms   *xi*

Introduction   1
Søren Dosenrode

PART I: THE HISTORY AND STRUCTURE OF THE EMU

1. The Negotiations Leading to the Creation of the ECB   9
   Erik Hoffmeyer

2. The Euro-Zone in a Political and Historical Perspective   17
   Kenneth Dyson

3. The Economic and Monetary Union's Institutional Framework   41
   Søren Dosenrode

PART II: THE EMU AND THE DYNAMICS OF EUROPEAN INTEGRATION

4. EMU and the Dynamics of European Integration   71
   Loukas Tsoukalis

5. What Makes a European Monetary Union Without a Parallel Fiscal Union Politically Sustainable?   87
   Sverker Gustavsson

PART III: EMU, EU AND DEMOCRACY

6. Democracy, EU and the EMU 121
   Morten Kelstrup

7. Will Monetary Unification Make it Easier or More Difficult to Democratize the European Union? 147
   Philippe C. Schmitter

8. The European Central Bank and Democracy: the Political Framework of Economic Policy in the EMU 165
   Henrik Plaschke

PART IV: THE WELFARE STATE AND THE EMU

9. Money's not Everything – The EU and the Danish Welfare State 195
   Peter Abrahamson and Anette Borchorst

10. EMU – A Defense Mechanism for the Nordic Welfare State 221
    Wolfgang Zank

PART V: THE EMU – A POLITICAL CONSTRUCTION

11. Political Implications of the Economic and Monetary Union 247
    Søren Dosenrode

APPENDIX

Appendix *265*
Index *273*

List of Figures

Figure 3.1	The European Central Bank (ECB)	49
Figure 3.2	The organization of the European Central Bank	55
Figure 4.1	Public opinions: for and against the EMU	80
Figure 5.1	Possible outcomes of the Stability Pact as seen by David McKay in his 1999 article	96
Figure 5.2	Four possible outcomes when considering democracy as important as the Stability Pact	99
Figure 9.1	Three ideal typical welfare models	200

List of Tables

Table 10.1	The Danish public sector during the years of 'euro policy', general indicators	226
Table 10.2	The development of the Danish welfare state, selective indicators	226
Table 10.3	Danish employment and unemployment in absolute figures	227
Table 10.4	Inflation and unemployment in Denmark, 1960-82	228
Table 10.5	Interest rates and inflation in Denmark, 1988-98	229
Table 10.6	Nominal and real long-term interest rates for Mediterranean countries and Ireland	238
Table A1.1	Total social expenditure 1990-98	265
Table A1.2	Total social expenditure at fixed prices 1990-98, index 1990 = 100	266
Table A1.3	Total social expenditure at fixed prices 1998 in PPP	267
Table A1.4	Functional distribution of total social expenditure in per cent 1998	268
Table A1.5	Financing of total social expenditure 1998	269
Table A1.6	Wealth, poverty, redistribution and inequality in Europe mid-1990s	270
Table A1.7	Ratio of services versus transfers in three welfare regimes	271

List of Contributors

PETER ABRAHAMSON, Ph.D. is Associate Professor and Head of Department of Sociology, University of Copenhagen, Denmark.

ANETTE BORCHORST, Ph.D. is Associate Professor, Institute for History, International and Social Studies at Aalborg University.

SØREN DOSENRODE is Dr.Phil. and Jean Monnet Professor of European Politics and Administration at the University of Aalborg where he is Director of the Institute for History, International Studies and Social Studies. He is a member of the Danish Advisory Council for European Politics as well as its editor.

KENNETH DYSON, Ph.D. is Professor of European Studies at the University of Bradford, a Fellow of the British Academy, and an Academician of the Learned Societies of the Social Sciences.

SVERKER GUSTAVSSON, Dr.Phil. is Jean Monnet Professor at the Department of Government of Uppsala University, Sweden.

ERIK HOFFMEYER, Professor, Dr.Polit., Royal Director and Head of the Directors of the National Bank of Denmark 1965-94, Honorary Professor in Economics at the University of Southern Denmark from 1998. Danish Governor in the International Monetary Fund 1965-94. Head of the European Central Bank Executive Board 1975-75, 1979-81, and 1991-92.

MORTEN KELSTRUP is a Senior Research Fellow and Program Director at Copenhagen Peace Research Institute and Jean Monnet Professor at the Institute of Political Science, University of Copenhagen.

HENRIK PLASCHKE is Associate Professor and Jean Monnet Professor of European Studies and Political Economy at the European Research Unit, Institute for History, International and Social Studies at Aalborg University. His research interests include theory and methodology of political economy, international relations and European integration (particularly macroeconomic and monetary issues).

PHILIPPE C. SCHMITTER, Ph.D. is Professor of Political and Social Science at the European University Institute in Florence.

LOUKAS TSOUKALIS, Ph.D. is Professor at the European Institute of the London School of Economics and Political Science.

WOLFGANG ZANK, Dr.Phil. is Senior Research Fellow, Institute for History, International and Social Studies at Aalborg University. Besides his academic work, he has written many contributions to the German weekly 'Die Zeit'.

List of Acronyms

CAP	– Common Agricultural Policy
COREPER	– Committee of Permanent Representatives
EC	– European Community
ECB	– European Central Bank
ECOFIN	– Council of Economic and Finance Ministers
EEC	– European Economic Community
EMCF	– European Monetary Co-operation Fund
EMI	– European Monetary Institute
EMU	– Economic and Monetary Union
EMS	– European Monetary System
ERM	– Exchange-Rate Mechanism
ESCB	– European System of Central Banks
EU	– European Union
GDP	– Gross Domestic Product
IGC	– Intergovernmental Conference
OCA	– Optimal Currency Area
SEA	– Single European Act
TEU	– Treaty on European Union

Introduction
SØREN DOSENRODE

> *The single currency is the greatest abandonment of sovereignty since the foundation of the European Community [...]. It is a decision of an essential political character [...]. We need this united Europe [...]. We must never forget that the Euro is an instrument for this project.*
>
> Felipe Gonzales' statement from May 1998

The Economic and Monetary Union

The Economic and Monetary Union (EMU) began working January 1st 1999 and from 2002 the euro is replacing the national currencies of the EMU's 12 member states: a unique step in European history, which will affect not only Europe, but the outside world, too. Borders, foreign policy and currency are 'sacred' signs of sovereignty[1] but now the third stage of the Economic and Monetary Union has been implemented, with a common currency and a supranational bank, replacing the national banks and currencies. What has persuaded 12 European states to take such a dramatic step?

Let us look at four commonly heard arguments, knowing well that the list is by no means exclusive (depending on the theoretical eyes of the spectator, (s)he will tend to emphasize the liberal or realist arguments for creating the EMU).

2   *Political Aspects of the Economic and Monetary Union*

EU-Internal Motives

1) to further the integration process;
2) to create prosperity within the EU/completing the Internal Market;
3) to secure that Germany did stay within the EU after the reunification, and that a reunited, strong Germany did not get an undisputed hegemonic status (French point of view) and to calm down nervous partners (German point of view).

EU-External Motives

4) to create a bulwark against the negative consequences of globalization, and work for the construction of a fair international economic system respectively to challenge and outweigh the economic hegemony of the US: or said in another way, to strengthen the EC/EU as an international actor.

Creating the EMU has been interpreted as a sign of wanting to take integration one step further. The German *Bundeskanzler* Helmut Kohl, together with the French President Francois Mitterand and the President of the EU Commission Jacques Delors, one of the strongest advocates of European integration during the last two decades of last century, expressed this clearly in 1992:

> A European army and a European police force lie at the end of the road to European Union [...]. The Maastricht Treaty introduces a new and decisive stage in the process of European Union, which with a few years will lead to the creation of the United States of Europe [...]. We want the political unification of Europe. If there is no monetary union, then there cannot be a political union, and vice-versa.

According to the 'logic of integration' a state-like entity needs a monetary (and fiscal) union, including the strong national symbols of its own currency. Having established the Internal Market, the EMU could be interpreted as the next stone in the building of the European federation. This interpretation is prevailingly liberal, just as the next one.

'The plans concerning an economic and monetary union became important again in 1988. This was among other things due to the effort to harvest the full advantages of the Internal Market.' (Økonomiministeriet & Finansministeriet, 2000: 16). The EMU was marketed as the natural corollary to the Internal Market, securing monetary stability, and following from this: prospering trade, investments and employment.

A realistic approach stresses the power-political aspects. As the cold war ended, the 'German question' turned acute, both for Germany and its EU-partners. For Germany's EU-partners, the question was double: on the one hand they wanted to anchor Germany within the EU, to prevent it from feeling the temptation of 'going it alone', seeking partners in Eastern Europe, thus potentially creating instability in Europe. On the other hand a re-united Germany within the EU would be a dominant power, both in terms of people, land and economy. For Germany the primary wish was to get re-united, and for *Bundeskanzler* Kohl, the secondary wish was to secure Germany in the EC. The price which Germany paid was the EMU in other words giving up the *Bundesbank's* hegemony over Western Europe's economies.

Globalization has given highly developed countries, like the Western European ones, a number of opportunities but it also contains various dangers (monetary speculation, 'unfair' competition, uneven development, and a social list, just to mention a few) and it is hard to control these. Together the populations of the EU member states correspond to 6.3 per cent of the world population, and the joint production correspond to 28 per cent of the world's production. The Single European Act (SEA), establishing the Internal Market and the introduction of the euro by the EMU have cemented the EU as the world's largest trading block, with 20 per cent of world trade (Hvidbog 2001: 138-141). A realist interpretation would stress that this gives the EU a strength making it impossible for the US to act as an undisputed economic hegemony. It also allows the two, eventually together with Japan, to set the frame for the global economy without consulting the other involved actors. A liberal analysis would agree but stress the possibility to repel the negative effects of globalization, and to work for a more just world, where all would get a share of the benefits of globalization. One finds both arguments in the debate on the EMU, EU and globalization.

This rudimentary examination of motives has shown that it is impossible to separate the economic from the political motives. The motives for the EMU were both economic and political, internal and external (especially chapters 2 and 3 will look deeper into this matter). Of course it is so, one might say, but the debate leading up to the Danish referendum in September 2000 was from the outset dominated by the attempts to reduce the question of EMU-membership to an economic-technical question. And that was our argument for writing this book: we wanted to analyze the *political* aspects of the EMU.

Structure of the Book

This book is structured so as to address essential aspects of the political aspects of the EMU. In doing so, it basically takes a 'Euro-centric' perspective. As mentioned above, the establishment of an entity which alone contributes 20 per cent to world trade has large global consequences, as the power this entity possesses may be used selfishly or in solidarity i.e. it may be used to challenge an American hegemony, to collaborate with it *contra mundo*, or to work for some kind of just division of the world's goods. But this discussion must wait for another publication.

The first part of the book introduces the developments leading up to the creation of the EMU and its first years of performance (Hoffmeyer and Dyson) as well as the institutional set-up of the EMU (Dosenrode). After the introductory part, three important topics are analyzed: integrational dynamics (part 2), democracy (part 3) and welfare state (part 4).

Under the overall headline 'The integrational dynamics of the EMU' the second part of the book discusses questions such as the 'impact of the EMU on EU-integration' (Tsoukalis), and the 'sustainability of the EMU without a fiscal union' (Gustavsson). The next part of the book concerns the democratic aspects of the EMU and inevitably the EU. In the first article, the central questions of democratic legitimization within the EU are discussed with a certain emphasis on the role of the EMU in this context (Kelstrup). Then Schmitter discusses the impact of the EMU on both the integration process and on the process of democratization of EU-institutions. Then follows an analysis of the political framework of the economic politics within the EMU (Plaschke). The fourth part discusses the consequences of the EMU for the Nordic welfare state (Abrahamson & Borchorst and Zank). The last topic has gained extra importance with the Lisbon-process (2000 forward), where the European Social Model has been on the agenda, including the welfare state models. In the last chapter, Dosenrode sums up some of the discussions of the book and analyzes the state of the European Union today (2002).

The 'Historical' Background of this Book

As the Danish government decided to have a referendum on membership of the third phase of the Economic and Monetary Union (EMU), the Danish Advisory Council for European Politics decided to ask their editor to publish two volumes on the political and economic aspects of Danish membership of the EMU. The purpose of the two reports was to give a scientific analysis of the economic and political aspects of a

Danish membership respectively. The reports were meant to be independent; i.e. neither support the government's recommendations nor the adversaries of membership.

The report on the political aspects of an EMU membership was especially welcomed as unique in the debate, which had until then been kept on a technocratic-economic level.

After the referendum in September 2000, which ended with a 'no' to the Danish EMU-membership, there have been requests from 'non-Danish speakers' to make an English version available. Luckily my colleagues from the original version answered positively when I asked whether they would like to participate in a new international version. Making the book 'international' has actually changed it so much, that it is virtually a new book. Apart from a few hints, the specific Danish questions have been removed, unless they were expected to have a broader interest such as the contributions on the Nordic welfare state and the EMU. New chapters have been added and a few have disappeared.

I would like to thank Professor Timothy Shaw for his kind interest in the book as well as for his advice. I am grateful to Ashgate for their quick and professional handling of the manuscript. Ms Julie Larsen MA has had the troublesome task of preparing a camera proof manuscript, and has done so in good spirit and most professionally. Last but not least I would like to thank the Institute for History, International and Social Studies (IHIS) at Aalborg University as well as the Danish Advisory Council for European Politics for their economic support. The Danish Advisory Council for European Politics has initiated a project on Denmark and the EMU, from which this book takes its departure.[2]

I dedicate this book to my wife Andrea Dosenrode, Lic. Iur.

Notes

1 Concerning borders, the intra-EU borders were *de facto*, if not *de jure*, abandoned with the Schengen-agreement; and the EU has its Common Foreign and Security Politics which has gained strength over the last few years (since Amsterdam and Helsinki).
2 Dosenrode (2000).

References

Dosenrode, Søren (ed.) (2000): *Danmark og ØMU'en – Politiske aspekter (vol. 1), Danmark og ØMU'en – Økonomiske aspekter (vol 2)*, Århus: Systime.
Hvidbog (juni 2001): Danmark og Europa – udvidelse, globalisering, folkelig forankring, Udenrigsministeriet.
Økonomiministeriet & Finansministeriet (2000): *Danmark og Euroen (2000) – Konsekvenser ved forskellig tilknytning til Eurosamarbejdet.*

Part I

The History and Structure of the EMU

1 The Negotiations Leading to the Creation of the ECB

ERIK HOFFMEYER

Introduction

It can be argued that negotiation about a common responsibility for monetary policy within the Community has been an ongoing process since the late 1960s and that the end result – a common central bank dedicated primarily to price stability – was a surprising but probably unavoidable outcome.

It is true to say that the major players were France and Germany to such an extent that all initiatives and decisions emanated from the relation between these two countries and never from other members. The basic strategies in the two countries were formulated already at the beginning of the late 1960s and remained unchanged until the end in spite of changes in the political landscape in both countries. In particular it is interesting that parties that were in opposition in France often were critical towards the French strategy but converted quickly when they came to power.

The literature abounds with material about relations between French and German politicians, their advisers, the monetary authorities etc.[1] These are valuable contributions to understanding the mechanism of decision making and to some extent also the motivations.

In this brief essay I will concentrate on how the strategies were used in the negotiations on the important initiatives.

EMU: A German–French Project

The Treaty of Rome (1957) had two basic objectives. One was to create a system of free trade among members and the other was a more vague commitment to coordinate economic policy in various fields as a step to closer political integration. Decision making on monetary and exchange rate policy should for example be integrated. But how?

To begin with there was a tendency to consider these matters as extremely complicated and a field where central banks were the experts. They were silent and competent so it would be highly likely that they could coordinate policy in such a way that tensions between members could be avoided.

Proposals in the beginning of the 1960s on a wider area of policy cooperation could not be supported by politicians except to establish a Committee of Central Bank Governors in 1964 with the explicit task of coordinating monetary policy by consultations before any decisions were taken by the national central banks – so far as possible.

It was an explicit instruction by the politicians to the central banks and the wish was repeated several times during the years. Reality was, however, different.

Already in 1966 the president of the German *Bundesbank* made it quite clear that the German monetary authorities were not willing to cooperate on such a scheme. Monetary policy was the responsibility of the individual country and the internal and external defense of the currency was a national affair. This meant that compromises with other member central banks were not possible.

Only the German and Dutch central banks made such statements. Other member central banks would not be able to go so directly against the political demands. The German attitude led to the doctrine of monetary indivisibility which meant that any change in monetary decision making from the national to a common level had to be made by a change of the Rome Treaty. Gradualism within the system was ruled out. This meant that there was never a discussion in the Committee of Governors about monetary policy measures to be taken but only what had happened and there was hardly any occasion where German monetary measures were questioned. If there was a reservation it was always formulated in extremely polite language. It may sound odd but it was a recognition of the fact that coordination of policy was a political task.

The political importance of a change came in late 1968 when a French devaluation of 10-15 per cent was negotiated at an international meeting in Bonn. German politicians made it a big publicity show with open disagreement within the German government. The outcome was that the public got the impression that the political strength of Germany was returning – it would no longer be an economic giant but a political dwarf.

President de Gaulle was quick to sense that a French devaluation under those circumstances would be humiliating and stopped the negotiations. Since then the increasing dominance of the D-mark has been a controversial element in French-German relations. The French wanted a change in the German attitude that would prevent tensions between the French franc and the D-mark with France being the loser.

They wanted an active German effort to contain market pressure against the French franc and in favor of the D-mark. This could be achieved by monetary police measures and by market intervention in franc which was then kept in German reserves. The German position was that tensions could be avoided if French stabilization policy was at the German level – meaning convergence towards German performance.

The story about the Brandt – Pompidou and the Schmidt – Giscard d'Estaing initiative has been told so many times that it is sufficient to just sketch the essential elements. The German chancellor Willy Brandt made the EMU (economic and monetary union) a German government proposal at the Hague meeting in 1969, presumably in order to reassure other Community members – in particular France – that his reconciliation policy towards the East did not reduce Germany's firm commitment to the West. His proposal was referred to the Werner Committee where the German and Dutch attitude left a heavy imprint.

EMU was possible on certain conditions, namely convergence of economic performance and transfer of national sovereignty to common institutions responsible for fiscal and monetary policy. To this was added a strong statement on the necessity of political union.

The French would favor a monetary union only where monetary and exchange rate policy would be handled in common but other elements of policy being left to national authorities. A European Monetary Fund might gradually take over responsibility for the common monetary policy.

The plan to establish an EMU ran into political difficulties in both France and Germany and economic performance did not converge. There remained however the reduction of margins between the member currencies. It was a limited step that soon disintegrated as the big members left when tensions towards the D-mark became strong.

Next came the Schmidt – Giscard d'Estaing initiative in 1978. From the German side it was driven mostly by a wish to influence the international monetary system whereas the French side in addition wanted a clear reduction in the strength of the D-mark. The elements were identical with the philosophy of the Werner Report, namely convergence of economic performance and a common fund that should be responsible for relations to non-Community countries and support national monetary institutions that remained independent.

This two-tier system was a questionable proposition, but it never came into being for largely the same reasons as the first proposal. The French tried again and again in the 1980s to persuade the German political authorities to come to an understanding on improved cooperation on monetary and exchange rates policy. They did not succeed as the *Bundesbank* and the German finance ministry steadfastly rejected any proposal that might transfer the smallest bit of decision making to common deliberations.

The French political pressure increased strongly in 1987 and 1988 but still on the old model of a monetary cooperation that could hardly be called an economic and monetary union or even a monetary union. It was strongly supported by the transition to a stability oriented economic policy since 1982-83.

The German chancellor Helmut Kohl was probably uncertain about the dimensions of an EMU but maintained the old German attitude that economic convergence and political integration (union) were indispensable for a realization of an EMU. After much maneuvering the Delors Committee was established in 1988 to report on the feasibility of creating an EMU. The answer – delivered in April 1989 – was 'yes' on condition of convergence of monetary and other macroeconomic policies over a period until the final stage. This answer could not be considered a surprise to persons that had followed the debate over the previous decades.

The surprise was what was put under the carpet and what was not. In the open was, as a condition, an independent common central bank in the final stage, modeled on the *Bundesbank*. This was a recognition of the fact that the Germans would never accept a central bank under political authority.

Under the carpet were two issues. One was how an EMU could work without transferring authority to a common institution responsible for fiscal policy. This was not debated but assumed. The second was whether a parallel political union was in the long run a prerequisite for the existence of an EMU. This was not debated but disposed of by stating that it would be necessary to develop an innovative and new approach.

It has often been suggested that the Delors Report aimed at binding the central bank governors. It is, however, hard to see what binding elements there are in the mentioned statements. The *Bundesbank* was not bound by the report and has later stated its view that political union is indispensable for an EMU. Most members of the committee (including the German) believed that an EMU was a goal far away – not to be realized in our lifetime.

In the Delors Report there was a recommendation for the Committee of Governors to try to coordinate monetary policy in advance. An endeavor was actually undertaken to compare forecasts of the development of money supply in the participating countries. There was, however, no real substance in this undertaking, as Germany was the only country that put great weight on money supply as an important target.

After the fall of the Berlin Wall in November 1989 the speed of what happened became incredible. For Germany unification became a top priority whereas strong reservations were held in the Soviet Union, the United Kingdom and France. They were concerned about a dominant Germany that might return to nationalism that had created so many difficulties in the past. The US primary objective was to keep Germany as an ally within NATO. The US decided to support German unification with this basic aim in mind.

The relation between Kohl and Mitterand became heavily strained when the clearly opposing interests came into the open. Mitterand demanded an unequivocal decision on establishing an Intergovernmental Conference (IGC) among members of the European Union with the task of preparing a change of the treaty to make an EMU possible. Kohl stuck to the traditional German position that an EMU could only be developed in parallel with a political union, as it had been expressed in the Werner Report. He furthermore did what he could to expedite German unification, which by the way happened much faster than he had expected. The issue was settled at the heads of state and government (summit) meeting in Strasbourg on 8 December 1989 where Kohl was heavily criticized for his statement in the German parliament on German unification. In the end agreement was reached on the French request of establishing an IGC on an EMU before the end of 1990, whereas political unification was not mentioned.

The two aspects had been split and Kohl mentioned a few days later in a talk with the US foreign minister that he had taken this step against German interests in order to assure other members of Germanys European commitment. In other words Germany had undertaken an obligation to work in good faith for an EMU without a concomitant process of political unification.

The old disagreement since the Werner Report had for the time being been settled along the French view. Later on in 1990 it was agreed between France and Germany that a parallel IGC on political union should be established. This happened but with the surprising result that Germany could not present any clear model for political unification. It turned out to be an empty box.

It is sometimes suggested that an important difference between the work on an EMU and political unification was that the latter had no analytical work like the Delors Report to rely on. The difference is rather connected with the fact that the EMU had been debated for 20 years and the strategies between France and Germany had been clearly defined. The issue of political union had gone from the wide ranging plans of a united Europe on the US model to something much looser but difficult to define.

The work on a treaty on EMU – as part of the Rome Treaty – began with draft proposals from France and Germany. The French accepted an independent central bank but with political interference on the broad goals of policy – including exchange rate policy vis à vis external countries. The common central bank should be established already in stage 2. The German version that had been negotiated between the finance ministry and the *Bundesbank* was heavily weighted with convergence criteria and difficult voting requirements for moving into stage 2 and the final stage 3. Central bank independence should be accepted but transfer of sovereignty should not take place until the final stage 3. It was as if everything had moved back to base 1.

In contrast with the Germans the French would not fully accept the doctrine of monetary policy indivisibility and had not strong inclinations of precise convergence criteria. Both were vague on the question of coordinating fiscal policy that later on to some extent was dealt with in the Stability and Growth Pact. The negotiations proceeded and became dominated by the views of German monetary authorities.

First, the Committee of Governors under German chairmanship and German dominance drafted the statutes of the common central bank. The new central bank was modeled over the *Bundesbank*. Price stability should be the overpowering goal – other goals could only be supported within the primary target. The common central bank should not be established until the final stage – no transfer of sovereignty until then.

Second, the question of political influence on the broad targets for monetary and exchange rate policy (*gouvernement économique*) was not accepted.

Third, quite forbidding convergence criteria were requested on wide ranging fields: price performance, market interest levels, exchange-rate stability, public sector deficit, and public sector debt. Performance should be at the most stability oriented level and it was widely expected that only very few countries would be able to meet the requirements. It was, however, agreed as a general compromise that such criteria could not be used in an automatic way but would require the exercise of judgment. So after all there was a loophole.

It has been demonstrated how earlier attempts to create an EMU faltered for political or economic reasons so there was much debate on how the project could be made irreversible. Irreversible is a hazy concept that was not discussed in the IGC that prepared the text for the treaty, but it was on the minds of politicians – both Kohl and Mitterrand. How could a defeat of the plan be avoided? There are several versions about how the question of irreversibility was handled and how the final decision was made. One version is that Padoa-Schioppa, adviser to the Italian Prime Minister,

Andreotti, attended a meeting of the Giscard–Schmidt committee in Brussels shortly before the Maastricht meeting on 9 December 1991. A fixed date was discussed and this prompted him to prepare a text for Andreotti proposing a fixed date. Another version mentions a meeting at the end of November where Guigou suggested to Mitterrand that a fixed date in the treaty was the best way to make the process irreversible. A third version is given by Niels Ersbøll, Secretary General of the Council, who accompanied the Dutch chairman of the European Council, Lubbers, on his visit to colleagues just before Maastricht.

At talks with Kohl he was asked whether they had ideas how to make the process irreversible. Ersbøll suggested that the same model as in the Rome Treaty regarding the establishment of a tariff union should be used. If agreement could not be reached an alternative procedure with a fixed time limit would be used. Kohl accepted this.

At the start of the meeting in Maastricht, Mitterrand proposed fixing a date for entry into the third stage, at the latest, 1 February 1999. This was accepted even though it had not been negotiated in the IGC or in the ECOFIN. It turned out to be solely a decision of the heads of state. It meant that an EMU would be realized by those countries that were judged to fulfil the convergence criteria. Even though the exchange-rate system broke down in 1992 and 1993 convergence improved in almost all member states. It happened to such an extent that the European Council decided to accept all members – except Greece – that wanted to join the EMU from 1 January 1999.

It is often assumed that many members worked hard to be able to fulfil the convergence criteria. This is really not a true picture of what happened. Stability development in prices and interest rates was quite widespread in the industrial countries, irrespective of whether they were applicants to the EMU or not. There were some difficulties with the public budget requests in various countries which were widely publicized. They were, however, of minor importance and in several cases solved by unorthodox book-keeping practice.

EMU – A German or French Success Story?

An EMU has been on the political agenda for 30 years. It is remarkable that the initiatives have invariably been taken by the heads of state in France and Germany. They have been defeated by the monetary bureaucracies in Germany and political reservations in France against transfer of sovereignty. This was, however, overcome in the Maastricht Treaty.

The German strategy prevailed regarding central bank independence, and convergence towards the most stable level but parallelism between EMU and political unification was separated at the Strasbourg meeting December 1989 and eventually abandoned. The French strategy prevailed in limiting transfer of sovereignty to the central bank issue but had to abandon political influence on the new central bank.

The European Council (heads of state) became the decisive factor in the decision-making process – the split between economic and political union and the solution of the irreversibility problem. Kohl and Mitterrand were both convinced that the dominance of the D-mark was a severe threat to a peaceful equilibrium in Europe. Both have succeeded in abandoning the D-Mark but the model chosen can only survive so long as political support is available (cf. Tsoukalis, chapter 4).

Note

1   References can be found in the analyses of Dyson and Featherstone (1999); Gros and Thygesen (1998); Hoffmeyer (2000); Ludlow (1982); and Tsoukalis (1977).

References

Dyson, Kenneth and K. Featherstone (1999): *The Road to Maastricht*, Oxford: Oxford University Press.
Gros, Daniel and N. Thygesen (1998): *European Monetary Integration*, London & New York: Addison-Wesley Longman.
Hoffmeyer, Erik (2000): 'Decisionmaking for European Economic and Monetary Union', *Occasional Paper 62*, Washington D.C.: Group of Thirty.
Ludlow, Peter (1982): *The Making of the European Monetary System*, London: Butterworth Scientific.
Tsoukalis, Loukas (1977): *The Politics and Economics of European Monetary Integration*, London: George Allen & Unwin Ltd.

2 The Euro-Zone in a Political and Historical Perspective
KENNETH DYSON

The complexity of the causes and effects of Economic and Monetary Union (EMU) in Europe makes for difficulties in ensuring that full justice is done to this historic issue in public debate, especially in referenda. These difficulties are exacerbated in a landscape of modern political communications in which messages are reduced to short 'soundbites' and in which entertainment values predominate (Postman, 1985; Dyson, 1996). The aim of this chapter is to rescue the complexity of EMU from a political debate that threatens to be myopic and one-dimensional and to reduce what is happening to amusing caricature. This aim's importance derives from the 'history-making' character of decisions about EMU. EMU is, above all, crucial to power and how it is exercised in contemporary Europe. It is also about the fundamental values according to which we wish to be governed.

The issue of whether EMU makes sense and of whether to join in completing the process is all the more difficult to handle because EMU is not just bound up in complex cause-effect relationships that elude existing economic models and theories. Thus, for instance, there will be effects on growth and employment both from entering the Euro-Zone and from remaining outside. But it is difficult to estimate these effects with any degree of reliability. To complicate the issue, the process of EMU has two other characteristics: contingency and constitutive effects. As in other systems, natural as well as social, the operation of EMU represents a fusion of causes and contingency, yielding a high degree of uncertainty about its future (Dyson, 2000a; Dyson, 2001a). Its operation will display randomness and indeterminacy. But before rejecting it as too uncertain a venture, one should note that the status quo is also beset by great uncertainties. The case for EMU rests on its role in reducing some threatening uncertainties (e.g. about how a unified Germany will use its economic power in Europe and about dependency and vulnerability of European states in a fast-changing global economy). EMU will not remove this contingency. It should, however, help in better dealing with it, notably as a large economic block less vulnerable to external trade and price shocks. Not least, through a system of sharing power in joint economic and monetary decision making the behavior of large, powerful states becomes more controllable. In this sense EMU favors smaller states to a greater extent than the earlier Exchange-Rate Mechanism (ERM), in which the status of the D-Mark as the anchor currency endowed the German *Bundesbank* with a dominant position. The *Bundesbank's* perception of the requirements of the German economy with respect to price stability drove policy across the system, with potentially deleterious effects on other states – as after German unification (Dyson, 1994; Kaltenthaler, 1998). Within the ECB the *Bundesbank* was reduced to an equal vote with Luxembourg and other states.

EMU also has constitutive as well as causal effects (Dyson, 2000b; Dyson, 2001a). In other words, it changes the way in which elites define national interests and form identities. It is in this sense a cultural and not just material phenomenon. EMU is about more than simply price and wage transparency, new liquid financial markets in euros and corporate restructuring. Above all, it rests on a set of shared beliefs in 'sound' money and finance, beliefs that are institutionalized through provisions in the Maastricht Treaty of 1993 and in the Stability and Growth Pact of 1997 (Dyson, 1994; Dyson, 2000a). These provisions privilege price stability as a value and identify the role of fiscal policy as to flank the European Central Bank (ECB) in single-mindedly pursuing this value. The paradigm of 'sound' money and finance structures how economic and monetary policies are debated in the Euro-Zone, gives political direction to policy development, and provides a legitimating formula by reference to which economic and monetary policy responses are judged appropriate or inappropriate. It creates a logic of appropriateness. In these respects beliefs matter. As far as the Euro-Zone is concerned, this paradigm identifies growth and unemployment as fundamentally 'supply-side' matters. It prioritizes liberalization of product, service, capital and labor market and flexible wages as the fundamental requirements for optimizing these two values. In short, it assigns responsibility for growth and employment to governments and to the social partners, not to central bankers.

EMU, States and Social Democracy: Challenge and Opportunity

This section argues that, beneath these complex cause-effect relations, contingencies and constitutive effects, it is possible to discern a pattern. In launching the single European market program, and equipping the EC with the authority and instruments for this purpose, the Single European Act of 1987 provided the basis of legitimacy for the EC to consolidate as a 'regulatory' state (Majone, 1996). In essence, the EC's specialized function is to regulate the European market, attending to the efficiency of its operation. This regulatory function is compatible with a technocratic form of legitimacy. With the Maastricht Treaty, and the Stability and Growth Pact, the EC was armed with the authority and instruments to operate as a 'stabilization' state (Dyson, 2000a). Its function is to ensure economic stability in Europe through the independent action of a new technocratic institution, the ECB, and through an institutionalized process of budget consolidation.

These twin functions of regulation and stabilization are mutually compatible and reinforcing. They underline the extent to which the EC has become an institution preoccupied with the efficiency of the European market. EMU created a new interest in extending the European agenda of market efficiency to include labor markets, wages and the welfare state. Flexible wages and labor markets, labor mobility and welfare-state arrangements that encouraged employment were seen as indispensable for efficient adjustment to economic shocks (e.g. caused by differential productivity growth in the Euro-Zone). National and regional economies can no longer rely on lower interest rates or currency devaluation to restore growth and employment.

This technocratic conception of EMU is not seen as anti-democratic by its exponents (cf. especially Kelstrup and Plaschke in this book). It is about safeguarding the long-term viability and strength of liberal democratic states by improving their capacity to deal with economic shocks and avoid economic instability (Issing, 1999). EMU strengthens the problem-solving capacity of member states in relation to economic stability and sustainable economic growth without a 'boom-bust' cycle. This theoretical position has its main intellectual roots in German Ordo-liberalism and in the lessons drawn from the effects of hyper-inflation on the Weimar Republic. It transferred with the *Bundesbank* model into the design of EMU (Dyson and Featherstone, 1999).

But Ordo-liberalism presupposes 'strong' states, willing and able to act to reform labor markets, wage bargaining and welfare provision. The paradox is that states are not simply losing powers over interest rates and exchange rates. They are being asked to become more politically active in taking on powerful domestic interests, including often their core constituencies of supporters. In practice, by 2001 the French, German and Italian governments were still displaying timidity about pensions and labor-market reforms. What emerged was a gap between the underlying political assumption of Neo-liberal/Ordo-liberal economic theory (the 'strong' state) and the consensual nature of most EU states whose institutional arrangements favored negotiated and relatively slow-moving change (Lijphart, 1977). The model of negotiated change involves the incorporation of potential losers and those able to veto into the process of reform, with the state taking on some of the costs of adjustment. This model finds its justification in a concern to preserve social stability and cohesion, and in a belief that social stability and cohesion are important collective goods for the effective economic performance of capitalism. In other words, economic policy beliefs and the institutional beliefs embedded in national political systems (and classically represented by Christian and social democracy) are potentially in conflict.

The result is scope for tensions between the ECB and member-state governments about the scope and pace of domestic policy change. The threat of rising interest rates puts governments under greater pressure to act in order to avoid reverses to growth and employment and a more difficult budgetary situation. Their preference was, however, for negotiated change in the form of social pacts in which wage moderation by organized labor was exchanged for job-creation and training measures by the state and state action to supply collective goods (including social stability) as a means of creating a climate in which capital was likely to increase investment. This tension was not least apparent with respect to Germany. Germany had exported the Ordo-liberal ideas of the *Bundesbank* and the Federal Economic and Finance Ministries to EMU. But the Rhineland capitalism model had not been exported, with its stress on long-term relations in financing industry and on cooperative relations between employers and labor. The Schröder government sought to revive this model through the 'alliance for jobs' as an instrument for creating consensus around supply-side reforms to improve the competitiveness of the German economy. In consequence, change was slow and discreet rather than bold and rapid.

This tension between EMU and member-state governments reveals the complex changes at work. On the one hand, governments are under pressure – not least from global financial markets – to manage domestic opinion and consensus formation in the direction of accepting the assumptions of the neo-liberal economic model. Here the effects of EMU are bound up with the effects of globalization and the single European market program in strengthening competitive pressures and giving a new weight to demands from the business and financial sectors for a supportive framework of stability. They would face the same problems from globalization and the single European market, irrespective of EMU.

The process of domestic opinion management was by no means easy either for center-right governments (witness the problems of the government of Alain Juppé in France, especially the wave of strikes and demonstrations in December 1995, and the 'reform blockade' facing the Kohl government between 1996 and 1998) or for center-left governments, faced with opposition from core supporters both in social democratic parties and in trade unions. In fact, social democratic governments might be better placed to secure wage moderation and deliver consent for public expenditure cuts (Ross, 1997). Despite their differences of emphasis, Tony Blair's Third Way, Gerhard Schröder's *Neue Mitte*, Lionel Jospin's regulated globalization and the Dutch Polder Model can be seen as center-left political formulae that express a social democratic acceptance of market-driven adjustment in a global economy (e.g. Giddens, 1998; Hombach, 1998; Jospin, 1999; Visser and Hemerijck, 1997). At the same time they remain contentious within domestic left-wing politics, especially with those who favor bolder and more radical policy measures to promote redistribution and intervene directly in the economy. By 2001 social democratic parties were beginning to fear electoral risks from abstention by their core supporters.

On the other hand, the specialization of the EU on economic efficiency, regulation and stabilization accentuates the importance of the European state as the site for tackling issues of growth, employment and redistribution through the state's primary role in economic and social policy. Redistribution in particular is too problematic a function for the EU. It depends on a role in taxation and spending, and a level of politicization of issues, for which the EU – with its democratic deficit – is not designed. The principle of 'no taxation without representation' suggests that a wholly new structure of democratic governance at the EU level would be required to support such a role. Quite simply, monetary union is not embedded in a structure of political union, with an 'economic government' (rejected by the Germans) and a strong European Parliament (rejected by the French). There is no fiscal transfer system at the EU level redistributing income between individuals. What EMU means is a politicization of state policy as member-state governments are pushed to tackle labor-market, wage and welfare-state reforms as well as accelerating liberalization of product markets and services. These issues are highly charged politically, upsetting many vested interests.

What emerged by 1997-98, with the Jospin government in France, the Blair government in Britain and then the Schröder government in Germany, was an interest in trying to give a new coherence to state economic policy in the fields of growth, employment and social justice.

Social democratic governments sought to identify and exploit a 'policy space'. For Schröder the mechanism is binding trade unions into a neo-corporatist 'alliance for jobs', aiming to focus government, employers and trade unions jointly on the requirements of improving competitiveness, notably wage moderation. For Jospin the mechanism is state-led action, especially the 35-hour working week as a means to create jobs and improve labor-market and wage flexibility. For Blair the emphasis is on 'new growth' theory as a means for justifying government intervention, e.g. in welfare-to-work measures and public investment in training and infrastructure. How governments seek to exploit 'policy space' reflects differences in national institutional and political circumstances, for instance the lack of a strong integrative trade union movement in Britain and the traditional power of the trade unions in Germany and of the state in France. Governments are also sometimes less than wholehearted in their pursuit of a distinctive social democratic 'policy space'. Thus the Blair government paid more attention to using budget consolidation as a means to create a room for maneuver for redistribution than to applying new growth theory in the form of bold new training and infrastructure programs (Wickham-Jones 2000: 16). But what is clear are the efforts of different national governments to carve out a new 'policy space' within the framework of EMU, focusing on their role in growth, employment and redistribution. As regulation and stabilization become the prime tasks of the EU, so the role of states in social justice takes on a higher profile (Dyson, 2000a; Dyson, 2001a). This development offers a new opportunity to social democratic parties to reconcile 'modernization' (represented by market efficiency and economic stability) with social justice (cf. Zank in this book). By 2001 social democratic governments are still seeking out a coherent set of policies to deal with this situation. The special Lisbon European Council of March 2000 was a tentative step in this process.

The Historical Significance of EMU: (1) The Political Dimension in its Origins

It is also important to examine the complex causes and effects of EMU in historical perspective. In identifying its causes an historical examination reveals the important role played by both the political motives of actors and deeper political developments. Politics has, in other words, played the leading role (a topic that is handled in greater detail later in this chapter).

This first major attempt to launch EMU as the leading Community project was at the Hague Summit of EC leaders in December 1969, attended by President Georges Pompidou for France and Chancellor Willy Brandt for Germany, both new in office and both keen to make a mark. In sponsoring EMU Pompidou was most influenced by geostrategic arguments of a political nature. EMU dealt with two problems of political power that disturbed the French elite: the hegemonic position of the US in international monetary arrangements; and the way in which German economic power was outstripping French and threatening to 'unbalance' the Franco-German relationship (Dyson, 1994; Dyson and Featherstone, 1999). Two events had been of particular concern to Paris: the 1968-69 currency turmoil, in which the French franc was seen as the victim; and the new *Ostpolitik* (policy towards the East) of Brandt which threatened to strengthen German presence in this region and divert German attention away from the EEC. Hence EMU was vital for two political reasons: to bind Germany closer into the EEC and to share monetary power with Germany at a time when Germany threatened to become less predictable; and to create a currency block able to bargain on a basis of equality with the United States, especially about reform of the Bretton Woods system (cf. Hoffmeyer in this book). Furthermore, EMU served a domestic political purpose: it cemented a political opening of Gaullism to the political center, thereby strengthening Pompidou's position. Brandt's motive in endorsing the French initiative was also grounded in his conception of European security. *Ostpolitik* was intended to strengthen that security, but it could only do so if it went in parallel with moves to deepen Western integration. EMU was a testament to German good will on European unification.

It is conventional to attribute the failure to implement the design for an EMU by stages outlined in the Werner Report of 1970 to the economic unraveling of the Bretton Woods system. The result was a major diversion of attention away from EMU and a new climate of economic and monetary uncertainty that induced greater caution. But politics was again central. Pompidou ran into major opposition within the Gaullist Party to the threat to national sovereignty from the Werner Report. The French government was soon clarifying its unwillingness to see rapid and parallel progress between economic and monetary union, with a strong economic 'pole' at the EC level. The German government saw the principle of parallelism as central to the Werner Report so that monetary and political union would march in tandem. Hence by 1971 the German government had lost its faith in the exercise (Dyson and Featherstone, 1999).

Despite this setback French concern about German economic power and its political implications remained a constant factor, uniting the presidencies of Pompidou (1969-74), Valéry Giscard d'Estaing (1974-81) and François Mitterrand (1981-95). An ardent European, Giscard d'Estaing sought out opportunities to pursue EMU, especially after 1976 when a new government under the pro-European Raymond Barre took office. In taking the initiative in 1978 that led to the European Monetary System (EMS) agreement, German Chancellor Helmut Schmidt was accepting some of the political analysis of the French, especially about the irresponsible use of US economic and monetary power and the need to insulate Europe from its destabilizing effects.

That the ERM survived and prospered owed much to President Mitterrand's decision in March 1983 to keep France within the mechanism and to ensure that France lived within its constraints. This decision was fundamental to domestic economic policy under the French Socialists: a policy of expansion was replaced by budgetary 'rigor' and the 'strong' franc, eventually conceptualized as 'competitive disinflation'. It was also the vital underpinning for his European policy that was pursued with great vigour from 1984 onwards. French presidents had long recognized that a strong domestic economy was the precondition for playing an effective role on the international and European stages. Mitterrand had learnt this lesson painfully between 1981 and 1983. Between 1983 and 1987 French economic performance converged rapidly towards that of Germany, creating a new climate of trust and an opportunity for new progress on EMU. But this economic convergence had its basis in a political decision of March 1983 'for Europe'.

In the relaunch of EMU in 1988 the prime mover was Germany as both holder of the EC Presidency and the main European economy. Again, politics was decisive. The fact that Hans-Dietrich Genscher, the German Foreign Minister, took the initiative ensured that both geopolitical calculation and security policy beliefs were central to German thinking about EMU. EMU was 'nested' in a view of the long-term incompatibility of a dominant German role in the ERM with stable political relations in the EC (Dyson and Featherstone, 1999). Repeated controversies about decisions of the Bundesbank as the lead central bank were too politically costly for Germany. In addition, the new opportunities offered to German policy by Gorbachov's new policy of reform and openness needed a major initiative to reassure Germany's partner states in the EC that Germany was not available to be seduced away from the EC as a price for a future German unification. Domestically, Genscher's political weight within the Christian Democrat-Liberal coalition had been reinforced by the 1987 federal elections. This essentially political analysis of the rationale for EMU was accepted by the Federal Chancellor's Office in May-June 1988 (Dyson and Featherstone, 1999).

But crucially, other than a date for starting stage 1 of EMU in 1990 and a commitment in principle to convene an intergovernmental conference (IGC) on EMU, no precise timetable was agreed at the Madrid European Council in June 1989 to carry forward the work of the Delors Committee on how to realize EMU. Delors' expectation was an IGC to coincide with the completion of the European single market program in 1992-93, followed by slow progress. But the political events surrounding German unification in 1989-90 radically altered the parameters within which decisions about accelerating EMU were taken at the Strasbourg European Council in December 1989. A timetable for negotiations was put in place. Chancellor Kohl's political motive was revealed in his formula that German unification and European unification were 'two sides of the same coin'. EMU was of vital strategic interest as a clear statement of German commitment both to make European unification 'irreversible' and to step up the speed of progress, especially by linking EMU to parallel negotiations on political union. The crucial agreement at the Maastricht European Council in December 1991 was to fix a final date for the transition to the third and final stage, 1 January 1999. This decision was taken at the highest political level, outside the view of the EMU negotiators (Dyson and Featherstone, 1999).

An analysis of the complex causes of EMU draws out the importance of economic developments in making agreement possible. In particular, clear and demonstrable evidence of convergence in economic policy ideas and in economic performance was necessary. Here the key development was an emerging consensus around the values of the 'sound' money and finance paradigm. This consensus facilitated an unexpectedly rapid agreement in the Delors Committee, especially on the design of stage 3 with an independent ECB (Dyson, Featherstone and Michalopoulos, 1995; Verdun, 1999). The definition of relevant convergence criteria (inflation, budget deficit, public debt, exchange-rate stability and long-term interest rates) was shaped by this paradigm. But, if a necessary condition, these economic factors were not sufficient. Both the timescale and key elements of the content, especially relating to process, were determined by political factors and motives. In particular, the changed parameters of European security with the end of the Cold War and German unification, and with the new opportunities available to Germany, altered political definitions of national interest in relation to EMU. In a context in which the economic implications were unclear, there was greater scope for geopolitical arguments and security policy beliefs to shape the EMU policy process.

A key factor in putting EMU on the agenda in 1969-70, 1978 and 1988-91 was the Franco-German relationship. Privileged by both sides, this relationship was seen by Bonn and Paris as both vital in its own right as a means of reconciling historic enmities that had lain at the heart of Europe's security problems in the nineteenth and twentieth centuries and as the 'motor' of European unification. In this framework, resting on the Elysée Treaty of 1963, the French President and German Chancellor were able to give a political direction to EMU based on European security policy. Once the Franco-German Economic Council had been established in 1987, the French and German Finance Ministers saw it as in their interests to ward off interventions from their heads of state and government by strengthening their own cooperation. Hence, paralleling the IGC in 1991 was a series of top-secret Franco-German bilaterals designed to iron out major disagreements. Right up to 1998 the Franco-German relationship provided the political 'motor' for EMU. Thereafter, in working out the scope for, and nature of, economic policy cooperation, a more complex pattern of bilateral relations developed on a more issue-specific basis. The Franco-German relationship lost its centrality for EMU once the Euro-Zone had been established. Thus there was no joint Franco-German paper for the Lisbon European Council of March 2000 on coordinated action to strengthen Europe's competitiveness. Within the framework of the Euro-Zone a new scope opened for smaller states to gain influence by seeking out a cognitive leadership based on their better economic performance than large states, especially when there was ideological proximity between the states (Dyson, 2000c). Thus the German government began to take a much closer interest in policy transfer from Denmark and the Netherlands (Bundesministerium der Finanzen, 2000: 11).

The Historical Significance of EMU: (2) Effects

An historical perspective on EMU also draws attention to the extent to which its effects did not just begin on 1 January 1999 when stage 3 started with an independent ECB conducting a single monetary policy. Its effects on states like Denmark, Greece and Sweden predated their possible entry, in a manner not noticeably different from such states as France and Italy which joined at the beginning of stage 3. In any case, membership of the ERM2, linking their currencies to the euro, ensures that they will continue to be subject to the EMU process. In moving from ERM2 to Euro-Zone membership these states are substituting a sharing in decision making in the ECB and in consultation in the Euro Group for being 'policy takers'. Escaping the EMU process would entail exit from ERM2, an option that was not for instance on the Danish referendum agenda in 2000. Exiting

ERM2 would, in any case, be a choice for embracing the logic of dependency of small states in global markets.

From its establishment in 1979 the ERM served as a training ground for EMU, with the German *Bundesbank* acting as team trainer. In consequence, the key turning points for European states have varied, depending on when, and if, their membership of the ERM required domestic policy reforms. For Denmark, like the Netherlands, the critical juncture can be dated to the early 1980s, as the central bank governor sought to alert political and group leaders to the domestic implications of external exchange-rate discipline and to the value of price stability. In the case of France the main turning point was March 1983 when President François Mitterrand exchanged domestic economic policy reform (budget discipline) for continuing influence on European political and economic unification through continuing membership of the ERM. Italy's key transitions came in 1992 (under the shock of humiliating exit from the ERM) and in 1996-97 (when it was faced by the prospect of exclusion from the EMU 'club'). Hence states paid, often painfully, much of the political and economic price for EMU during the twenty-year period of the ERM. That price included a protracted period of output and employment loss in the 1990s as states pursued budget consolidation to qualify for stage 3. EMU's deflationary impact in the 1990s will in retrospect be viewed either as a one-off adjustment to inherited budget difficulties, consequent on 'irresponsible' fiscal policies to cope with the oil crises of the 1970s (the neo-liberal interpretation), or as evidence of a built-in deflationary bias in the whole construction, consequent on a 'rigid' adherence to 'sound money' policy beliefs (the neo-Keynesian interpretation). What seems clear, however, is that the costs of EMU precede the benefits. In this sense a decision to stay in the process (in ERM2) but not go the full way (enter the Euro-Zone) is a choice for maximizing the costs and minimizing the benefits.

Two states fit less well into this picture. Britain was a member of the ERM for only a brief interlude (1990-92), with negative associations. The decision to join at an overvalued exchange rate, at a time of accelerating inflation, and with the effects of German unification beginning to materialize, was a case of political bad timing. ERM membership was linked to output and employment losses; whilst exit unleashed bitter political recriminations notably directed against lack of support from the *Bundesbank*. These negative associations, which had serious long-term consequences for the image of economic competence of the Conservative Party, produced an alienation of right-wing opinion from EMU and more generally from the European integration process. British detachment from

EMU was also consequent on the absence of linkage between the program of neo-liberal economic reforms of the Conservative governments of Margaret Thatcher (1979-90) and John Major (1990-97) and the ERM. The determinants of reform were essentially domestic and influenced by the importing of US policy ideas. In consequence, the Labour governments of Tony Blair from 1997 saw the problem of EMU entry in terms of a Euro-Zone that was inadequately committed to structural economic reforms. The agenda of exporting British ideas about structural reforms to product, capital and labor markets was pursued through the British EU Presidency in 1998 (the so-called 'Cardiff' process) and through the special Lisbon European Council in March 2000. It also informed the substance of the five economic tests for entry spelt out by Chancellor Gordon Brown in October 1997, focusing on greater economic flexibility. For the British government EMU was about an unfinished economic policy revolution in Europe, designed to boost productivity and lower the rate of unemployment at which non-accelerating inflation was possible. Hence the relationship of the British government to EMU was at best ambiguous, at worst sceptical. In its view, the major adjustment to make EMU work had to be made by the Euro-Zone economies, in the form of supply-side flexibility especially in wages and labor markets, rather than by the British economy. This confidence reflected a preference of the Blair government, similar to that of the previous Major government, for importing ideas from the United States as opposed to continental Europe. Underpinning this preference was the impact of the City of London as a global financial center which took US deregulation and the practices of US financial markets and players as its benchmarks (Dyson, 2000b). The attraction of strengthening the Euro-Zone by bringing the City of London within its borders offered a potentially strong negotiating advantage to Britain compared to other states seeking entry.

For Germany too the decision to opt for EMU in 1988-91 was not linked to pursuit of an agenda of domestic structural reform. It involved the objective of exporting the German model of monetary stability to the EU in order to reassure an anxious German public that the new single currency would be at least as stable as the D-Mark. The result was an EMU agreement at Maastricht that confirmed German values. It was further underpinned by German success in getting the ECB sited in Frankfurt, in changing the currency's name from ECU to euro, and in securing the Stability and Growth Pact as a means of ensuring that member states pursued budgets that were in balance over the economic cycle. It was not envisaged that EMU would require major domestic policy reforms. However, by the time of the Red-Green Chancellorship of Gerhard

Schröder in September 1998 it was apparent that, whilst Germany may have exported its monetary policy model in the form of an independent ECB, the situation was very different with respect to economic policy. The economic implications of the Euro-Zone, especially stronger competition, raised new and serious questions about the sustainability and relevance of the German model of Rhineland capitalism, with its stress on cooperation between capital and labor and its regulation of economic behavior. The Euro-Zone was associated with intensified calls for structural economic reforms in Germany embracing labor markets, wages and the welfare state. In economic policy 'Model Germany' had given way to a new interest in benchmarking best practice elsewhere, especially in Denmark and the Netherlands, and importing policy (e.g. on wages).

It is important to gain a historical perspective on the processes of change associated with EMU over a longer time period rather than to see it as a sudden, once-off event. At the same time, as the German case and entry for states like Denmark and Greece exemplify, the establishment of the Euro-Zone still represents an historically important event. The Euro-Zone unleashes powerful new forces for change. Institutionally, these forces are most clearly embodied in the ECB, a supranational institution that is independent not just in pursuing the objective of price stability but also, and crucially, in defining what that objective is. The ECB's governing council has set this objective as a rate of increase of 'less than' 2 per cent in the harmonized index of consumer prices. This tough standard is anchored in an institutional philosophy of 'sound' money and finances, endowing its pronouncements on policy with a robustness that echoes the *Bundesbank*. The result is an ECB-centric Euro-Zone, in which the strongest supranational institution – the ECB – is wedded to a single objective, price stability (Dyson 2000a). Other objectives, notably growth and employment, are assigned to EU governments and to the social partners and seen as independent of monetary policy. Hence the ECB has strenuously pressed the need for structural economic reforms on member states, notably to labor markets, wages and pensions, blaming them for low growth and high unemployment. The ECB can be seen as possessing instruments, notably interest rate policy, to coerce states to import best practice in market liberalization. In doing so it appears as part of a powerful transnational coalition embracing multinational companies, threatening states with withdrawal of inward investment, and the global financial markets, threatening an exit of capital. By 2000-1 an ECB interest rate that exceeded that required by their national economies increased pressure on states like Germany and Italy to step up the scope and tempo of structural economic reforms.

A single currency also means deeper structural changes affecting how markets operate. Above all, the introduction of the euro involves a new transparency about costs and prices, and about how wage bargaining and public policy affects costs and prices (e.g. through taxes and social charges on businesses). It also means new highly liquid financial markets, especially for eurobonds. These changes mean much greater competitive pressures, a more ruthless climate of merger and acquisition activity, and a process of consolidation in financial markets (e.g. of stock exchanges). The effects are seen in more assertive demands from business associations and firms for supportive taxation, welfare-state and labor-market reforms and for productivity-related wage bargaining. In essence, the arguments presented by the ECB and the positions adopted by firms and business associations are broadly similar – liberalization of product, capital and labor markets and flexible wages. Hence, pressures from above – the ECB – and below – the business lobby – point in the direction of market liberalization.

EMU can be seen as wrapped up in a long-term trend, discernible from the late 1960s, for economic policy to be embedded in a new economic paradigm of 'sound' money and finances that legitimates both a more central role for central bankers and a more assertive role of capital in shaping values and practices. This paradigm was institutionalized at the EU level by the Maastricht Treaty and by the Stability and Growth Pact. Hence, whilst the discourse of growth and employment has taken a new prominence, especially with social democratic-led governments in the ascendancy since 1997-98, this discourse has been fitted into the dominant economic paradigm rather than served as a means of catalyzing change in that paradigm. The Macro-Economic Dialogue, introduced by the Cologne European Council of June 1999, does not involve the explicit, *ex ante* coordination of monetary policy with growth and employment objectives. Similarly, the Employment Policy Guidelines that were introduced in the new employment chapter of the Amsterdam Treaty of 1997 are subject to consistency with the Broad Economic Policy Guidelines, which are in turn subordinated to the primacy given to price stability in the Maastricht Treaty. In consequence, the new initiatives designed to give a social democratic face to EMU do not represent paradigm change in the underlying assumptions about economic and monetary policies. Such an assault came from Oskar Lafontaine as German Finance Minister, questioning the strict interpretation of the Stability and Growth Pact and seeking a stronger coordination of economic and monetary policies at the EU level. His early resignation in March 1999 revealed the limits of a social democratic reform politics. At the same time the Lafontaine experience drew attention to the importance of a politically sensitive interpretation of independence by the ECB.

Hence the historical significance of the Euro-Zone lies in consolidating and strengthening the power of the 'sound' money and finance paradigm and in raising the question of whether social democratic governments can seek out a 'policy space' for developing new and distinctive policies for growth, employment and social justice. A combination of institutional innovation – the ECB – with structural changes in markets – especially financial markets – has reinforced the pressures on governments to pursue structural economic and budgetary reforms. But this ideational shift predated EMU and was independent of it. Joining the Euro-Zone was in this sense a decision to accelerate and intensify a process that was already underway. The Euro-Zone's key impact as a variable was on the timing, rhythm and tempo of these reforms (Dyson, 2001a).

At the same time historical change is more complex and multidimensional than such an analysis suggests. In an additional sense the Euro-Zone represents an important structural change in the context in which European states make economic policy. By entering a large currency area, they divest themselves of the balance of payments' constraint and the vulnerability of the domestic currency that had inhibited economic policy in the past. As part of the Euro-Zone, trade as a proportion of GDP fell markedly closer to the levels in the United States and Japan (Dyson, 2000a). Hence internal economic policies were less dependent on, and sensitive to, currency fluctuations. Just how liberating this change was depended on the extent to which external (i.e. non-Euro-Zone) trade mattered in relation to national GDP. For a country like Ireland, for instance, the weak euro meant potentially serious inflationary consequences from rising import prices and an export boom resulting from a high proportion of non-Euro-Zone trade. But, subject to this constraint, EMU had something of a liberating effect. National governments could be tempted by a sense of a greater freedom of maneuver as a consequence of this structural change in external dependency. This process was visible in Germany. With the national economy boosted by a weak euro through higher exports, the Schröder government was under less pressure to tackle problems like labor-market reforms with vigor and urgency.

Politics, Economics and Markets

Like the creation of earlier currency unions EMU can be understood to only a limited extent by the concepts and approaches of economics. EMU's fundamental importance is as a political and historical process, driven by political motives and a sense of 'making history'. Economic theory has been used in this process in two ways: to inform decisions about how EMU is best constructed so that it is technically viable (witness the influence here of the 'credibility' theory of inflation in supporting an independent ECB); and to legitimate essentially political decisions to move ahead with EMU (hence the European Commission's 'One Market, One Money' report followed rather than preceded these decisions) (Dyson, 1994; Dyson and Featherstone, 1999). Economics was important in a third sense – by providing theories that were used to cast doubt on the wisdom of the enterprise. In particular, 'optimum' currency area theory suggested that the EU as a whole lacked the economic attributes of an economic zone able to function efficiently and effectively in the absence of exchange-rate adjustment and differential interest rates. Labor markets were too inflexible and labor not mobile enough to ensure a prompt response to asymmetric shocks within the euro-zone. This problem was exacerbated by the lack of a fiscal federal union that would be able to transfer resources to areas suffering from structural difficulties, like low productivity and high unemployment.

But the typically gloomy and at best sceptical conclusions of economics tend to ignore the political dynamics of EMU and the way in which politically-induced change – like creating a currency union – can alter the parameters of economic (and political) behavior in ways that economic models fail to capture. It is likely that the new experience with EMU will reshape economics to at least as great an extent as economics shapes EMU. A politically-inspired EMU is creating a new economic reality, most prominent of which in the short term is a powerful new eurobond market that provides a new platform for acquisitive merger, acquisition and joint venture activity on a European scale. In particular, monetary union has unleashed a learning process about the nature and scope of economic policy cooperation. As outlined below, its effects were evident at the special European Council in Lisbon in March 2000.

EMU is also a stimulus to reflect on the complex interaction between politics and markets. It is conventional to argue that business has a privileged position vis-à-vis the state, especially because it can threaten to relocate investment and hence punish recalcitrant governments by job and tax-revenue losses (Lindblom, 1977). Hence, pursuing this logic, globalization is associated with deregulation and with a 'race to the bottom' in taxes, putting welfare states under increasing pressure. This argument has not changed with EMU. States are under acute pressure to reform welfare states so as to reduce costs on business, to lower corporate taxes, and to liberalize product, service and labor markets. The symptom of this pressure was a weakening euro in 1999-2000 occasioned by a movement of capital out of the euro. Restoring market confidence became a key objective of EU governments, for instance by the ambitious communiqué of the special Lisbon European Council with its targets, deadlines and review process for revitalizing the European economy. EU governments appeared defensive and reactive to markets. This posture was historically conditioned by the heritage of high debt levels, consequent on the use of deficit financing especially in the 1970s, and independent of EMU. In short, it would have been the modus operandi without EMU.

But EMU is no simple story about a logic of neo-liberal economics. Within the confines of the 'sound' money and finances paradigm, EMU can be seen as the reassertion of a new political determination by EU states. Firstly, they showed their ability to make, and abide by, an historically momentous decision – to complete EMU by 1 January 1999 latest. 'History-making' decisions are properly the business of states. Market reactions were taken into account in designing EMU, for instance the convergence criteria for entry into stage 3. But in formulating the objective politics was determining. EMU was embedded in a larger political narrative about the conditions for European security in the face of rapid change, notably consequent on German unification in 1989-90. It was about a political reaffirmation of German commitment to a 'Europeanized' Germany. EMU was also about Franco-German rapprochement and the continuing demonstration of the Franco-German role as the 'motor' of European unification. Finally, it was about increasing Europe's weight in the management of the global economy. In seeking to pursue these objectives and play a global role the EU may have demonstrated a 'capabilities-expectations' gap. But the key point is that a dimension of independent political determination underpinned EMU.

Secondly, through the Stability and Growth Pact of 1997 EMU became a mechanism for states to retrieve collectively a new freedom of fiscal maneuver by a process of budget consolidation. In that way national 'automatic stabilizers' could operate more efficiently. By reducing debt servicing costs there would be new scope to vary tax and spending policies to achieve ideological objectives, reward core supporters and win domestic elections. High deficit spending and rising public debt were not an essential element of social democracy. Budget consolidation was also a precondition for exerting influence within the Euro-Zone. As new French Finance Minister in 2000, Laurent Fabius was sensitive to his weak position consequent on a French budget deficit that was perceived by his peers in ECOFIN as too lax for France's position in the economic cycle.

Finally, how states responded to the liberalizing pressures from globalization and EMU remained deeply conditioned by national models of capitalism. These models are entrenched in domestic institutional arrangements, for instance in labor markets and wage determination and in the management of the welfare state (Dyson, 2001a). Within the EU at least three main models can be identified: market capitalism, state-led capitalism, and managed capitalism. They are represented respectively by Britain, France and Germany. Globalization and EMU represented powerful pressures for convergence. However, convergence was less apparent in processes of domestic economic policy management, policies and outcomes. During the 1990s there was no real evidence of a 'race to the bottom' in either taxation or welfare state spending (Dyson, 2001a). The most interesting institutional development was a resurgence of interest in national policy concertation, for instance in Denmark, Ireland, Italy and the Netherlands (Compston, 1998; Dyson, 2001a). This interest in negotiating domestic structural reforms through social pacts underlined the entrenched power of the managed capitalism model. It remained the centerpiece of the Schröder government's management of economic reforms in Germany (Dyson, 2001b).

Despite the entrenched power of domestic institutional arrangements, it would be foolish to underestimate the power of markets. This power was, for instance, manifested in the ERM crises of 1992-93. Markets are clearly important, not just as external disciplines on the EMU process but also as internalized values within that process, conditioning how the Euro-Zone is designed and operates. There was, however, a political agenda at work, and ERM crises did not disrupt the politically defined path to EMU. This political agenda was linked to a belief in the political values of European integration – making European unification 'irreversible' in the language of Helmut Kohl and François Mitterrand. It was reinforced by the shock of German unification in 1989-90. The role of European integration in binding German power into Europe and 'Europeanizing' Germany assumed a new topicality. Agenda change was also linked to a political belief that EMU could be used to lever domestic structural reforms on recalcitrant interests: EMU as a domestic discipline and catalyst for reform, for instance for the Greek and Italian technocratic elites. Above all, budget consolidation through peer review of national convergence programs opened a fresh vista of domestic fiscal flexibility and a rebalancing of the relationship between politics and markets. In short, not only was politics determining in the creation of EMU but also EMU offered an opportunity for reasserting political priorities.

Paradigm Shift: From 'Hard' to 'Soft' Economic Policy Coordination

Above all, EMU registers a fundamental shift in European societies since the early 1970s. At that time Keynesianism was still ascendant. It formed the intellectual basis for the Werner Report of 1970. This report made no reference to an 'independent' European system of central banks. It spoke of a 'strong' monetary pole. But this pole was to be balanced by the parallel development of a 'strong' economic policy pole, coordinating fiscal policies, and by the involvement of the social partners at the European level. There was no inhibition in talking about 'coordination' of fiscal, monetary and wage policies, even from the German side where Karl Schiller, the Economic Minister, was the advocate for the introduction of Keynesian ideas in the form of an 'enlightened' social market economy and an 'optimal' policy mix. There was a close intellectual similarity between Schiller's Stability and Growth Law of 1967 and the substance of the Werner Report.

The fundamental shift in economic policy beliefs that had occurred by the time of the relaunch of EMU in 1988 reflected deeper structural changes in society, in particular the growth of a larger proportion of the population with significant ownership of assets and hence with an interest in protecting their value from erosion by inflation. This change went along with the huge growth of financial conglomerates handling savings. Global financial markets grew at an extraordinary pace, making territorial definitions of sovereignty increasingly irrelevant (Cohen, 1998). Hence, for reasons of domestic politics, as well as for reasons of change in international financial markets, state elites were forced to reflect on the appropriateness of Keynesian beliefs. This reflection was triggered by evidence that Keynesianism lacked the policy instruments to deal with emerging economic problems of the 1970s, especially the combination of growing unemployment with rising inflation. In this context of crisis of the prevailing economic paradigm monetarist ideas gained a new appeal. They prioritized price stability and argued that unemployment was independent of monetary policy, having its basis in supply-side conditions in the economy. The 'sound' money and finance views of central bankers and financial market players were given a new respectability and legitimacy.

Against this background the intellectual consensus that lay behind the Delors Report of 1989 was very different. The principle of an independent ECB, committed solely and exclusively to price stability, became the anchor for the whole design of EMU. Though Delors sought to give more attention to economic policy coordination, this topic was very secondary. In his White Paper of 1993 on Competitiveness, Growth and Employment

Delors tried in vain to revive the theme of economic policy coordination. But the Broad Economic Policy Guidelines introduced in Article 103 of the Maastricht Treaty, and the related process of multilateral surveillance of member-state economic policies, remained only weakly developed. With the Euro-Zone there was some attempt to strengthen them, notably at the Helsinki European Council in December 1999, by a greater emphasis on structural reforms and on issuing specific guidance to individual states. But this development was consistent with the 'sound' money and finance paradigm. As we saw above, neither the Employment Policy Guidelines, post-Amsterdam, nor the Macro-Economic Dialogue, post-Cologne, represented a shift towards explicit, *ex ante* coordination of economic, monetary, exchange-rate and wage policies (cf. Dosenrode (chapter 11) in this book).

What had emerged by 2000 was a new emphasis on 'soft' coordination. This took the form of a methodology of 'benchmarking' best practice in economic policy, with the assumption that states would learn from each other and from examples outside the EU and translate those lessons into domestic policies. 'Benchmarking' was a means for coordinating economic policies in the absence of a direct ceding of economic policy competence to the EU. Given the sensitivity of tax issues to national sovereignty, and especially the intimate connection of tax and representation, this formula represented a means of squaring coordination with the continuing realities of national responsibility for economic policy. But it begged a serious question about whether it could be operationalized in the context of the extent to which particular policies and practices are 'institutionally locked', for instance in labor markets and wages (Soskice, 1997). Policies and practices thrive in certain cultures and contexts, making them hard to export. Thus the Dutch model of negotiating change through social pacts was in principle transferable to Germany. But it faced the constraint of the constitutionally enshrined principle of freedom of collective bargaining, which meant that the federal government could not induce agreement between employers and trade unions by the threat of intervention in wages policy. The constraint on exporting this model was even greater in the case of Britain, which lacked an encompassing labor movement that had the authority to strike and deliver on deals (Wickham-Jones, 2000).

In consequence, economic policy coordination is the more uncertain part of EMU. It reflects the asymmetry in its design, with monetary union supranational and economic policy intergovernmental (Dyson, 2000a). This asymmetry in turn expresses the shift from a Keynesian to a neo-liberal economic paradigm. European states are in effect competing to establish the best practice in tackling problems of growth and employment. In this sense coordination is the product of a competitive search for best solutions, based on the assumption that good practice will drive out bad. At the same time a continuing belief in the integrity of the European social model leads to a widespread political concern to establish minimum standards, for instance in social protection and in taxation. This concern is fuelled by fears that competition to attract inward investment could easily lead to a reduction in business taxes, a shifting of taxation onto employees and an erosion of the revenue basis of welfare states. The consequences would be felt in weaker social cohesion and a whole host of criminal, public-order and social exclusion issues that would burden states. Hence there is a deep political reluctance to see economic policy coordination as simply an outcome of competition. But the difficulties of putting flesh on this approach have been most clearly revealed over the issue of harmonizing taxation of income from savings. This issue brings the European social model into conflict with the neo-liberal model of freely operating capital markets.

Conclusion

EMU is above all a powerful historical process in which the relationship between the EU and member states is being reconfigured. Four key themes emerge. Firstly, a division of labor is emerging between an EU specializing in the economic stabilization function and market regulation function and member states whose function is to attend to growth, employment and redistribution. Put simply, the EU deals with efficiency, member states with social justice. For that underlying institutional pattern to work member states will need to maintain a political consensus about the value of economic stability, thereby facilitating the ECB's independence in the pursuit of its objective. In turn, EMU must provide member states with a more secure and a sustainable basis for them to deliver social justice through redistributive programs and to promote growth and employment. There will inevitably be conflicts about how best to realize social justice and how best to promote growth and employment as well as about the implications and requirements of economic stability (e.g. for labor markets and wages). Above all, the politics of EMU will gravitate around the appropriate balance between the European social model and the neo-liberal economic paradigm.

Secondly, the EMU process places a new pressure on European states to be active in reforming labor markets, welfare states and wages policy. In doing so it draws out a tension between the specific institutionalized ideas and practices of European states (for instance, in the case of managed capitalism stressing consensus through negotiated change in which potential losers participate) and the belief of the neo-liberal paradigm in 'strong' states able to press through reforms in the name of the principles of economic stability and of open competition and free markets. The ECB, multinational corporations and global financial markets represent a powerful coalition pushing for domestic reforms, with powerful resources to deploy (interest rates, disinvestment, capital flight). In facing them domestic institutional difficulties and crises (e.g. associated with the profit levels of companies and the job losses affecting organized labor) open up opportunities for domestic change agents to overcome traditional veto players. At the same time more fundamental institutional beliefs, notably about the values of social cohesion, stability and consensus, are likely to endure. The outcome is more likely to be a reconfiguration of domestic institutional arrangements, giving them a new dynamics, than institutional convergence around an imported Anglo-Saxon model.

The third theme is more a question and challenge: whether and how European states will be able to identify and develop a 'policy space' within the framework of EMU (cf. Plaschke in this book). They are constrained in doing so by an EMU design that seeks to make it robust in global financial markets by institutionalizing the 'sound' money and finance paradigm. Opening up a 'policy space' for a reformist politics is dependent on three key factors:

- success in achieving budget consolidation linked to the idea of intergenerational equity and creating a greater room for fiscal maneuver;
- putting in place domestic frameworks for negotiated change that bring on board potential losers and deliver concerted action by states, employers and trade unions in keeping down unit labor costs, notably through wage moderation;
- significant increases in public investment in infrastructure, especially education, training, research and development, and technology transfer, essentially collective goods that both employers and trade unions desire.

Seizing such an opportunity for states in the Euro-Zone involves a strengthening of the provision of collective goods and a more active management of domestic opinion formation through negotiated change. Seen from this perspective, states like Denmark and Sweden have little to fear from entry. Only in this way can the EMU project be made social democratic or at least compatible with polities in which social democracy has shaped the political culture.

Finally, membership of the Euro-Zone offers a greater opportunity for smaller states to influence economic and monetary policy processes and outcomes in the EU than they enjoyed within either ERM1 (before 1999) or ERM2. They gain an equal voting right with large states like Germany in the governing council of the ECB (where monetary policy decisions are made). No less importantly, in an institutional framework of collective deliberation and decision there are opportunities for cognitive leadership based on the quality of arguments. In short, 'insider' status can be combined with 'benchmark' status, resting on evidence about economic performance especially in promoting sustained growth and reducing unemployment, to establish credibility and reputation. This credibility and reputation offers a major resource in 'two-level' bargaining within the Euro-Zone. It makes for persuasive argument rooted in the 'model' character of the domestic economy for other member states. It also can be translated into a domestic political and electoral asset from playing a cognitive leadership role in Europe. The Euro-Zone is pre-eminently a forum for economic policy transfer and benchmarking. States like Denmark and the Netherlands have in this context a greater influence than their size would suggest.

References

Bundesministerium der Finanzen (2000): *Arbeitsplätze Schaffen – Zukunftsfähigkeit Gewinnen. Jahreswirtschaftsbericht 2000 der Bundesregierung*, Berlin.
Cohen, B. (1998): *The Geography of Money*, Ithaca NY: Cornell University Press.
Compston, H. (1998): 'The End of National Policy Concertation? Western Europe since the Single European Act', *Journal of European Public Policy*, vol. 5, pp. 507-26.
Dyson, K. (1994): *Elusive Union: The Process of Economic and Monetary Union in Europe*, London: Longman.
Dyson, K. (ed.) (1996): *Culture First: Promoting Standards in the New Media Age*, London: Cassell.
Dyson, K. (2000a): *The Politics of the Euro-Zone: Stability or Breakdown?* Oxford: Oxford University Press.
Dyson, K. (2000b): 'Europeanization, Whitehall Culture and the Institutional Veto Role of the Treasury: A Constructivist Approach to Economic and Monetary Union', *Public Administration*, vol. 78, pp. 897-914.
Dyson, K. (2000c): 'EMU as Europeanization: Convergence, Diversity and Contingency', *Journal of Common Market Studies*, vol. 38, pp. 645-66.
Dyson, K. (ed.) (2001a): *European States and the Euro: Europeanization, Variation and Convergence*, Oxford: Oxford University Press.

Dyson, K. (2001b): 'The German Model Revisited: From Schmidt to Schröder', *German Politics*, vol. 10.
Dyson, K. and K. Featherstone (1999): *The Road to Maastricht: Negotiating Economic and Monetary Union*, Oxford: Oxford University Press.
Dyson, K., K. Featherstone and G. Michalopoulos (1995): 'Strapped to the Mast: EC Central Bankers between Global Financial Markets and Regional Integration', *Journal of European Public Policy*, vol. 2, pp. 465-87.
Giddens, A. (1998): *The Third Way: The Renewal of Social Democracy*, Cambridge: Polity.
Hombach, B. (1998): *Aufbruch – Die Politik der neuen Mitte*, Düsseldorf: Econ Verlag.
Issing, O. (1999): 'The ECB and its Watchers', Auszüge aus Presseartikeln, Frankfurt: Deutsche Bundesbank, 17 June, pp. 10-19.
Jospin, L. (1999): *Modern Socialism*, London: Fabian Society.
Kaltenthaler, K. (1998): *Germany and the Politics of Europe's Money*, Durham: Duke University Press.
Lijphart, A. (1977): *Democracy in Plural Societies: A Comparative Exploration*, New Haven: Yale University Press.
Lindblom, C. (1977): *Politics and Markets*, New York: Basic Books.
Majone, G. (1996): *Regulating Europe*, London: Routledge.
Postman, N. (1985): *Amusing Ourselves to Death*, London: Methuen.
Ross, F. (1997): 'Cutting Public Expenditures in Advanced Industrial Democracies: The Importance of Avoiding Blame', *Governance*, vol. 10, pp. 175-200.
Soskice, D. (1997): 'Stakeholding Yes; the German Model No' in G. Kelly et al. (eds), *Stakeholder Capitalism*, Basingstoke: Macmillan, pp. 219-25.
Verdun, A. (1999): 'The Role of the Delors Committee in the Creation of EMU: An Epistemic Community', *Journal of European Public Policy*, vol. 6, pp. 308-28.
Visser, J. and A. Hemerijck (1997): *A Dutch Miracle*, Amsterdam: Amsterdam University Press.
Wickham-Jones, M. (2000): 'New Labour in the Global Economy', *The British Journal of Politics and International Relations*, vol. 2, pp. 1-25.

3 The Economic and Monetary Union's Institutional Framework[1]
SØREN DOSENRODE

Introduction

The purpose of this chapter is to analyze the Economic and Monetary Union's (EMU) institutions. The main emphasis is laid on the European System of Central Banks (ESCB) and its interaction with the traditional EU institutions. The focus is upon the monetary aspects of the EMU which played a dominant part in the Maastricht Treaty compared to the general economic side which was not developed until after Amsterdam (e.g. the Employment Pact, see below) and does not, to the same extent, include the new formation of own institutions, but functions within the 'normal' framework of the EU. Therefore, this chapter will contain, among other things, a short review of the contents, objectives, developments from 1990-2002 of the EMU, the ESCB (its structure and tasks) as well as interaction with the other institutions, including the Council of Ministers in particular in its composition of Ministers of Economic Affairs and Ministers of Finance (ECOFIN) and the Economic and Financial Committee. An underlying issue is the coordination of the Union's economic and monetary policies.

At the European Council's meeting in Hanover in June 1988, the Heads of State and Government stated that the Single European Act ('The Single European Market', etc.) had been part of the process that was to lead to an economic and monetary union. Jacques Delors, the President of the Commission of that time, was asked to preside over a task group that was to submit specific proposals for the establishment of an EMU.

That was the last part of a history that in terms of ideology goes back to Jean Monnet[2] and first saw the light of day with the establishment of the Committee of Central Bank Governors in 1964. Among other things, the purpose of this committee was to discuss all important monetary policy measures before they were introduced and to the largest possible extent coordinate the nations' monetary policies.[3] The first breakthrough in terms of practical politics with regard to the establishment of an EMU came during the meeting of the Heads of State and Government in The Hague in December 1969 when they decided to work for an EMU. Pierre Werner, Luxembourg's Prime Minister of that time, was asked to examine the possibilities of establishing an EMU and presented a report in June 1970. According to that the Community was to constitute within ten years (translated from Danish):[4]

> [.1.] an area within which persons, goods, services and capital can move freely [...]. 2. [The Community] will form an independent monetary area in the international system, characterised by the complete and irrevocable convertibility between currencies, abolition of the currencies' fluctuation margin, fixing of invariable currency parities; which are necessary conditions for the establishment of a common monetary unit and comprise a common central bank system. 3. in the economic and monetary area [the Community] will have competence and responsibility that make it possible for its institutions to ensure the administration of the union. With a view to that the necessary decisions on the necessary powers shall be assigned to the Community's institutions.

The long quotation above is a good indication of what the 'common European' conception of an EMU's contents is: a single market (later realized by The Single European Market or Internal Market, and accompanying policies, e.g. competition policy, structural policy), a common monetary area with own monetary unit and a degree of common administration and coordination of the Union's economic and monetary policy.

At the Council meeting in March 1971, a resolution was adopted on implementation of the objectives in the Werner Report, and again at the summit meeting in Paris in 1972 (with Danish participation), the Council confirmed its intention to implement the EMU which was to be finalized on 31 December 1980.

As the Werner plan was not realized, other measures were introduced instead, e.g. 'the snake collaboration' in 1972. In 1974, the Commission was allowed to make recommendations to a member state on its economic policy; the European Monetary System in 1979, etc. But Werner's EMU idea remained in the background and was a source of inspiration to the Delors Group, even though there were also deviations (e.g. in the Werner Report there were no convergence requirements and no free movement of capital before the EMU had been implemented).

John McCormick described the principal lines in the Maastricht Treaty's EMU like this:[5]

> Economic union implies agreement on economic policies (which in practice means the establishment of a single market), while monetary union means the agreement of fixed exchange rates and a single currency.

Recent years' development has resulted in the economic side of the EMU being improved too (e.g. with the Employment Pact, and the Lisbon-proceeds). In that connection especially the French Government has talked about making the EMU 'walk on two feet' and thus implied that, at the beginning, the EMU was to a large extent related to the monetary aspect, but that the economic aspect must be given just as high a priority as the monetary aspect in future.

Objectives and Instruments Behind the EMU

The motives for establishing and finalizing the Economic and Monetary Union can be divided into several groups (cf. the introduction as well as chapters 1 and 2). The overall objective is to further the European integration process as indicated by the following quotations. In Copenhagen in 1990, Jacques Delors, President of the Commission, said when it was discussed whether to implement monetary policy nationally or supranationally:[6]

> The first solution is not the way that the Community functions. Its entire structure and basic structure aim at decisions being made jointly. In fact its strength emerges from the fact that the various Member States [...] make decisions jointly. In that way they surrender a certain part of their sovereignty for their common good.

At the same time, in 1991, Otmar Issing,[7] the German Federal Bank's chief economist and member of the board and presently member of the Executive Board of the European Central Bank, spoke about the integration policy objectives of the EMU: 'There is no example in history of a lasting monetary union that was not linked to one State'.

These thoughts about the objectives of the EMU, from its time of establishment, have been followed up by European leaders until today. For example, Federal Chancellor Schröder declared at the end of 1998:[8] [9]

> The European Single Currency is but a stepping stone to a political union [...].
> We will only succeed in shaping a common Europe by developing further towards a political Union.

Romano Prodi, President of the EU Commission, said:[10]

> We must now face the difficult task of moving towards a single economy, a single political entity [...]. For the first time since the fall of the Roman Empire we have the opportunity to unite Europe.[11]

But, besides the overall integration policy, the project contains other motives that all play an important role. The EMU is to be viewed as an instrument to diminish the EU's dependence on the USA and generally strengthen the EU as a global actor:[12] an attitude assumed by France in particular. Also, the EMU is intended to be a bulwark against the negative aspects of globalization.

Internally, the French-inspired EMU project can be understood as a realization that it was not possible to control the German *Bundesbank* which exercised a clearly regional hegemony. A common currency and central bank would, from the French point of view, solve that problem.[13] As mentioned in the introduction, the question of how to tie Germany to western Europe was an equally important motive for creating a strong Union with an EMU.

In terms of economics, the Single Market and the rest of the EMU were to ensure economic prosperity and stability. One rationale behind the EMU was to create stable economic and monetary conditions and thus create more predictability for the various investors and the market in general. The euro was to promote growth and welfare.[14] To put it a little simplistically, the EMU can be considered a French idea realized by Germans (cf. chapter 2).

To be able to realize the vision of a strong EMU it was decided, cf. the report from the Delors Group, to create a strong independent European Central Bank.

Developments 1989-2002

The EMU project was based on the above-mentioned report from the Delors Group and the so-called Delors Report, which was very much a monetary project, but had developed in the economic area too, following the Maastricht Treaty. The road to the euro, which was the name of the new currency, was divided into three phases as suggested in the Delors Report. As the first phase did not require any amendments to the Treaty, the European Council decided in June 1989 to implement it on 1 July 1990. The Committee of Central Bank Governors which had increasingly gained influence since its establishment in 1964 was commissioned to hold consultations and further the coordination of the Member States' monetary policies with a view to obtaining price stability. As time was pressing, the Committee of Central Bank Governors also took the responsibility for initiating the preparations for the next two phases.

To be able to continue to phase 2^{15} and phase 3^{16} of the EMU it was necessary to amend the EC Treaty, and an intergovernmental conference (IGC) was convened in 1990-91 which was extended to include the political aspects of a European union.[17] To realize the EMU project the Maastricht Treaty protocol:

- laid down the institutions that were to be created, and the relationship between the new and the old EU institutions was (rudimentary) established; and
- established the road to a common currency.

Due to the Danish 'no' vote to the Maastricht Treaty, among other things, the EMU project was delayed, and 'phase two' could not be initiated until 1 December 1994. The start of phase two was marked by the establishment of the European Monetary Institute (EMI) and the simultaneous dissolution of the Committee of Central Bank Governors and the European Monetary Co-operation Fund (EMCF).[18] EMI's two main tasks were:

1) to strengthen the cooperation between the central banks and the coordination of their monetary policies; and
2) to make the necessary preparations for the establishment of the European Central Bank System to be able to pursue a common monetary policy and introduce a common currency in the third phase. The currency was named 'euro' in December 1995.

To become a member of the EMU the candidates had to meet the so-called convergence criteria that were incorporated in the Maastricht Treaty (The Treaty on The European Union (TEU) Art. 121):

1) a high degree of price stability;
2) sustainable public finances;
3) compliance with the normal fluctuation margins in the EMS Exchange Rate Mechanism for at least two years without devaluation;
4) the long-term interest rates must be relatively stable.

On 2 May 1998, these criteria were tested by the 12 Member States that wanted to join the EMU, and 11 states were admitted; Greece could not at the time, Denmark, Great Britain and Sweden would not. There was now a euro-zone consisting of 11 EU Member States and a group of four non-euro members.

On 28 May 1998 the Heads of State and Government from the 11 EMU countries appointed the President and Vice-President of the European Central Bank as well as the four remaining members of the Executive Board.[19] They were to take up the posts on 1 June 1998 and thus set up the ECB. With the establishment of the ECB, EMI gradually reduced its activities, and on 1 January 1999 the exchange rates of the 11 states were irrevocably pegged to one another and marked the beginning of the EMU's third phase. In early 2002, the euro replaced the national currencies in the EMU Member States.

The 'E' in EMU

As indicated above, the monetary aspect of the EMU, the 'M', got the most attention in the initial phase of creating and structuring the EMU. But there was the 'E', too. The Economic aspect has gained in importance over the past five years.

As members of the EMU's third phase, the individual states have promised to pay deposits to comply with the so-called 'Stability and Growth Pact' that was launched in 1995 by Theo Waigel and in its substance adopted at the European Council meeting in Dublin in December 1996. At that time, it was only called 'the Stability Pact'. The main objective of the pact is to lay down guidelines for the individual state in order for it to pursue an economic and monetary policy and thus avoiding the stability of the euro zone being threatened by national measures. The pact mentions 'responsible fiscal policy' and that the countries as a principal rule are to aim at a balance in their public budgets. If the pact is not observed, a number of sanctions are laid down; from reprimands to payment of deposits for the confiscation of these; i.e. to fines.[20] That the 'Stability Pact' later on changed its name to the 'Stability and Growth Pact' arose from the election in France where the conservative Government was superseded by a socialist Government which already in opposition had thundered against a Pact it regarded as far too stringent and one-sided as it mainly dealt with monetary policy.[21] Prime Minister Jospin was afraid that the Pact would prevent an active policy against unemployment. The result of the long and tough negotiations about amendments to the Pact clearly shows the power structure of the EU: at first, the substance was not amended, but the parties agreed to call it 'the Stability and Growth Pact' and to incorporate a general commitment to work for a high level of employment in the TEU's Art. 2.

In other words, Jospin saved his face without Germany allowing a weakening of the contents of the original pact. Since then the change of power in Germany, from a conservative-liberal government to a social democratic one the way was prepared for the development of the economic side of the EMU with special emphasis on the so-called 'Employment Pact'.

As mentioned before, the Employment Pact did not turn up out of the blue. France had for a long time exerted pressure to strengthen the economic side of the EMU. In Amsterdam in June 1997, France succeeded in having a resolution adopted on 'Development of the Economic Pillar'[22] which together with the Amsterdam Treaty's chapter on employment paved the way for the following process.

Unemployment as a real problem had been recognized in the course of the 90s, and at the extraordinary meeting in the European Council in Luxembourg in November 1997, the Council adopted a coordination process which in outline was to the effect that once a year the Council of Ministers was to prepare general guidelines for the employment policy which the individual Member States were to implement nationally.[23] The next step was the ECOFIN meeting in Cardiff in May 1998 when the Council of Ministers agreed to make the Member States' markets more efficient, and, analogous to the Luxembourg process, to adopt annual guidelines at Council level to be implemented nationally.

The financial crisis in October 1998 made a number of Governments propose various far-reaching motions to stimulate economic growth and thus employment. The ECB had a bearing on a number of these motions, but it reacted negatively to them.[24] That emphasized the inconvenience of the 'E' and the 'M' in the common EMU not having a reasonable *gremium* to discuss common problems. The summit meeting in Cologne in June 1999 resulted in two things: first, it was agreed to promote the dialogue between the Council of Ministers (in various compositions), the ECB and the labor market parties. It was agreed to create a forum for dialogue between equal parties with the purpose of discussing growth, employment, and price stability. Secondly, the said dialogue was harmonized with the coordination processes from Luxembourg and Cardiff. This construction was called 'The Employment Pact'.[25]

With this development, the economic side of the EMU has been promoted so that in time it can be compared to the monetary side if the process continues as is indicated by the Council of Minister's meeting in Helsinki and Lisbon.[26] Institutionally, in a traditional sense, it is still the monetary part of the EMU which is politically the stronger one and also more controversially seen from a political point of view (see Dyson in this book).

The New Institutions – and Their Interaction with the Old Institutions

There was clearly a need for new institutions on the monetary side of the EMU and they were envisaged in the Maastricht Treaty (during the interim period: EMI, and then the European Central Bank). On the other hand, it was not anticipated to establish new large institutions for the economic side of the EMU:

- because the original plan envisaged that all EU Member States would become members of the EMU as soon as they met the admission requirements;
- because the economic side of the EMU on the one hand, already functioned within the 'normal EU framework' (mainly within the framework of the ECOFIN Council), and on the other hand, the increased need for coordination could (one expected) be handled without any large new institutions; and
- because the economic aspects in 1990-92 were not weighted as high as today.

As Great Britain, Denmark and Sweden did not want to participate, and Greece could not, an unforeseen situation arose which was attempted to be solved with preliminary meetings before the ECOFIN meetings when the Euro 11 Group meet.[27]

The following deals, *inter alia*, with the European System of Central Banks (ESCB), the ECOFIN preliminary meetings, and their interaction with the other relevant EU institutions.

ESCB

The European Central Bank (ECB) in Frankfurt am Main is the essential part of the European Central Bank System (ESCB). Article 107 in the Maastricht Treaty lays down that the ESCB consists of ECB and the national central banks (cf. Figure 3.1).

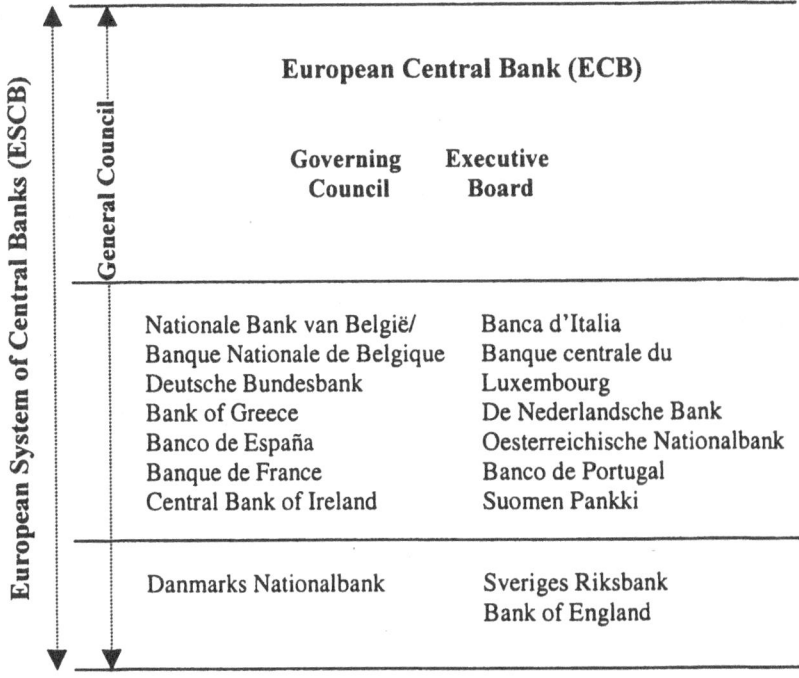

Figure 3.1 The European Central Bank (ECB)
Source: http://www.ecb.int./about/image/escb.jpeg

The ESCB is governed by the ECB's decision-making bodies, i.e. the Governing Council and the Executive Board. The ESCB's paramount objective is to prevent inflation and to maintain price stability[28] and this treaty obligation has first priority in the ECB's daily policy.[29] If it is possible without undermining the price stability objective, the ESCB must also support the union's general economic objectives, that is:[30]

> [...] to promote economic and social progress and a high level of employment and to achieve balanced and sustainable development, in particular through the creation of an area without internal frontiers, through the strengthening of economic and social cohesion and through the establishment of economic and monetary union ultimately including a single currency in accordance with the provisions of this Treaty; (...)

The Task of the ESCB

To be able to carry out its main task, i.e. to ensure low inflation, the ESCB has been assigned the following rights and duties: 1) to formulate and implement the Community's monetary policy.[31] In other words, it has been attempted to take this out of the direct political void and pass it on to officials in the form of the Governors of national central banks and the ECB's officials. The EU's monetary policy is thus attempted to be depoliticised, taking into consideration that politicians who are to be re-elected can be tempted beyond their powers to pursue an inflationary policy in order to reduce unemployment in the EU, for example:[32] by making the monetary policy 'technocratic', the politicians also succeed in avoiding the responsibility for making unpopular decisions. If the EU 2) is to negotiate agreements on monetary issues or exchange rate schemes with third countries or international organizations, the ECB is entitled to be consulted, and ECB has a general right to make transactions in foreign currency.[33] The ESCB holds and administers, as a third element 3), the Member States' official currency reserves.[34] Finally 4), it is the ESCB's task to promote the flexible function of the payment systems.[35] In addition, the ECB is entitled to be consulted with regard to common acts that affect its competence, etc. The performance of these very extensive tasks is sought to be ensured by providing the ECB with wide-ranging independence that looks like that of the EU Commission.[36] TEU Art. 108 lays down:

> When exercising the powers and carrying out the tasks and duties conferred upon them by this Treaty and the Statute of the ESCB, neither the ECB, nor a national central bank, nor any member of their decision-making bodies shall seek or take instructions from Community institutions or bodies, from any government of a Member State or from any other body. The Community institutions and bodies and the governments of the Member States undertake to respect this principle and not to seek to influence the members of the decision-making bodies of the ECB or of the national central banks in the performance of their tasks.[37]

It is a very strong independence where the ECB is more independent that the central banks in Japan and in the USA. This independence is undoubtedly real,[38] but besides the socialization effect which will arise in the interactions already envisaged in the Treaty on the European Union, the ECB will inevitably be involved in various networks to be able to carry out its tasks. It will need information and allies in the power-political game that takes place in Brussels. A number of contacts are institutionalized and open (e.g. the ECB President's participation in the some of the ECOFIN preliminary meetings, the ECB's participation in the Economic and Financial Committee and the right of the President of the Council of Ministers and a commissioner to participate in the meetings of the Governing Council). Other contacts will inevitably take place unofficially and thus without transparency. The danger of this situation is that these contacts are not controllable and therefore can easily result in the presumption that the ESCB/ECB favor some interests at the expense of others.[39]

The Institutions of the ESCB

As mentioned before, it was envisaged that the ESCB was to consist of all the Member States' central banks and the ECB. The overall management was to consist of the Governing Council and the Executive Board. The Governing Council consists of the Governors of the national central banks and the ECB's Executive Board, i.e. President, Vice-President and the four remaining members, but Art. 113 (TEU) adds to this, that the President of the Council of Ministers as a member of the Commission may participate although they do not have any right to vote. As it turned out that initially four EU-Member States would not be members of the EMU's third phase, the General Council of the ECB was created. It consists of the governors of the national banks of all the EU-Member States as well as the president and vice-president of the ECB.[40]

The Governing Council's task is to adopt the guidelines and take the decisions necessary to ensure the performance of the tasks entrusted to the ESCB:[41]

> [...] The Governing Council shall formulate the monetary policy of the Community, including, as appropriate, decisions relating to intermediate monetary objectives, key interest rates and the supply of reserves in the ESCB, and shall establish the necessary guidelines for their implementation.

In accordance with the guidelines laid down by the Governing Council, the Executive Board is to implement the monetary policy of the EU. The federal structure becomes evident as it appears from Article 12 of the Statute that:

> To the extent deemed possible and appropriate, [...] the ECB shall have recourse to the national central banks to carry out operations which form part of the tasks of the ESCB.

The Governing Council meets at least ten times a year, but in reality the frequency is much higher; e.g. in 2002, 25 meetings are scheduled.

The President of the Council has a right to participate in the meetings of the Governing Council and a right to submit a motion for discussion. This is potentially a strong instrument for coordinating the economic policy of the EU with the monetary policy of the ESCB. This potential was stressed by the Heads of State and Government at the summit in Luxembourg in December 1997,[42] but has according to Smaghi and Casini[43] never been pursued; the presidency of the Council of Ministers only turn up twice a year, thus loosing an important possibility of influencing the agenda of the ESCB. An additional disadvantage is that the potential direct line of information from the ESCB via the Presidency to the ECOFIN is not exploited.

To secure the political independence of the Executive Board, its members are appointed for an eight-year period that cannot be extended. The Executive Board members are appointed by the Heads of State and Government on the recommendation of the Council after consulting the European Parliament and the Governing Council. The appointment of the ECB's first President, the Dutchman Duisenberg, probably ended with an agreement that he would retire to make room for another (French) candidate before the termination of his term in office. This compromise was seen by commentators as a potential undermining of the ESCB's future work which, besides exhibiting disagreement among the 15 Heads of State and Government, also indicated that the Member States intended to interfere in the running of the ESCB.[44] With the decision of Great Britain, Denmark and Sweden not to apply for admission to the EMU's third phase, an institutional problem arose which was sought to be resolved by establishing the General Council that, besides the 11 EMU countries' national bank Governors and Vice-Governors, the ECB President and Vice-President, also consists of the national bank Governors and Vice-Governors of the four non-members.

The tasks of the General Council[45] are mixed, but one function is to be contact forum for the ESCB and the four outsider central banks, i.e. all central banks in the EU and the ECB. In addition, there are a number of consulting rights, among other things relating to the annual report, proposals for community acts within the jurisdiction of the ECB, including legislation governing the supervision of credit institutions and the stability of the financial system, the key for capital subscription, etc. However, the evaluation from senior officials with direct knowledge of the General Council is that its influence is marginal. An indication of this is its low frequency of meetings (four planned meetings in 2002) compared to the 25 of the Governing Council and the 11 planned press meetings.

The new, subordinate and implementing role of the national central banks is emphasized in Article 14 of the Statute which lays down, among other things:

- each Member State shall ensure that the statutes of its national central bank is compatible with the TEU and the Statute and that the term of office of a Governor of a national central bank is no less than five years;
- that a national Government cannot relieve a Governor of a national central bank from office at its own convenience – a decision to this effect may be referred to the European Court of Justice by the Governor concerned and;
- that the national central banks are subordinate to the ESCB.

The position of the national central banks can be summarized in the following way: their independence is increased and ensured towards their national Governments; this increased independence has been simultaneously surrendered to the ESCB with the proviso that the Governor of the national central bank has a seat in the ESCB's Governing Council (parallel to the EU Member States giving up sovereignty to the EU, but are seated in the 'EU Government', the Council of Ministers).

The Organization of the ECB

Article 10 of the ECB's 'Rules of Procedure' lays down laconically that, having consulted the Governing Council, the Executive Board decides upon the number, name and respective competence of each of the work units of the ECB. Furthermore, it is established that the Executive Board decides upon and distributes the approximately 17 areas of responsibility. Potentially, this approach gives a high degree of flexibility with regard to adaptation of the structure of the organization to possible new needs (e.g. six permanent distributions of the areas of responsibility has been established and named something like 'Director for Monetary Policy', 'Director for External Relations', etc).

On the other hand, this approach means that strong personalities with the ability to find allies can be very influential on the Executive Board *qua* the portfolios they have composed for themselves and their allies. Thus, there is an imminent danger that the Executive Board will be split between the 'extremely heavy' members and other potentially marginalized members. Add to this that the ECB to a large extent will be exposed to external pressure from the national Governments in the appointment phase. As regards flexibility in the administration, experience from the organization theory shows that it is very difficult to change already incorporated forms, for which reason the potential flexibility is to be taken with a grain of salt.

As it appears from the organizational chart below (Figure 3.2), the ECB consists of the following primary units. The President, Willem Duisenberg heads the 'presidential services' that can support his overall management and help him not to get buried in details. These are the Directorate for External Relations, the Secretariat and the Divisions for Language Services and Audit. The Vice President, Christian Noyer, also heads the traditional services such as the Directorate General for Administration and Personnel and the Directorate General for Legal Services. Eugenio Domingo Solans has been given mainly technical duties: the Directorate General for Information Systems, the Directorate General for Statistics and Banknotes. Where the President's and the Vice-President's portfolios reflect traditional organizational theory (important internal tasks which at the same time ought to give them time to overall coordination, management of the organization and very important: external representation), Solans' portfolio is to be regarded as relatively weak on the face of it. The same cannot be said of the remaining three. Put on a tentatively power continuum, Sirkka Hämäläinen and Tommaso Padoa-Schioppa lie reasonably side by side, clearly after Otmar Issing, who has the distinctly strongest portfolio after the President and perhaps the Vice-President. Hämäläinen has the Directorate General for Operations and the Directorate for Controlling and Organisation in his portfolio, whereas Padoa-Schioppa has the Directorate General for International and European Relations, the Directorate General for Payment Systems and the ECB Permanent Representation in Washington DC in his. Both are important, heavy portfolios. As mentioned before, Otmar Issing has the 'strongest' portfolio, perhaps stronger than that of the Vice-President. He has the following units in his portfolio: the Directorate General for Economics, the Directorate for Monetary Policy and the Directorate for Economic Developments as well as the Division for Fiscal Policies and the Directorate General for Research. All of them are central units that strengthen Issing's position considerably.

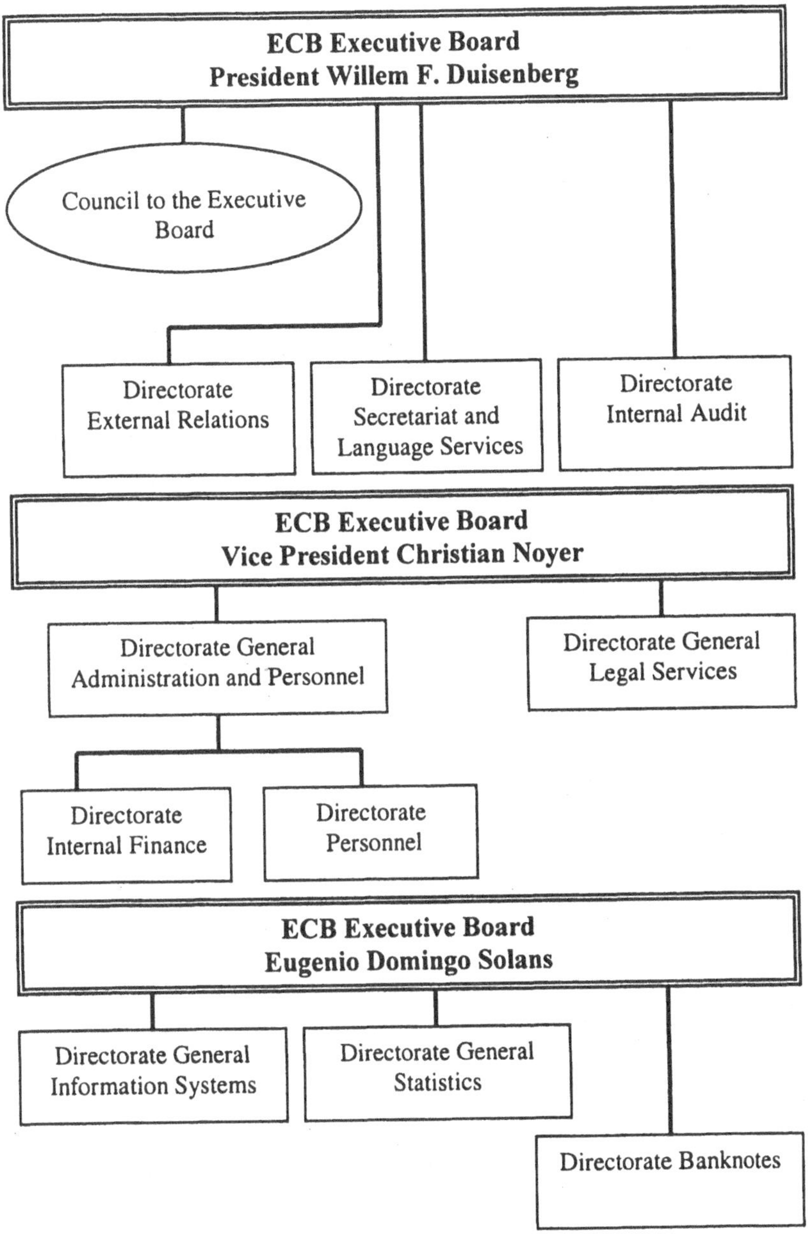

The Economic and Monetary Union's Institutional Framework 55

```
┌─────────────────────────────────────────┐
│         ECB Executive Board             │
│     President Willem F. Duisenberg      │
└─────────────────────────────────────────┘
        │
   ╭─────────────╮
   │ Council to the Executive │
   │      Board      │
   ╰─────────────╯
        │
   ┌──────────┐   ┌──────────┐   ┌──────────┐
   │Directorate│   │Directorate│   │Directorate│
   │ External │   │Secretariat│   │ Internal │
   │ Relations│   │    and    │   │   Audit  │
   │          │   │ Language  │   │          │
   │          │   │ Services  │   │          │
   └──────────┘   └──────────┘   └──────────┘

┌─────────────────────────────────────────┐
│         ECB Executive Board             │
│    Vice President Christian Noyer       │
└─────────────────────────────────────────┘

   ┌──────────────────┐        ┌──────────────┐
   │ Directorate General │     │ Directorate General │
   │ Administration and │     │  Legal Services  │
   │     Personnel      │     │                  │
   └──────────────────┘        └──────────────┘

   ┌──────────┐   ┌──────────┐
   │Directorate│   │Directorate│
   │ Internal │   │ Personnel│
   │ Finance  │   │          │
   └──────────┘   └──────────┘

┌─────────────────────────────────────────┐
│         ECB Executive Board             │
│       Eugenio Domingo Solans            │
└─────────────────────────────────────────┘

   ┌──────────────┐   ┌──────────────┐
   │Directorate General│ │Directorate General│
   │Information Systems│ │   Statistics    │
   └──────────────┘   └──────────────┘

                      ┌──────────────┐
                      │  Directorate  │
                      │   Banknotes   │
                      └──────────────┘
```

Figure 3.2 The organization of the European Central Bank
Source: http://www.ecb.int/about/pdf/org

56 *Political Aspects of the Economic and Monetary Union*

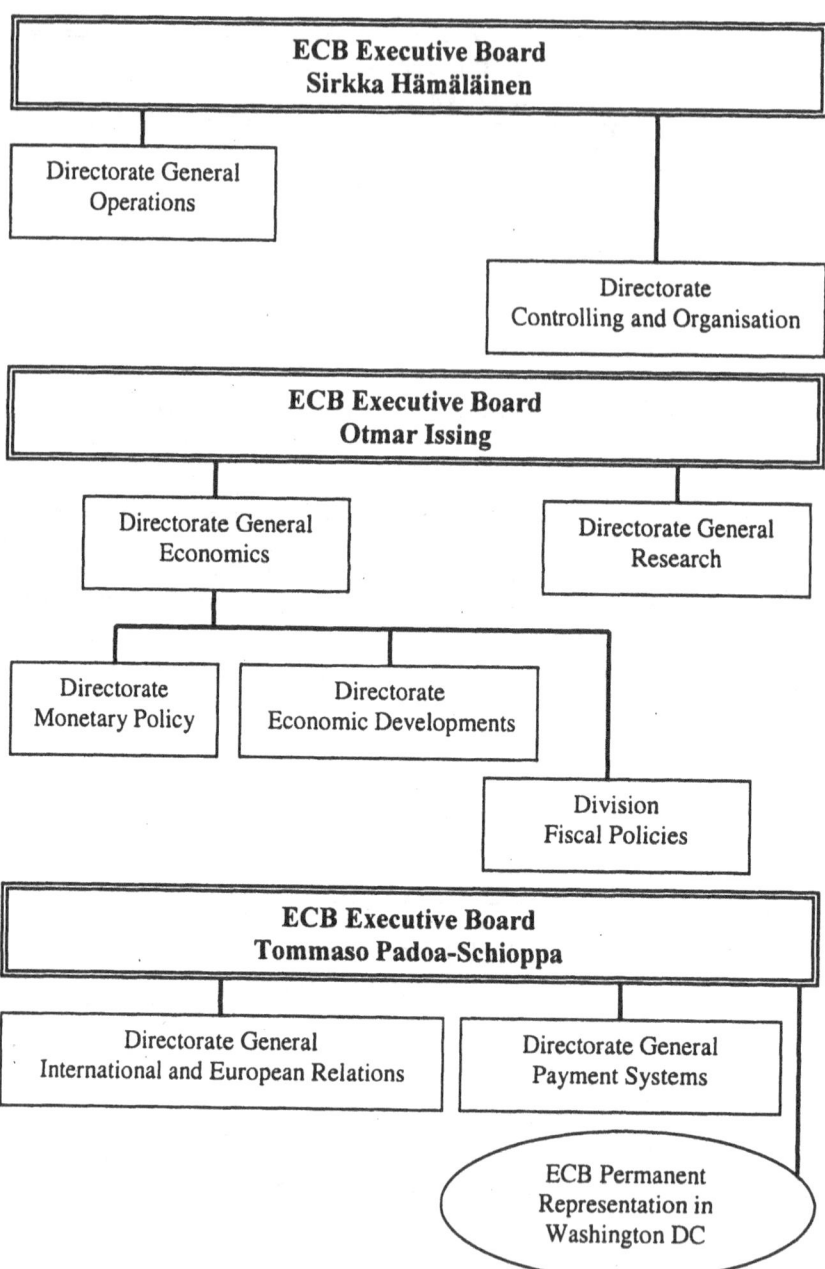

Figure 3.2 (continued)

By August 31 the ECB had approximately 1020 employees, distributed on a number of Directorates General, Directorates and Divisions. Besides the permanent organization, there are a number of ESCB committees[46] that consist of officials from the ECB and the 12 national banks (when the task groups discuss themes that also affect the three outsider EU Member States, they are invited to participate in the work). These task groups are established when the Governing Council believes that there is a need to discuss a theme more thoroughly. The President is usually an official from the ECB who also functions as secretariat for the task groups. The only task group which is explicitly mentioned in the text is the Committee for the Prevention of Fraud. That is a clear signal to the public that the ECB does not want the same (fatal) problems as the EU Commission had under Jacques Santer.

There is a very large parallelism in the way that the other institutions of the ECB and the EU are organized. In the following sections I turn to the role of the EU-institutions in relation to the ESCB.

The European Council

As argued elsewhere[47] it is possible to regard the Union as an embryonic state where the Council of Ministers is a form of government, especially when it meets as the European Council 4-6 times a year. In other states of a federal nature the Government has the whole or a part of the overall responsibility for the country's economic and monetary policy, cf. the country's constitution.

Article 4 (TEU) gives the European Union a very powerful position: 'The European Council shall provide the Union with the necessary impetus for its development and shall define the general political guidelines thereof'.

Practice has shown that the 'general political guidelines' can be very detailed. With regard to the economic policy the European Council has a very clear mandate:[48]

> The European Council shall, acting on basis of this report from the Council [here ECOFIN], discuss a conclusion on the broad guidelines of the economic policies of the Member States and of the Community.

With regard to the monetary part of the EMU, the fundamental idea was that it had to be safeguarded by the ESCB without 'political intervention'. As mentioned before, the powers of the European Council are officially confined to appoint the management for the ECB. However, as economic and monetary policies to a large extent interact, it is not realistic to believe that there will not be a form of mutual interaction. It has often been pointed out that the objectives confirmed by the treaties concerning a high level of employment and low inflation will not always be compatible. The European Council – especially in a social democratic composition as today (year 2002) – will have a tendency to give a high priority to employment and adjust the economic policy accordingly, as indicated by e.g. the decision to launch the Employment Pact at Cologne 1999, and by creating the so-called Lisbon process (began March 2000). It is therefore not entirely unrealistic that these two institutions can pursue opposite policies without the possibility of stopping them – with unintentional consequences. The interaction between 'Government' and 'Central Bank' lacks a 'conciliation procedure'.

Council of Ministers: ECOFIN and the EURO 12 Group

When the Council of Ministers meets in its composition of Minister of Economic Affairs and Ministers of Finance, the meetings are called ECOFIN meetings. This composition has a number of tasks in connection with the EMU as the Council is responsible for setting out the EU's broad, macroeconomic lines[49] or rather it is responsible for preparing proposals for the European Council and concretizing its decisions. Naturally, such decisions also have implications for the EMU, and for the ESCB. Besides the overall economic guidelines, ECOFIN also has a number of tasks that are directly related to supervision, among other things, whether the individual Member States behave responsibly with regard to the EMU, and if not the use of Article 99.4 (TEU):

> Where it is established [...] that the economic policies of a Member State are not consistent with the broad guidelines [... or that they risk jeopardising the proper functioning of the Economic and Monetary Union], the Council may [...] make the necessary recommendations to the Member State concerned. [...]

As regards economic and monetary issues on an international level, the Council has the power to negotiate and enter into agreements with third countries and international organizations.

The Council negotiates after having consulted the Commission and the ECB who are bound by the negotiating result obtained by the Council.[50] For example, the Council can, after having heard the recommendation of the Commission or the ECB, enter into formal agreements on an exchange rate system for the euro towards non-community currencies. If there are no exchange rate systems, the Council can prepare general guidelines for the monetary policy in relation to these currencies (Art. 111.1 & 2, TEU). Moreover, the Council can negotiate agreements on monetary questions with several third countries or international organizations.

Buiter considers this a potential threat to the substance of the ECB's independence, and mentions that it gave Oskar Lafontaine and Dominique Strauss-Kahn a possibility to suggest exchange rate target zones.[51] Still, the European Council in Luxembourg, December 1997, decided, however, that the Council only was to set out the general guidelines in exceptional cases. Therefore, it was decided to limit the Council's right to 'interfere' in the monetary policy, thus disarming Buiter's fears.

Besides the mentioned tasks, there will of course be a number of other issues that are significant, either directly or indirectly, to the EMU. The Cologne process is especially important in this connection. As mentioned before, the Cologne summit in June 1999 decided that the dialogue between the ECB and the Council of Ministers had to be strengthened. ECOFIN and the Council of Ministers of labor and social ministers were commissioned to hold a meeting twice a year with the purpose of promoting the macroeconomic dialogue, together with the ECB, the Commission, and the labor market parties. This development has strengthened ECOFIN and especially the Euro 12 Group a lot in the whole EU hierarchy.

There was no institutional problem with regard to ECOFIN and the EMU as long as all EU Member States were presumed to be members of the EMU, but in the present situation it has occasioned political controversies. Great Britain, for instance, has insisted that all ECOFIN themes, including those specifically relating to the EMU, and non-EMU members were to have full participation in decision making, among other things, from the point of view that the EMU as a real existing factor would affect the whole EU and not only the EMU countries. This attitude was not accepted by the EMU member countries which insisted on their right to decide themselves. The 'compromise' from December 1997 was a triumph for the EMU countries that were permitted to hold 'Euro 11 meetings'.[52]

The Presidency's conclusion from the Luxembourg council are very obliging towards the Euro Group:[53]

> The Ministers of the States participating in the euro area may meet informally among themselves to discuss issues connected with their shared specific responsibilities for the single currency. The Commission, and the European Central Bank when appropriate, will be invited to take part in the meetings.

During these meetings general themes as well as the euro zone's relations to 'external parties', the three Member States and the surrounding world, were discussed.

Contrary to the original idea (officially at least), the agenda has been extended drastically, and the *gremium* has discussed structural and social policies. The Governor of the ECB as well as the Governors of national central banks participate in most of the meetings which gives the meetings a very important consulting and coordinating function. Basically, the preliminary meeting should only discuss and consult and leave the decisions to be made after a renewed discussion at the ordinary ECOFIN meeting. However, it does not take too much imagination to picture that when the 12 euro states, and the Governor of the ECB and the Governors of the national central banks, have agreed on an position, it will be very difficult for the three outsider countries to change it at the subsequent meeting. The only three things that speak in favor of the possibility of altering a consensus that has already been obtained are:

1) Great Britain's economic and monetary weight in the actual EU system;
2) that Germany and the Netherlands do not want the Euro-12 to develop into a *gouvernement économique* which could threaten the independence of the ECB, and;
3) the general ethos in the Council of Ministers that each others' desires and problems are to a large extent taken into consideration.

Still, this does not change the fact that the Euro-12 is a very important, properly the most important forum for coordination between the ECB and the 12 EMU states. Nugent wrote that the Euro 12 meetings are not well-defined[54] and that it is a relatively new process which can still be developed in various directions. Three years later, there are clear signs of formalization and institutionalization so that it is correct to talk about a new (informal) institution which competes with the ordinary ECOFIN meeting, and in certain situations even outdoes it.

Smaghi and Casini concludes the following:[55]

> The Euro-11, created to develop informal discussions between the finance ministers of the Member States adopting the euro, the ECB and the European Commission, actually represents the most important forum for dialogue and for discussion on macroeconomic items in the euro-zone.

The Economic and Financial Committee

As mentioned before, especially the French Government wanted a political counterweight towards the very strong ESCB, among other things, from the point of view that the ESCB's objects clause to pursue a low inflationary policy could lead to unwanted consequences, e.g. with regard to the employment policy. The strong French desire was not met due to German opposition. Still, France has declared that both ECOFIN and the Economic and Financial Committee[56] could be the seeds of such a counterweight.

The Economic and Financial Committee is fundamentally a task group under the Council of Ministers like many others. However, it is a very special task group. Firstly, it is mentioned in the TEU (Art. 114.2) where it receives its mandate, and secondly, its members were originally imagined to be high-ranking persons, two from each country (one from the board of the national central bank and a permanent secretary from the Ministry of Finance), and two from the ECB and the Commission respectively.

The Economic and Financial Committee has the following tasks:[57]

- to deliver opinions at the request of the Council or the Commission, or on its own initiative for submission to those institutions;
- to keep under review the economic and financial situation of the Member States and of the Community and to report regularly thereon to the Council and to the Commission, in particular on financial relations with third countries and international institutions;
- [...] to contribute to the preparation of the work of the Council [...];
- to examine at least once a year the situation regarding the movement of capital and the freedom of payments, as they result from the application of the Treaties and of measures adopted by the Council [...].

Clearly, the committee can carry out a potentially important control and coordination function within a very broad framework. Add to this that the committee prepares the meetings in the Euro 12 Group (this means that the three outsider countries are well-informed on the agenda at the meetings of the Euro 12 Group although they have not any influence on the substance), and that it also prepares the Unions participation in G-7 meetings. With the members who were originally intended for the committee, it goes without saying that it could have been a potentially powerful instrument for nation state control with the ESCB in general and the ECB in particular. However, it was not the Governors of the national central banks who got a seat on the committee, but their deputies or their deputies. Likewise, the ECB does not send its President. One of the reasons why the committee is not to be regarded as the seed of a political control body at present is that Germany, for instance, will not allow the national Ministers of Finance to interfere in the monetary policy and that it does not wish to undermine the independence of the ECB. Still, the EFC is an important forum for exchanging views on the economic policy of the Member States and it gives the ECB a possibility to contribute to the discussion.

As a result of the Cologne process the committee was charged with the extra task of preparing 'the macroeconomic dialogue'. In collaboration with the Employment and Labour Market Committee and the labor market parties (the ECB and the Commission are already members of the committee), the technical sides of the dialogue are planned and discussed.

The EU Commission

The Commission plays an important, but not prestigious, part in connection with the EMU. In connection with the economic policy it has already been mentioned that ECOFIN submits a proposal to the European Council. This proposal is based on a recommendation from the Commission.[58]

In addition to that, the Commission functions as a 'watch dog' towards the Member States. The Commission is to monitor the economic development in the individual Member States and report to the Council.[59] If it turns out that a Member State's economic policy is not compatible with the general guidelines set out by the European Council, or if there is a risk that a Member State's economic policy jeopardizes the EMU, the Commission must recommend to the Council that it should consider the matter.[60] This monitoring function also applies to the monetary area[61] where the Commission is to keep a special eye on the Member States' budget situation. If the Member States do not observe the budget discipline, the Commission writes a report to the Council of Ministers which is to act accordingly.

The European Parliament

The European Parliament, the Union's democratic 'element', has no direct powers with regard to the EMU and is not represented in e.g. the Economic and Financial Committee.[62] However, it has a right to be informed and consulted which commits the Council, the Commission, and the ECB to keep the EP informed of what is going on with regard to the EMU and in some cases consult it. The president of the ECB has indicated to the EP that he is willing to appear four times a year before the Parliament additional to the one obligatory appearance. This must be considered a gesture indicating a certain wish to acknowledge the Parliament as the EU's democratic body and could be considered a stretched out hand for further collaboration.

Conclusion

The Economic and Monetary Union has entered into its third and final phase which means that the exchange rates between the participating Member States have been definitively pegged to one another, and a European System of Central Banks has been established with the purpose of deciding and implementing the Union's monetary policy. For this task a number of institutional arrangements have been established, especially for the monetary policy, but the economic policy is to an increasing extent becoming involved too. The EMU as a 'policy area' has become large and complex and has contact surfaces with a number of institutions.

When so many instances are involved in a system like the Economic and Monetary Union, the question of coordination and interaction arises, and we have already mentioned it a couple of times. The relevance of this question is increased when the political and economic extent of the whole project is so large as is the case here. In addition, but outside the scope of this analysis, the question of the democratic control of the whole EMU project emerges.[63]

If one only looks at the monetary side of the EMU, it is evident that the ESCB has been able to create an efficient institutional system that functions within the parameters laid down in the TEU. The basis for the large independence of the ESCB and the ECB is the political desire to ensure a stable price development, i.e. low inflation. In that connection both Mitrany's suspicious nature towards politicians and the diplomats' ability to think of anything but the national interest,[64] and the convenience, for politicians, of being able to disclaim the responsibility for any unpopular decisions are felt.

However, the establishment of the Euro-12 Group as a result of the three countries that are not forming part of the EMU's third phase has been an institutional half measure with political consequences. The establishment of the Euro-12 Group has led to a new 'unofficial' forum being created of an institutional nature with great power and not subject to the same rules as a 'normal' ECOFIN meeting. The meetings of the Group imply a real risk of undermining the ECOFIN meetings as there is a tendency to use them for coordinating other policy areas than those originally planned.

Formally, there is no great need for coordination between the Council of Ministers and the ECB. The ECB must ensure a low inflation independently. But in reality it is difficult to isolate monetary policy from the rest of economic policy. But it is indeed a heavy task to try to coordinate the economic policy of 15 states with the monetary policy of the ECB. The first compliance with this fact could be seen in the establishment of the Economic and Financial Committee which hierarchically is arranged as a task group under COREPER, but potentially can exert influence on the level with COREPER. The question was whether the tasks of this committee confirmed by the treaties were 'enough' to ensure the necessary coordination in the whole EMU structure. Developments until 'Cologne 1999' shows that this was not the case. There was an obvious need to ensure a dialogue and coordination of the 'E' and the 'M' in the EMU. The European Council in Cologne took the consequence and created a forum for discussion between the Council, the Commission, an the ECB social partners.[65] As mentioned before, the background was an economic crisis; and a crisis is what it takes to see whether the structure holds. As the situation is today – 2002 – one can stress the following trends:

- that the interaction between the Council of Ministers, the Commission and the ESCB has increased;
- that there is no indication that this interaction will not be intensified (it has to);
- that the simple institutional 'set-up' functions, but also that: 'The degree of dialogue and cooperation between budgetary and monetary authorities prevailing in EMU seems to be inferior to the one existing within most countries before EMU'.[66] This implies that there is room for improvement;
- that the economic part of the EMU has developed and will continue to do so.

This leads to the assumption, that the informal structures already developed will have to be formalized – as was the case with the EPC and the CFSP. The trick will be to secure the independence of the ECB on the one hand, and at the same time the coordination of the economic and monetary policy of the Union on the other.

Notes

1. The author would like to thank a number of senior officials for their kind assistance. I respect their wish for anonymity. Likewise, the author thanks Poul Thøis Madsen for his comments on this chapter.
2. 'The fusion [of economic functions] would compel nations to fuse their sovereignty into that of a single European state', 3 April 1952.
3. According to an old member of the committee these plans never succeeded, among other things because the German Federal Bank neither wanted nor was allowed to commit itself to others.
4. Resolution of 8-9 February 1971 submitted by the Council and representatives of the Member States' Governments concerning the phased implementation of The Economic and Monetary Union, Forlaget Mikro (1972: 64).
5. (1999: 195).
6. Ministry of Economic Affairs (1990: 12).
7. The German Federal Bank's Council (1991).
8. Cf. also the statement of Helmut Kohl in the introduction of this book.
9. Federal Chancellor Schröder in the German Federal Diet, 10 November 1998.
10. In the European Parliament, 13 October 1999.
11. See Communication from the Commission: Strategic Objectives 2000-2005, Shaping the New Europe (COM 2000, 154 final).
12. The latter aspect was stressed by Mrs Hämäläinen, member of the Executive Board of the ECB in a speech at the Finnish Culture Institute in Stockholm, 12 February, 2001: 'Globalization has increased competition in all areas, including areas which traditionally are under the direct control of governments, [...]. European integration can be seen as one way of trying, in a healthy and coordinated manner, to counter-balance the growing pressure from market forces'.
13. This realization followed after a decade of frustration for various French Governments which all had pressed for giving the EU a *'gouvernement economique'* to ensure political coordination and control of the economic and monetary policy. These attempts were met by German opposition regularly. The only way to coordinate European monetary policy was, cf. high-ranking officials, to follow The German Federal Bank.
14. Nugent (1999: 332).
15. Phase 2 meant, among other things, that the national central banks were to be secured independence and monetary financing of budget deficits was to stop.
16. Phase 3 laid down, among other things, that the exchange rates were pegged irrevocably to one another, that the monetary policy was transferred to ESCB and that a common currency was introduced at the beginning of 2000.
17. Actually it was two parallel conferences, but the result was one treaty: The Maastricht Treaty.
18. Protocol (no. 4) to the Treaty on the European Union, on the Statute for the European Monetary Institute.
19. The composition of the Executive Board reflects the conditions in terms of practical politics in the EU; the four great powers that participate in the EMU's third phase all have a seat (France, Italy, Spain, and Germany). According to senior officials there is no reason to assume that Great Britain would not get a seat on the Executive Board if the country was to decide to participate. This means that there will be one seat left for a representative of a small state.
20. For a discussion of the consequences of the Stability Pact and, for that matter, the political consequences of the EMU, see Madsen & Plaschke (1998).
21. See Nugent (1999: 79).

22 Council Resolution 97/C236/02.
23 DN: DOC/97/23 and DN: DOC/97/24.
24 See DUPI (2000: 82).
25 C/999/1500.
26 Council/99/999.
27 Until it became clear how many states participated in the EMU's third phase, it was called the Euro X Group. When it became evident that 11 states participated, the name was changed to the Euro 11 Group; with Greece's membership, the name was changed to the Euro 12 Group; it is also referred to simply as the Euro Group.
28 TEU Art. 105.1 'The main objective of ESCB is to maintain price stability [...]'.
29 Duisenberg's statement delivered to the European Parliament 3 July, 2001.
30 TEU Art. 2.
31 TEU Art. 105.2.
32 Economists are discussing the dominant role of monetary policy, especially the administration of the money supply. Economists inspired by monetarism have a tendency to attach great importance to the development in the money supply, whereas Keynesian-inspired economists tend towards giving its importance a lower priority. Reference is made to the Council of European Policy's account of the economic aspects of the EMU.
33 TEU Art 105 & 111.
34 TEU Art 105.
35 TEU Art 105.
36 TEU Art. 213.2.
37 In the Danish central administration there is a persistent rumor abroad to the effect that the National Bank of Denmark does not do anything drastic without consulting the Ministry of Economy. It is worth noting, however, that the Minister and the Governor of the National Bank speak to each other as peers. If the rumor is true, the National Bank would, on the one hand, strengthen its independence on a national level after a possible Danish accession to the EMU, but at the same time be subject to the ECB (cf. De Haan & Eijffinger's analysis (2000)).
38 For a discussion of the ECB's independence, see De Haan & Eijffinger (2000).
39 A solution to this problem would be – although it is difficult for a bank – to implement rigorous transparency, possibly in the form of public lists of which meetings that high-ranking ECB officials participate in. But with the Buiter–Issing exchange in memory this does not seem likely (Buiter, 1999; Issing, 1999).
40 Art 45, Statute of the European System of Central Banks and of the European Central Bank.
41 Protocol no. 3 on the statute for the European System of Central Banks and the European Central Bank, Art. 12.1.
42 DN: DOC/97/24, annex 1: 'The Council should therefor play its full part in exploiting the channels of communication provided by the Treaty. The President of the Council. using his position under Article 109b of the Treaty, should report to the Governing Council of the ECB on the Council's assessment of the economic situation of the Union and on economic policies of the Member States and could discuss with the ECB the views of the Council on exchange-rate developments and prospects.'
43 (2000: 382).
44 This fear has not been confirmed (see below as well as Plaschke in this book). Buiter comments on the appointment process that it is quite natural that it is political, but regrettably that it turned out to be national interests prevailing and not European (1999: 185).

45 Cf. 'Rules of Procedure of the European Central Bank', Articles 12 & 13.
46 Rules of Procedure of the European Central Bank, Article 9.
47 See e.g. Dosenrode & Dosenrode (2001) and chapter 11 in this book.
48 Art. 99.2.
49 Cf. TEU Art. 99.2.
50 TEU Art. 111, especially (3) and (4).
51 (1999: 190).
52 The idea of the Euro 11 Group (now Euro 12 Group) came from Theo Waigel, German Minister of Finance, in 1995, but was abandoned again. It was re-launched by French Minister of Finance Arthuis in 1996 in the form of a 'stability council', an idea that was received with scepticism as it had to have political powers. However, the states involved agreed to continue to negotiate the idea. The outcome was the Euro 11 Group with not quite as many far-reaching powers as requested by the French.
53 DOC/97/24, point 60.
54 Nugent (1999: 294).
55 (2000: 383).
56 In the transition period this committee was called 'The Advisory Monetary Committee'.
57 TEU Art. 114.2.
58 TEU Art. 99.2.
59 TEU Art. 99.3.
60 TEU Art. 99.4.
61 TEU Art. 104.
62 Buiter discusses among other things the legitimacy of the EMU and concludes (1999: 200): 'It is essential, however, that the European Parliament act as an effective watchdog over the ECB. The legitimacy of the ECB will depend on the extent to which it is effectively accountable to the European Parliament'. See also De Haan & Eijffinger (2000), and Kelstrup and Plaschke in this book.
63 Reference is made to Chapters 5-8 in this book.
64 David Mitrany is the founder of 'functionalism' and the inspiration for Jean Monnet, among others. His most important work was 'A Working Peace System', Chicago (1943).
65 C/99/1500, point 19.
66 Smaghi & Casini (2000: 388).

References

Birkelbach, Davignon og Werner Rapporterne – Aldo Moros erklæring (1972): København: Forlaget Mikro.

Buiter, Willem H. (1999): 'Alice in Euroland', *Journal of Common Market Studies*, vol. 37, no. 2, June, pp. 181-209.

C/99/1500 (1999): *Presidency Conclusions Cologne European Council 3 and 4 June 1999.*

Conseil/99/999 (1999): *Presidency Conclusions Helsinki European Council 10 and 11 December 1999.*

Council Resolution 97/C236/02.

de Haan, Jakob & Sylvester C. W. Eijffinger (2000): 'The Democratic Accountability of the European Central Bank', *Journal of Common Market Studies*, vol. 38, no. 3, September, pp. 393-408.

DN: DOC/97/23 *Extraordinary European Council Meeting on Employment Luxembourg, 20 and 21 November 1997 – Presidency Conclusions.*

DN: DOC/97/24 *Luxembourg European Council 12 and 13 December 1997 – Presidency Conclusions.*

Dosenrode, Søren & Andrea Dosenrode (2001): Den Europæiske Stat – Nogle Refleksioner, *Økonomi & Politik*, vol. 74, no. 2, June.

DUPI (2000): *Udviklingen i EU siden 1992 på de områder, der er omfattet af de danske forbehold*, København.

Hämäläinen, Sirkka (2001): 'The euro and European integration', speech delivered at the Finish Culture Institute in Stockholm, February 12.

Issing, Otmar (1999): 'The Eurosystem: Transparent and Accountable or 'Willem in Euroland'?', *Journal of Common Market Studies*, vol. 37, no. 3, September, pp. 503-20.

Issing, Otmar (2001): 'The Monetary Union in a globalised world', speech delivered at Second Vienna Globalization Symposium, Institut für den Donauraum und Mitteleuropa, Wirtschaftskammer Österreich, Wien 11. Mai.

Madsen, Poul Thøis & Henrik Plaschke (1998): *Den Forbudte Debat om ØMU'en*, Århus: Rådet for Europæisk Politik & Systime.

McCormick, John (1999): *Understanding the European Union – A Concise Introduction*, London: Macmillan Press.

Ministry of Economic Affairs, see Økonomiministeriet.

Mitrany, David (1943): *A Working Peace System*, Chicago: Quadrangle Books.

Nugent, Neill (1999): *The Government and Politics of the European Union*, Fourth Edition, London: Macmillan Press.

Report by the ECOFIN Council to the European Council in Helsinki on Economic Policy Co-ordination (1999): *Review of Instruments and Experiences in Stage 3 of EMU.*

Smaghi, Lorenzo Bini & Claudio Casini (2000): 'Monetary and Fiscal Policy Co-operation in EMU', *Journal of Common Market Studies*, vol. 38, no. 3, September, pp. 375-92.

Trichet, Jean-Claude (2001): 'The Euro after Two Years', *Journal of Common Market Studies*, vol. 39, no. 1, March, pp. 1-14.

Werner (1972): see Birkelbach.

Økonomiministeriet (1990): Konference om Økonomisk og Monetær Union, Christiansborg den 3. maj 1990, Juni 1990, København: Forlaget J. H. Schultz Information.

Økonomiministeriet & Finansministeriet (2000): *Danmark og Euroen*, København.

Part II

The EMU and the Dynamics of European Integration

4 EMU and the Dynamics of European Integration
LOUKAS TSOUKALIS

On 1 January 1999, eleven countries of the EU (Austria, Belgium, Finland, France, FR Germany, Ireland, Italy, Luxembourg, the Netherlands, Portugal and Spain) entered the final stage of EMU, which led in 2002 to the replacement of the national currencies by the euro. They were joined by Greece on 1 January 2001. The participation of the remaining three countries of the Union, namely Denmark, Sweden and the UK, will depend on the outcome of referenda to be held in each country, the UK being expected to decide last.

EMU promises to be one of the most important events – arguably, the most important – in the history of European integration, with extensive economic and political ramifications (cf. e.g. Dyson in this book). If anything, it could, perhaps, be compared to the common foreign and security policy (CFSP) – money and defense being the two main attributes of national sovereignty. And we would then need to explain why monetary integration has reached the final (and irreversible?) stage, while the CFSP still remains more of a procedure than a policy.

Monetary integration in Europe has a long and checkered history, starting with the very cautious handling of monetary matters by the authors of the Treaty of Rome and ending (?) with the complete transfer of power in the conduct of monetary policy to the European level. Money has always been highly political and it has also been frequently used as an instrument for wider political objectives, even though markets and economic fundamentals have not always obliged by adjusting themselves to the exigencies of high politics. It may prove different this time round.

The Early History[1]

The first twenty years after the establishment of the European Economic Community (EEC) in 1958 were characterized by much talk and little action as regards monetary policy. The debate did, however, help to prepare the ground for the more substantial phase of monetary integration, which started with the setting up of the European Monetary System (EMS) in 1979.

The Treaty of Rome contained very little in terms of binding constraints in the field of macroeconomic policy. There was clearly no intention to set up a regional currency bloc. The Bretton Woods system provided the international framework and the US dollar the undisputed monetary standard. Moreover, Keynesianism was still at its peak. This meant that national governments were zealous in retaining the independence of their monetary and fiscal policies for the pursuit of domestic economic objectives, and a heavy armory of capital controls was considered as an acceptable price to pay for this independence.

Interest in monetary integration grew during the 1960s, largely in response to the increasing instability in the international system and the perceived need to insulate Europe from the vagaries of the US dollar. The French were more sensitive to those problems than the other Europeans, who were not keen on a confrontation with the United States. This complicated matters and helped to confine notions of a European interest to a general debate which remained far short of any kind of serious action by the Six. In any case the EEC lived under the illusion of having a *de facto* monetary union, during a relatively long period of unchanged exchange rates. The illusion was further strengthened by the setting up of the common agricultural policy (CAP), which was predicated on common prices across the EEC. This was a typical example of trying to put the cart before the horse.

The situation seemed to change in December 1969, when the political leaders of the Six adopted for the first time the target of a complete EMU. It was a political decision reached at the highest level, and it was directly linked to the first enlargement of the Community and the further deepening of integration. It was also the first important example of a Franco-German initiative, involving President Pompidou and Chancellor Brandt, although the common basis of this initiative proved subsequently to be very fragile. The negotiations which followed revealed the existence of a broad, even though superficial, agreement about the contents of the final stage, and little agreement about how to get there.

Solemn decisions were then taken at the highest level. They did not, however, prove strong enough to survive the adverse economic conditions of the 1970s. EMU became the biggest non-event of the decade.[2] The collapse of the Bretton Woods system brought down with it the fragile European edifice. Fixed exchange rates, with narrow margins of fluctuation, which had been seen as the most concrete manifestation of the first stage of EMU, proved incompatible with increasingly divergent economic policies and inflation rates. Thus, political commitments, taken at the very top and usually not translated into the appropriate economic policies, finally gave way under market pressure. After 1974, what was left of the ambitious plan for EMU was only a mutilated snake (the term used for the EC system of exchange rates) wriggling its way in the chaotic zoo of international exchange markets.

Despite the serious setbacks suffered in the attempt to move towards EMU in the 1970s, interest in the subject never disappeared. The minisnake was generally considered as only a temporary arrangement which would be improved and extended when the economic conditions became more favorable. It was succeeded by the EMS in March 1979, the product of another Franco-German initiative, from which only the British decided to abstain.

The EMS was a renewed attempt to establish a system of fixed, even though periodically adjustable, exchange rates between EC currencies. Concern about the proper functioning of the common market was combined with the desire to preserve common agricultural prices and thus do away with the system of monetary compensatory amounts. On the other hand, the initiative for the creation of the EMS was linked to the expectation that there would be no substantial reform of the international monetary system, and hence no prospect of a return to some form of exchange rate stability in the future.

Exchange rate stability was to be backed by an increased convergence between national economies, with the emphasis clearly placed on inflation rates. The EMS was considered as an important instrument in the fight against inflation, and its creation meant an implicit acceptance by the other EC governments of German policy priorities. The experience of the 1970s was seen as validating the German combination of an uncompromising anti-inflationary stance combined with a strong currency option. The EMS was also intended as a defensive mechanism against US 'benign neglect' as regards the dollar.

Last but not least, the EMS was directly linked to the wider project of European integration. It was seen as a means of strengthening Europe economically and politically through closer cooperation, at a time when

US leadership was seen as waning. Once again, monetary integration was partly – and in a rather vague manner – used by its supporters as an instrument for political ends; and this largely explains why the British chose to stay out.

The EMS prepared the ground for the much more ambitious project of EMU. Between 1979 and 1992, when hell broke loose in exchange markets, it was characterized by an increasing stability of exchange rates.[3] Greater stability in nominal intra-ERM exchange rates was achieved largely through a gradually accelerating convergence of inflation rates downwards. Price convergence and intra-ERM exchange rate stability relied basically on monetary policies and the almost exclusive use of short-term interest rates for exchange rate stabilization purposes. Price convergence, coupled with the growing credibility of stability-oriented policies, brought about the gradual convergence of nominal long-term interest rates downwards.

The ERM operated for many years as a system of fixed, but adjustable, exchange rates. Adjustments, soon the product of collective decisions, became smaller and less frequent as price convergence grew. Central banks made use of a combination of different instruments whenever bilateral exchange rates came under attack. Those instruments included changes in short-term interest rates, foreign exchange interventions, and capital controls, especially in countries such as France and Italy, which were later to abandon this policy instrument in the context of liberalization. Realignments were usually considered as an instrument of last resort. The everyday management of the system was left to central bankers, relying as much on informal networks as on established EC institutions and committees, and most notably the Committee of Governors of Central Banks.

Monetary stability was, however, also directly linked to the asymmetrical nature of the EMS. Despite special provisions, such as the creation of the divergence indicator intended precisely to prevent this, the EMS operated all along in an asymmetrical fashion, thus following the earlier example of the snake. The asymmetry of the EMS related in turn to the central role of the *Deutschmark* (DM). Asymmetry in a system of fixed (even if periodically adjustable) exchange rates is manifested in terms of an unequal distribution of the burden of intervention and adjustment, and also of influence in the setting of policy priorities.

However, asymmetry is not always bad, at least in economic terms. The EMS enabled countries, such as Italy, with a weak track record in terms of monetary stability, to borrow credibility by pegging their currencies to the DM. Participation in the ERM thus provided a convenient external constraint and strengthened the hand of institutions and interest groups inside countries fighting for less inflationary policies. This largely explains the popularity of the system with most central bankers, contrary to their earlier expectations. On the other hand, the asymmetry of the EMS became less acceptable in times of recession and growing unemployment, when the other European countries tended to adopt a less benign view of German leadership.

EMU: The Primacy of High Politics

The debate on EMU was initially revived by the single market, although no binding commitment had been undertaken in the Single European Act (SEA). An attempt was made, mostly by the Commission, to present EMU as the logical continuation of the single market program, with exchange rates as another non-tariff barrier to be eliminated. This was another example of the neo-functionalist strategy and the logic of spill-over. In the late 1980s, the EMS was still remarkably stable and Euro-euphoria was at its peak; hence the urgency felt in some European circles to win political commitment to the next stage of integration while the conditions remained favorable.

Monetary union would be the final and irrevocable confirmation of the reality of the single European market, and of a unified European economy. A common currency was seen as the means of welding national economies together; but also, very importantly, the means of accelerating the movement towards political union. And then came the breakdown of the old political division of the European continent, bringing down with it the communist regimes in Central and Eastern Europe as well as the disintegration of the Soviet Union. It also brought with it the unification of Germany, which finally acted as a powerful driving force for EMU.

For many people in Paris and Brussels in particular, the change of the European political scene called for a stronger Community and also a Community which would provide a stable and secure framework for a larger Germany. Money once again served as the main instrument. Wider balance of power considerations were thus added to what used to be an old and deep French concern with the asymmetrical character of the existing EMS, while most of the other EU countries had apparently reconciled themselves with the limitations on their monetary sovereignty.

Earlier initiatives in the field of European monetary integration had been largely motivated by external preoccupations; the instability of the dollar and US policies of 'unbenign neglect' had served as powerful federalizing factors in Europe. This was not true of the various initiatives which finally led to the new treaty provisions adopted at Maastricht for the establishment of EMU – or, at least, not to the same extent as in the past. True, the reform of the monetary system was not on the cards and the lack of unity among European countries remained an important factor behind the asymmetry in the international system. But this asymmetry was now less evident, the US Administration did not adopt the aggressive stance of its predecessors, and intra-ERM exchange rates appeared at the time less vulnerable to the gyrations of the dollar. Perhaps less preoccupation with external factors was also a sign of the new collective confidence of the Europeans.

The decision to liberalize capital movements, taken in 1998 as part of the single market program and also a long-established German precondition for any progress towards EMU, provided the catalyst. The combination of fixed exchange rates and free capital movements meant that national monetary autonomy would have to be abandoned.[4] This is also the main argument on which the Commission strategy was later based: another example of the Commission trying to make full use of functional spill-over.

Money was thus once again at the center of European high politics and commitment to monetary union was almost indistinguishable from the more general commitment to European unification. The second intergovernmental conference (IGC) on political union, called in June 1990, was directly linked to the EMU project. During the negotiations, the economic and political desirability of EMU was not seriously put in question. This matter was supposed to have been already settled. The political decision had been taken at the highest political level, and only British representatives were ready to express their doubts in public. The other doubters, and they did exist in significant numbers in the other countries, kept a low profile. They preferred to concentrate on specific problems instead of challenging the main principles and objectives. After all, much of the work had already been done by committees of experts. There was very little public debate on the subject of EMU prior to the signing of the Treaty, and one important reason was that it was still considered a matter for the *cognoscenti*.

The driving force for the re-launching of monetary union came from Paris, and to a lesser extent, Rome and Brussels. French governments had always been in favor of fixed exchange rates. They had never believed in the stability or efficiency of financial markets, which were often caricatured as a den of Anglo-Saxon speculators. For France, the move towards a complete EMU would help to end the asymmetrical nature of the existing system and would therefore secure for the country a stronger say in the collective conduct of European monetary policy. Last but not least, money provided the instrument for integrating the German giant more tightly into the Community system. Those objectives were largely shared by the Italians. As for the Commission, under the Presidency of Delors, it saw in EMU the consolidation of the internal market and the further strengthening of European political construction. It was the inevitable next step in the process of integration. The Commission provided valuable support, even though it played only a very limited role during the actual negotiations.

Initially, the Germans showed very little enthusiasm: the government and the central bank were happy with the status quo and any move towards monetary union was perceived, quite rightly, as leading to the erosion of Germany's independence in the monetary field. In purely economic terms, there was in fact precious little advantage for the Germans in a monetary union, assuming, of course, that some kind of a regional currency arrangement which helps to contain the overvaluation of the DM can be taken for granted. For most of the period of the EMS, the main gain for the Germans was the stability of exchange rates for approximately half of the country's external trade and the gain in competitiveness. This has always been a very important consideration, clearly more important for politicians and industrialists than for central bankers. On the other hand, there is no doubt that an EMS in which Germany sets the monetary standard was infinitely better for the Germans than a monetary union in which they would have to share with others the power to run monetary policy.

What finally tipped the balance was the perceived need to reaffirm the country's commitment to European integration in the wake of German unification. This is how the matter was presented in Paris. Thus, the German decision (Chancellor Kohl's to be precise) to proceed with EMU was highly political. Mr Kohl spoke of economic and monetary integration as a matter 'of war and peace in the 21st century';[5] and this statement is indicative of his approach to the subject. The combination of different factors, namely the relative weight of the country, its high reputation in terms of monetary stability, especially among European central bankers, and its strong preference for the status quo, strengthened enormously the negotiating power of Germany, thus enabling it in most cases to impose its own terms with respect to the transition and the contents of the final stage of EMU.[6]

Once a Franco-German agreement had been reached on the subject of EMU, the process appeared almost unstoppable, thus repeating earlier patterns of European decision-making. Italy was supportive, and it also provided much of the intellectual input. The Dutch shared much of the economic scepticism of the Germans, but their margin of maneuver was extremely limited. Belgium and Luxembourg were fervent supporters, although Belgium was at the same time extremely concerned in case a strict application of the convergence criteria kept it outside the privileged group, because of its very high public debt. Denmark felt almost like a natural member of the European currency area, although its politicians were not at all sure whether they would be able to carry the population with them into a monetary union; hence the 'opt-out' protocol.

The main concern of the other Southern countries was to link EMU to more substantial budgetary transfers and also to avoid an institutionalization of two or more tiers in the Community. As for Ireland, it benefited from the transfers and felt more secure than its Southern brethren that it would be among the first to obtain an entry ticket into the final stage. It would, however, have preferred that the other island separating it from the continent would also join since so much of its trade is still done with it.

On the other hand, Britain remained the only country where the government, itself internally divided, expressed grave doubts about the desirability and feasibility of EMU, on both economic and political grounds. The situation had apparently changed little since 1979. Realizing its isolation, the Conservative government made a conscious effort to remain in the negotiating table; and it sacrificed Mrs Thatcher in the process. It made alternative proposals, such as the 'hard ECU', which however failed to make much of an impression on the other partners. In the end, it reconciled itself with an 'opt-out' provision in the treaty.

Central bankers, who are absolutely crucial for the successful implementation of the EMU project, had been closely involved from an early stage, notably through their participation in the Delors Committee and subsequently in the drafting of the ECB statutes. They were also responsible for the everyday running of the EMS. In contrast, domestic interest groups, parliaments and the wider public played hardly any role during the negotiations. For the large majority of member countries, EMU became a political issue only after the signing of the Treaty; and popular reactions then came as an unpleasant surprise to most politicians.

Economics is an inexact science, and politics the art of the possible; hence the very imperfect product of Maastricht. The treaty met with little applause from European societies and international markets alike. What proved to be an agonizing process of ratification of the treaty coincided with the turmoil in the exchange markets, and the two became mutually reinforcing. The events of 1992-93 certainly did not augur well for the success of the EMU project. Hardly anybody would have dared to predict at the time that the final stage of EMU would in fact begin on 1 January 1999, with eleven countries participating. This became possible due to a dramatic transformation of the political and economic climate during the intervening period. The road leading to EMU was shaped by the continuous interaction between governments, markets, and societies. Governments operate at both the national and the European level (the subnational level being hardly relevant in the case of monetary policy), while financial markets are international and societies stubbornly national.

During the transition to EMU, most governments, acting separately or through European institutions, showed an absolutely remarkable commitment to this goal, not only in words but also in deeds. A number of important decisions were taken by successive European Councils, including most notably the plan for the changeover to the single currency, following the introduction of the final stage. Activity at the European level was continuously backed by political statements pointing to the inevitability of EMU and the appropriate macroeconomic policies which aimed at satisfying the convergence criteria. In this respect, the role played by Chancellor Kohl was absolutely decisive. The transition to EMU survived important changes of government in different member countries, which in itself says very much about the degree and cross-party nature of the political commitment in most EU countries, and hence about the solidity of the project (cf. Hoffmeyer in this book).

Also encouraged by the significant improvement in the economic environment, markets gradually began to believe in EMU. This helped to create a virtuous circle: the decline in inflation and budget deficits led to exchange rate stability and a reduction in nominal and real interest rates, both short and long, which in turn contributed to a further reduction in inflation and budget deficits.

European societies did not show the same degree of conviction or enthusiasm about EMU. This is perhaps understandable, since EMU was identified, at least in several countries, with deflationary policies at times of high unemployment, which hardly helped to make it an object of love for European citizens. In others, it was mainly perceived as leading to a substantial loss of national sovereignty; even though this loss of national sovereignty may be more a question of appearance rather than substance.

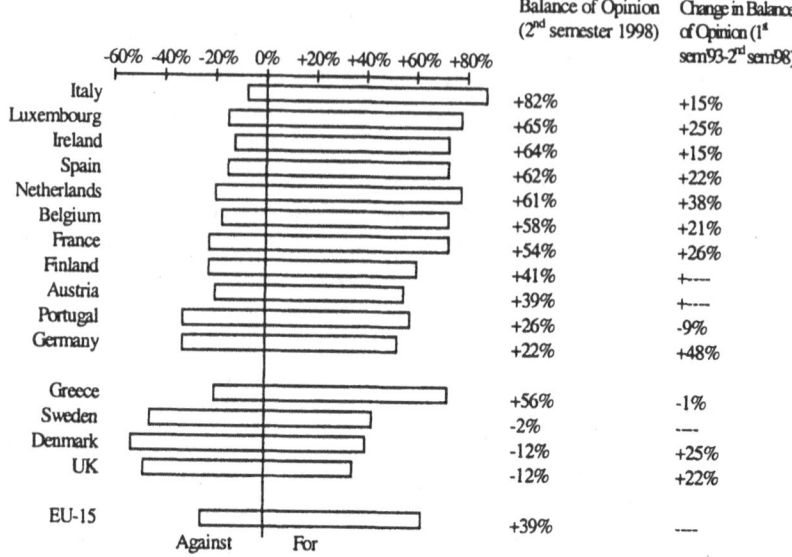

Figure 4.1 Public opinions: for and against the EMU
Source: Adapted from Dosenrode (2000: 104).

Nevertheless, opinion polls have regularly registered clear majorities for the Union as a whole in favor of EMU; and those majorities had been increasing as the big day approached (see Figure 4.1). The change in countries like Germany and the Netherlands, which had started with very low levels of public support for EMU, was quite dramatic; the shift in favor of EMU being of the order of 48 and 38 percentage points respectively between the first semester of 1993 and the second semester of 1998. This may serve as an interesting lesson about the ability of politicians to shape, as opposed to simply following, public opinion. If, for example, the German government had taken early opinion polls on EMU too seriously, the whole project would have never materialized.

Figure 4.1 also shows that the highest popular support for EMU appeared in countries with strong pro-integration majorities and/or high propensity to inflation and debt accumulation. Italy is the best example, with almost unanimous popular support for EMU. Ireland and Greece belong to the same category. On the other hand, negative attitudes continued to prevail in Denmark, Sweden and the UK until the end of the transition to EMU, although the balance of opinion had become more favorable during the intervening period of transition. Not surprisingly, these were also the countries where the governments had decided to postpone the decision, presumably hoping for a further shift in the future of public attitudes in favor of EMU. Sometimes, hard facts are much more convincing than any kind of argument.

Economic Risks and Political Stakes

The detailed provisions of the treaty, and the meticulous preparations which preceded the entry into the final stage of EMU, nevertheless left some fundamental questions unanswered. The Maastricht package was a political bargain, which deliberately left for later negotiation many of the wider ramifications of monetary union. The EU is not an optimal currency area; far from it. There are no adequate adjustment mechanisms, such as labor flexibility and large budgetary transfers, to act as effective substitutes for the exchange rate. The architects of EMU have produced a structure of arguably post-modern inspiration: a centralized monetary policy which operates against the background of a highly decentralized fiscal policy and an even more decentralized political system. This combination has no historical precedent, and it is also, arguably, unsustainable in the long run.

If economic cycles remain unsynchronized among individual economies within the euro-zone, the costs of the 'one-size-fits-all' monetary policy will be uneven. Yet the question of parallel measures to coordinate economic policies, or to provide compensatory budgetary transfers, has been side-stepped. The EU budget remains very small, and with no provision for a stabilization function. Nor is there much support in most member states for a larger common budget.

In a monetary union, there are strong arguments for greater flexibility of fiscal policy, to serve as an instrument of adjustment at the national and regional level. On the other hand, there is a risk of free-riding by national, or even regional, governments operating under the shield of the Union, assuming, of course, that markets cannot be relied upon to provide an effective restraint on government overspending (and undertaxing). The treaty provisions, and the Stability and Growth Pact which followed, were aimed essentially against 'free-riders' in the future monetary union. Their effectiveness and political feasibility, however, remain to be tested.

Behind the institutional structure established to manage the single currency lies the political issue of who is to determine macroeconomic priorities for the EU as a whole, and how. There is as yet no mechanism for this. The broad guidelines for the coordination of national policies, which

ECOFIN adopts each year, are too broad to have any noticeable effect on national economic strategies.

The pressure for a more effective coordination of fiscal policies, and macroeconomic policies in general, at the EU level is likely to increase (see Gustavsson in this book). This would, first of all, require the strengthening of the Euro-12 Council of Economics and Finance Ministers to provide a political counterweight to the bankers and a real dialogue between this Council and the ECB. EMU could then end up being Europe's answer to the globalization and inherent instability of financial markets by restoring some of the effectiveness of macroeconomic policy, which has been irretrievably lost at the national level.

After all, the EU is still a relatively closed economy in trade terms, very similar to the United States. The external trade of EU-15 in goods (excluding trade between the members of the Union) is still virtually the same as it used to be around 35 years ago, namely below 10 per cent of GDP. Some elements of Keynesianism could therefore be resurrected in the context of EMU; although, admittedly, this is something not envisaged by the authors of the Treaty on European Union, nor is it very compatible with current economic orthodoxy.

Holding the two intergovernmental conferences in parallel in 1990-91 was meant to stress the link between EMU and political union. The Treaty on European Union, however, delivered little of substance on political union; and the Treaty of Amsterdam, which followed it a few years later, has hardly contributed to the correction of the political deficit of the Union. Not much is expected either from the new intergovernmental conference which started in January 2000. European policy-makers seem to have left it to a future recession to test whether EMU will act as the catalyst for further political union, or whether monetary policy has been completely de-coupled from political authority.

Monetary union carries implications for a wide range of other policy domains, some not yet drawn into the EU framework, others already subject to EU regimes. The regulation of financial markets is one field for potential spill-over, especially given the rapid restructuring in this sector, partly a consequence of the move towards a single currency. Questions of tax harmonization, or of the prevention of harmful tax competition, are creeping on to the EU agenda. Taxes on capital, which is more mobile than labor across frontiers, are a particular concern to many EU governments. Fiscal incentives for investment are also a focus for controversy between advocates of harmonization and defenders of national fiscal autonomy.

On the other hand, the growing number of cross-border mergers and acquisitions is changing fast the corporate map of Europe. This will also have implications for EU competition policy. The loss of the exchange rate as a policy instrument at the national level, and the lack of any sizeable inter-country budgetary transfers to act as shock absorbers, will place the burden of adjustment on labor markets. Hence the emphasis has shifted to promoting greater flexibility in labor markets and social policies, even though definitions of flexibility differ widely.

Until the launching of the final stage of EMU, its external dimension had been largely ignored. Monetary union should imply a single external representative, but finance ministers of the major EU states are accustomed to playing a role on the international stage. The European Council has so far decided that the President of the Euro-12 Council will, together with the President of the ECB, represent the countries of the euro-zone in meetings of the Group of Seven (Eight, when Russia takes part), alongside – not instead of – colleagues from the larger member governments. Logically, the separate national representations of EU countries in international financial organizations, such as the International Monetary Fund (IMF) should in time give way to a single European representation. But the weak legitimacy of the EU, and the national sensitivities of the larger members, may make this a long-term prospect. The issue of common representation begs the question of what the external policy of EMU would be and how that might be defined.

This also relates to the exchange rate of the euro against other international currencies. Until the time of writing, the euro had suffered a long and continuous depreciation with respect to the US dollar, which could be at least partly explained in terms of interest rate differentials as well as different market expectations regarding growth prospects on the two sides of the Atlantic. Although being yet another example of overshooting in financial markets, the depreciation of the euro was also not unrelated to the inability of European policy-makers (be they central bankers or finance ministers) to present a coordinated, not to mention unified, stance.

The launch of EMU has opened up the prospect of a multi-tier EU. Three groups of countries have emerged: the Eleven, which tied their exchange rates irrevocably to the euro; Greece and Denmark, their currencies within the new ERM, and thus formally linked to the euro; and Britain and Sweden, which opted for an independent float. Having now fulfilled all the convergence criteria, Greece joined in 2001. If EMU proves successful, it will be extremely difficult for any member of the Union to stay outside this most important manifestation of economic integration for long. This is likely to prove a crucial factor in the debate currently taking place in those countries which chose to postpone the decision on joining. Thus, EMU may not after all constitute for long the example *par excellence* of variable geometry in the Union.

The shadow of eastern enlargement also hangs over the further development of monetary union. The *Deutschmark* already operates as a parallel currency in some parts of eastern Europe, including most of ex-Yugoslavia. Applicant countries may decide to move faster towards the single currency than most EU policy-makers either expect or wish. Those in Germany and France who had hoped to start EMU with a small and homogenous core of countries may find a lengthening queue of applicants pressing for inclusion.

Concluding Remarks

European monetary integration already has a long history. Earlier proposals had sketched out a broader program of parallel policies and institutional development than that which the EU accepted in the 1990s. The narrower agenda set out in the Treaty on European Union in some ways made agreement easier, but at the cost of leaving to be settled later a large number of politically sensitive issues – some potentially explosive.

The Treaty on European Union, and subsequent developments through the 1990s, have been strongly influenced by prevailing economic ideas, most notably the belief that there is no trade-off between inflation and unemployment. If and when economic conventional wisdom changes, treaties and institutions will have to face a difficult test of flexibility and endurance. The ECB, at the center of the new institutional architecture, will be tested most severely. It remains to be seen whether it will by then have found a credible political interlocutor in the form of a revamped Ecofin. Debate about macroeconomic choices, and about the balance between the instruments of economic policy, has been at the heart of national politics since the second world war. Some of those choices and instruments have now been transferred to the EU level, without the parallel institutions for generating a Europe-wide debate.

EMU is indeed a high-risk strategy. There is a serious economic risk involved in the irrevocable fixing of exchange rates, while other adjustment mechanisms are still very weak and economic divergence persists. Arguably, the instability of currency markets, combined with the high degree of openness of EU economies, left European policy-makers with little choice. There is also a political risk linked to the legitimacy deficit of the Union. And there is no easy exit option, if things go wrong. There is, however, the other side of the coin. If EMU works, it will most likely bring with it a much stronger and more integrated EU, in both economic and political terms. After all, the history of European integration has been marked by bold initiatives, which seemed to provide easy targets for various categories of Euro-sceptics. On most occasions, it was the latter who finally had to adjust to the ever-changing European reality.

Notes

1 See also Dyson and Hoffmeyer in this book.
2 See also Tsoukalis (1977).
3 Gros and Thygesen (1998).
4 See also Padoa-Schioppa (1994, chapter 6).
5 Quoted in *Financial Times*, 19 October 1995.
6 Dyson (1994); Tsoukalis (1997).

References

Dosenrode, Søren (ed.) (2000): *Danmark og ØMU'en. Politiske Aspektet*, Rådet for Europæisk Politik, Aarhus: Systime.

Dyson, K. (1994): *Elusive Union: The Process of Economic and Monetary Union in Europe*, London: Longman.

Financial Times (1995): October 19.

Gros, Daniel and N. Thygesen (1998): *European Monetary Integration*, 2nd edition, London and New York: Longman.

Padoa-Schioppa, Tommaso (1994): *The Road to Monetary Union in Europe: The Emperor; the King, and the Genies*, Oxford: Clarendon Press.

Tsoukalis, Loukas (1977): *The Politics and Economics of European Monetary Integration*, London: Allen and Unwin.

Tsoukalis, Loukas (1997): *The New European Economy Revisited*, Oxford: Oxford University Press.

5 What Makes a European Monetary Union Without a Parallel Fiscal Union Politically Sustainable?

SVERKER GUSTAVSSON

From the point of view of comparative federalism, monetary union without fiscal union constitutes a genuine puzzle. As far as federal experience goes, the suprastate is either limited to foreign and trade policy or fully-fledged in the sense that it includes a common currency and – as a consequence – a strong element of revenue sharing. One option is to have no monetary union at all. Another option is to have monetary union with a parallel fiscal union. In theory, there is no third alternative.

The Maastricht Treaty breaks with the idea of there being no third alternative. Seen from the outside, the current European construct is a full-scale experiment without precedence. The member states are firmly determined to have a common currency with no parallel fiscal union. That raises a question, which has not yet been discussed to the extent that it deserves. What is it that could possibly make such an unprecedented trajectory sustainable?

In the first part of this chapter I criticize what has been said about the sustainability of a monetary union without a parallel fiscal union. In the second part I suggest an answer of my own. Irrespective of whether such a consequence was intended or not, I argue, there are good reasons to believe that monetary union without fiscal union will lead to a strengthening rather than to a weakening of democratic government in the member states. That is so because the alternatives – fiscal federalism or authoritarianism – are so frightening.

In order to get to that point I have to start by describing this full-scale experiment in a way which is fruitful when it comes to questioning sustainability. From that point of view, I suggest, the *asymmetrical* character of the present union is its most striking feature.[1] Other federal structures – like the United States, Canada or Germany – are symmetrical. A unified monetary system is always accompanied by a corresponding mechanism for redistributing a considerable part of the gross national product across the federal territory. Roughly speaking, one *fifth* of the gross national product is being re-distributed via Washington, Ottawa, or Berlin in order to compensate for the social and economic rigidity caused by the equalization of exchange rates and interest rate levels across their territories.

Conversely, in the European case only somewhat more than one *hundredth* of the sum gross national product of its member states is being re-distributed through the cohesion funds, the common agricultural policy and the research programs managed by the suprastatal authorities in Brussels. All other contemporary constructs of this kind are monetary unions with a corresponding fiscal union. The European Union, however, is designed to work without the union having a right to tax 'its' citizens.

The asymmetry of the European Union's present system raises serious questions over its long-term sustainability. What allows this basic lack of proportion between monetary and fiscal powers to be a sustainable solution?

In the official view, the answer to this question is the 1997 stability pact and the supporting ideas of 'interlocked core executive governance' (Dyson, 1999: 116ff) and 'strengthening the Euro-Zone by policy convergence' (Dyson, 2000: 260ff). In that pact, the member state governments have promised each other not to help each other more than they are presently doing inside the small union budget, which is based on the principle of a membership fee.

In the absence of constitutional statehood and a fully developed mechanism of democratic accountability at the federal level, fiscal powers cannot be made part of the suprastatal structure the same way as the powers concerning the market and the currency have been centralized, the member state governments argue. A centralization of the fiscal powers would mean taking a definite step in the direction of statehood and democratization. In that case, the source of political authority would have to be found in a sovereign people of Europe rather than in the peoples of the member states.

Economic Analysis Alone is Insufficient

Academic prognoses regarding the long-term *sustainability* of a monetary union in the absence of a fiscal union have hitherto been carried out mainly by economists. There has been two main thrusts to their work. In part, they have been concerned with the question of how great an improvement in resource utilization may be expected to follow from reduced uncertainty in connection with exchange rates and levels of interest. Have the calculations behind the establishment of the common currency been properly carried out? Or have the efficiency gains been overestimated?

In addition, economists have wrestled with the question of whether or not the Union constitutes a so-called optimal currency area (OCA). According to an idea launched by Robert Mundell in the early 1960s, one must weigh two contrary considerations against each other when seeking to ascertain whether or not a given geographical zone constitutes an OCA. On the one hand, efficiency increases with the size of the unit. On the other, the need for equalization tends to increase with size as well, since larger areas will likely feature a wider variation in the economic development achieved by different zones.

Throughout the 1990s, economists have debated whether or not the European Union fulfils these so-called Mundell criteria. The discussion is a difficult one, for the different factors being weighed against each other are hard to express in quantitative terms. The interesting thing about this research, however, is not to be found in these methodological difficulties, but in the fact that the problem so plainly has a *political* import – a fact that the academic economists themselves are quick to recognize.

With great meticulousness and care, the economists list the changes that would be required to realize the efficiency gains that would accompany a given OCA balance. These changes must be reckoned as bitter medicine: they include a decrease in the job security of wage earners, the introduction of less favorable provisions in unemployment insurance, a neglect of infrastructure in regions judged economically less attractive, and other similar measures.

Such changes can, indeed, be introduced if the overall conditions are completely controlled. But how does the matter look in practice? Is it really possible to alter job-security provisions, labor-market institutions, and regional policy in the direction and to the degree presupposed by the OCA analysis? Are there not certain historically given external conditions – universal and equal suffrage, civic rights and freedoms – which powerfully inhibit the necessary balancing of the two contrary considerations featured in economic analyses?

The academic economists do not attempt, in other words, to hide the political aspects of the OCA problem. On the contrary, they underline precisely what needs to be discussed from such a perspective. Martin Feldstein, for example, ventures the following judgement in his 1997 article reviewing the field:

As economists, we can evaluate the likely effects of monetary union on employment, inflation, trade and overall economic well-being. But we should recognize that the officials who are pursuing monetary union are motivated by political considerations that transcend questions about the likely performance of the European Central Bank and whether the European economy satisfies the Mundell (1961) criteria of an optimal currency area. It is useful to explore these political considerations before looking at the likely consequences of EMU for the economies of Europe and the rest of the world.

My own judgment is that the net economic effect of a European Monetary Union would be negative. The standard of living of the typical European would be lower in the medium term and long term if EMU goes ahead than if Europe continues with its current economic policies of a single market for trade in goods and services, the free flow of capital and labor, adjustable exchange rates within broad bands, and domestic monetary policies aimed at low inflation. But in the end, it should be for the Europeans themselves to decide whether there are net political advantages of EMU that outweigh the net economic disadvantages. Unfortunately, the public discussion of EMU in Europe has not focused on this trade-off, because EMU is being marketed as a source of improved economic performance (Feldstein, 1997: 24 f).

The idea of a common currency unaccompanied by a fiscal union has been marketed as an economic gain. As a consequence of this, the question of whether or not the political advantages of such an arrangement outweigh its economic disadvantages has been asked all too rarely. Implicitly, then, Martin Feldstein is criticizing political scientists for neglecting this important question.

Picking up the Gauntlet

On the political science side of the disciplinary divide, meanwhile, there has been a strong tendency during the 1990s to uncritically accept a monetary union without a fiscal union. The first of our colleagues who posed the question as a serious academic problem was David McKay in 1996. Unafraid that his analysis might undermine the realization of the project, he discussed the political sustainability of such an arrangement, treating it as an analytical problem fully on a level with the question of said arrangement's economic impact.

In his 1996 book, David McKay attempts to explain the shift from pure common market centralization to a monetary union without a fiscal union in addition. Following Alan Milward and Andrew Moravcsik, his analysis is placed in the broader context of looking upon the political history of European integration as an historical attempt to strengthen rather than to weaken the member states and their democracies.

When, in the estimation of the member states, the balance of advantages and drawbacks shifted, McKay argues, 'the federal bargain' was re-negotiated through the Maastricht treaty. Such a re-negotiation took place not just within the individual countries but between them as well. The critical factor driving this change was a shift in the perceptions of the member states from fears over what they might lose from a further pooling of sovereignties to hopes over what they might gain from further political integration.

The governments of Europe re-negotiated the federal bargain when they framed the Maastricht Treaty. In their eyes, the difficulties they had encountered in the fight against unemployment – high inflation notwithstanding – justified a suprastatal and independent central bank. Democratic control over the value of money should be abandoned. The governments would then seek once again to combat unemployment. Now, however, they would be able to do so more effectively, because from here on out they expected to enjoy the eternal confidence of the financial markets.

Having explained why the member states shifted from market centralization alone to a monetary union without a fiscal union, McKay then raises the question of political sustainability as a general problem. What conditions are required for the survival of federations?

Bridging Administrative Levels

According to McKay, in order for a federation to survive political parties must be capable of bridging administrative levels: local, regional, state, and federal. Additionally, interest groups, mass media, and political parties must be centralized. Otherwise, the joint use of the tax bases cannot be rendered intelligible and legitimate.

A federation's sustainability is determined by the structure of its party system, McKay argues. In this, he connects his analysis with the work of William Riker, who had served as his inspiration. The latter's judgement on the matter is that:

> [in] a variety of governments, then, the structure of parties parallels the structure of federalism. When parties are fully centralized, so is federalism (e.g. in the Soviet Union and Mexico). When parties are somewhat decentralized, then federalism is only partly centralised.

Because of this perfect correlation of, at least, two extremes of party structure, the inference is immediate: one can measure federalism by measuring parties. The structure of parties is thus a surrogate of the structure of the whole constitution (Riker, 1975: p. 137).

The question, in other words, is how multi-level systems call forth and re-create consensus. How can citizens be induced – when deliberating together in municipalities, in regions, in states, and on the federal level – to think along similar lines when it comes to the content of legislation and the uses to which tax monies should be put?

Decisions that diverge all too greatly between levels, as to the way norm-giving and fiscal powers should be used, cannot be combined. For it is the same tax bases which are employed on all four levels, and it is the same citizens who must live according to the rules and stipulations laid down by the four barely coordinated power centers.

The fiscal side of things is particularly problematic here. The tax monies in their entirety constitute the sum of the use to which the fiscal power is used on all four levels. Without political parties which strive for internal consistency, and which are active in the formation of opinion on all four levels, no overarching policy capable of inspiring confidence can take form. This applies not only to the use of tax bases but also to legislation, in the degree that this means anything for the citizens on Election Day.

Variations in Political Visibility

The interest expressed by citizens in democratic accountability varies, I would argue, in accordance with the differential manner in which taxes, fees, and legal provisions are felt and are politically visible at the household level (Scharpf, 1999: pp. 30f, 2001: pp. 1ff).

Legal provisions bearing on conditions within families or affecting the status of employees at work are more easily 'seen', as are policies applied in connection with taxes and expenditures. Policies of this type are therefore harder to institute if those responsible for making them cannot be held democratically accountable. That portion of the norm-giving power, which bears on the mobility of capital, goods and services, on the other hand, is not so clearly visible at the household level. The regulation of the common market has not, therefore, called forth any drive for democratization.

So long as it is only power over the market that has been centralized, the Union organs do not compete with municipalities, regions, or the member states for the common exploitation of tax bases. When citizens see, however, that important fiscal questions are being decided at the suprastatal level, a fair measure of concord between the different political levels becomes a necessity. At that point, moreover, the debate becomes more engaging and concrete.

As long as the democratic deficit bears only on the legitimacy of rules instituted to regulate the market, the problem remains theoretical. As the question of how tax bases are to be used assumes increasing importance, however, we can expect an increased interest from the public. This is because there are alternative levels – municipal, regional, and national – at which the same fiscal resources can be put to work.

Unemployment, family-related legislation, and social-spending cuts are more acutely felt at the household level than are the abstract effects of a centralized competition law or common currency. Social consequences of these kind can be counted on to generate political demands of real weight.

Within a monetary union, regional differences become more clearly visible. Individual countries can no longer adjust to economic shocks by letting the value of their currency fluctuate. All that remains for individuals at the household level is to lower their standard of living or to move. The industrial structure, moreover, is in practice one-sided – within both individual countries and the Union as a whole – due to the exploitation of comparative advantages. Shocks originating in the international economy thus elicit demands for fiscal redistribution and a democratically accountable suprastate.

Yet a centralization of power over taxes and expenditures is extremely unlikely all the same. Power over the fiscal resources of the different nations could only – in a system characterized by far-reaching citizen rights and freedoms – be transferred to the Union with the greatest of difficulties. As long as the political system in the member states is based on universal and equal suffrage, it would be necessary to induce citizens in all fifteen states to decide – parallel with each other – to forswear the power to decide over the use of their own tax bases. A decision of such an import cannot easily be brought about, to put the point cautiously.

At the same time, a centralization of power over the currency cannot help but affect the different areas of the Union unevenly. Politicians will then be presented with a double demand. On the one hand, centralization cannot be allowed to result in a suprastatal right of taxation; on the other, it cannot be allowed to restrict democracy within the member states.

Monetary Unification Without Political Centralization

In the absence of centralized political parties capable of bridging the different levels, it is hard to see how this equation can be solved. It bears noting that a line of defense has been erected at the level of monetary union, even while no corresponding changes have taken place in parties, interest groups, or the mass media. Nor has there been any obvious increase in the preparedness of different electorates to countenance a redistribution of tax monies across borders.

> Uniquely in the history of federations, the bargain underpinning the European Union was policy driven and, as has been argued, will certainly produce pressures towards fiscal centralisation. In every other democratic federation this process has been facilitated by a centralizing party or parties operating through well-developed central political institutions. Politics has, therefore, been driving policy, rather than policy driving politics. What the rather dry and analytical term 'fiscal centralization' actually means is, of course, the willingness of the citizens of the component states of the EU to pay taxes to a federal government intent on redistributing revenues to disadvantaged countries and regions. This may be a permanent redistribution; the rich may never be paid back (McKay, 1996: p. 136).

The prospects for avoiding a monetary union that develops into a fiscal union will be determined, in McKay's view, by two factors. One is the willingness of citizens to countenance fiscal centralization. Will this willingness increase or diminish?

The other factor is the degree to which parties present a coherent program for all four administrative levels. How shall we interpret developments in this regard? Do we see before us centralization or decentralization? Are parties becoming more European in the view that they take of fiscal equalization? Is it not just as likely, in fact, that parties will be increasingly affected by municipal and regional considerations when it comes to their views regarding costly collective programs for health, education, and social care within the member states?

Upon having summarized the available facts, McKay concludes that there is very little reason indeed to believe the oft-presented claim that the scepticism exhibited by citizens in regard to European institutions is rooted in an information problem. On the contrary, the lack of enthusiasm appears to rest on much firmer ground than a monetary-union-without-fiscal-union agitator would prefer to believe. Citizens ask themselves, namely, what will happen if the arrangement undertaken cannot be sustained (an amply justified question in this case). 'In the final analysis, the viability of the union will be determined by the particular mix of costs and benefits which flow over time. Ultimately, it will be the willingness of some states and regions to subsidize others that will determine whether the union stands or falls' (McKay, 1996: p. 171).

In other words, the sustainability of a monetary union unaccompanied by a fiscal one is not, in the first instance, a question of economic but rather of political efficiency (see Hoffmeyer & Tsoukalis in this book). It is a question of convincing those who exercise universal and equal suffrage within the municipalities, the regions, the nations, and the European Union.

Democratic Threat Replaces Soviet Threat

McKay's point, reflected in the title of the 1996 version of his book is that the member states 'rushed' past the stage of political reflection that ought, in principle, to precede political decisions. What the governments did was to present citizens with a *fait accompli*. Before most people could grasp what was happening, they had been bound to a structure based on the proposition that the threat from the Soviet Union had been succeeded by another danger. The new fear was that it would not be possible to democratically formulate sound economic policy that dealt with the monetary and fiscal issues within the member states.

> [M]onetary union was seen as the solution to a quite different sort of threat – that stemming from a perception that, with the internationalization of capital, governments were increasingly unable to control inflation. The experience of the 1970s and early 1980s had convinced government and opposition parties alike not only of the evils of inflation, but also that the problem had to be solved by some external discipline (McKay, 1996: 172).

It does not appear to be the case that, in the spring of 1990, the politicians gave any thought to anchoring their decisions about the future shape of the Union to the public opinion of their peoples. Nowhere in materials from that period does McKay find any such evidence.

The leading statesmen appear to have been blissfully unaware of what was required in terms of legitimacy. It seems somehow to have escaped them that the solution they had chosen would have to be carried out in their own countries. They seem to have forgotten that member states were featuring far-reaching citizen rights and freedoms, universal and equal suffrage, a tax quotient of between 40 and 55 per cent of GNP, and political parties that consequently gave priority to municipal, regional and national questions. The risk of error is always serious when politicians make decisions 'in the absence of good information, or [when they] are driven more by ideology than by practical calculation' (McKay, 1996: 178).

Monetary Discipline, Loose Money or Fiscal Centralization?

Ten years on, we are nearing the moment of truth, McKay writes in a subsequent article in 1999. What will be the political effects and what is the likelihood of the one or the other result? In his latest article he seeks to answer this question by way of discussing three alternatives: monetary discipline, loose money, and fiscal centralization.

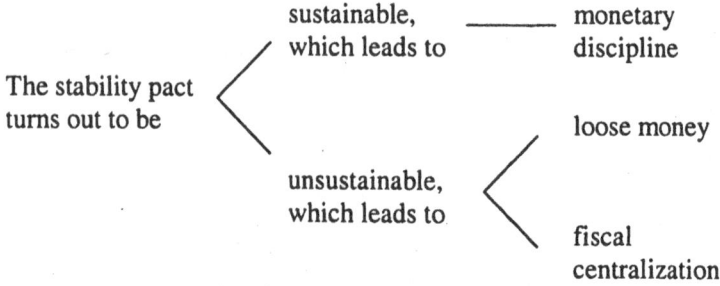

Figure 5.1 Possible outcomes of the Stability Pact as seen by David McKay in his 1999 article

In McKay's 1999 overview of possible outcomes, *monetary discipline* is the intended result of the stability pact. In this scenario, the stability pact forces through lower levels of compensation in social and labor-market insurance. The mobility of the labor force increases, and variations in wages become wider. Yet the social strains attendant upon reduced security and increased inequality are internalized in a disciplined manner by the public opinion, parties, and trade unions of the individual countries.

This is only one of the intended consequences. The stability pact also imposes restraints on the redistribution of funds among countries. As a result, the transfers of funds across borders must take place within the resources of the present structural funds, and within the bounds of balanced budgets within the member states. No transfers between countries are to take place beyond this. Nor can any member state seek respite from this discipline through borrowing.

Another feature of the picture here – and one tending to obscure the content – is the rhetoric that the Christian and Social democratic parties have developed in defense of a monetary union unaccompanied by a fiscal one. The object is not, to be sure, to create unemployment or to weaken the provisions of state-guaranteed welfare. But a retrenchment, it is thought, will make it easier over the long run to raise levels of employment and to defend social welfare. By shortening its lines of defense, the welfare state will be better equipped to withstand the strains. Success means preventing the rise of a democratic suprastate, and – at the same time – keeping power over taxes and expenditures within each one of the member states.

Having considered what would constitute a successful outcome regarding the adoption of a common currency unaccompanied by a fiscal union, let us now think about some less optimistic outcomes. There are two main ways such a project could fail.

In the first failure scenario, an absence of popular support combines with the absence of a fiscal union (and thus the competencies such an arrangement would entail) to cause a debilitating outbreak of inflation that engulfs the entire continent. This results in *loose money*. Opposition by the public and political parties to both austerity or redistribution measures generates this unhappy outcome. In the face of such a crisis the EU finds itself helpless, with no Union-wide inflation fighting means at its disposal. The suprastatal authorities have no significant budget of their own and they have no way of altering circumstances by conferring new prerogatives on themselves. Furthermore, there is not sufficient solidarity to permit redistribution. As a consequence the euro free-falls and becomes less attractive as a world currency.

McKay calls the second failure scenario, and third possible outcome, *fiscal centralization*. In this case, the lack of popular support is paired with such a strong aversion to inflation that the member governments choose fiscal union as the lesser of two evils. The need to collect taxes at the European level forces the member states to centralize power over the different national tax bases. Chillingly, this in turn would hardly be accomplished without democratization.

This outcome would create problems when it comes to defending – in municipal, regional, and national fora – cutbacks in the provisions for health, education, and social care that are provided on these levels. In terms of practical politics – since money must be taken from the lower levels to finance the suprastatal level – this problem seems impossible to solve. Citizens will be very defensive concerning any reductions in funding when it comes to the levels they know and love – municipalities, regions, and member states – and relatively uninterested in spending money at the Union level due to the relative weakness of an all-European identity. Yet the governments prefer running that risk to letting inflation loose, and thus jeopardizing municipal, regional, and national democracy over the long term.

McKay does not consider any of these three outcomes – monetary discipline, loose money or fiscal centralization – to be more likely than the two others. There are too many factors, he argues, and they are too uncertain. We do not know which considerations the participating governments will prioritize in the end. In order for strict prediction to be possible, the actors in question must have discernible and fixed preferences.

First Order Elections and Institutions

Preferences might change – both in reaction to subsequent events and on account of a growing understanding on the part of the actors and citizens regarding the relationship between the various desiderata. Yet a reasonable forecast, McKay concludes, would be that citizens will attempt to use 'legitimated first order (national) elections and institutions to express their disquiet. Clearly, such actions could constitute a serious challenge to the integrity of the EMU project' (McKay, 1999: 485). In municipal, regional, and national fora, politicians will continue to be held accountable for unemployment and for cuts in social spending.

Citizens will find it hard to accept, in other words, that they should abstain (and for their own good) from holding their national politicians accountable. Politicians may protest ever so vigorously that their hands are tied, that they cannot be held responsible for unemployment or for spending cuts, and that the power to decide over such matters has been formally delegated to the Union authorities. But as long as no mechanism has been established by which the Union-level authorities can be held accountable – as a unit, and on a single occasion throughout the Union – they will continue to confront a serious problem of legitimacy. The notion of democratic accountability is deeply and widely held, not least as a consequence of two world wars and a cold war.

The events of the former century make it hard to accept a system in which leaders cannot be held answerable for their actions. The most ingenious technical solutions in the world cannot suffice to solve the problems arising in connection with the establishment of a monetary union in the absence of a fiscal one. For the solution to be sustainable, it must be broadly accepted.

Creating a common currency in the absence of any redistributive mechanisms places heavy demands on the citizenry. Under such an asymmetrical structure, the critical decisions will be made by the Council, which cannot be held accountable as a collective. Indeed, this may be the reason why said structure was erected in the first place. The member state governments might have needed a suprastate to blame.

Democracy is as Important as the Stability Pact

In view of the general importance David McKay ascribes to *legitimacy* in his 1999 article, it is striking that his classification of possible outcomes does not consider democracy. Monetary discipline, loose money, and fiscal centralization are all potential outcomes in terms of the stability pact rather than democracy.

What is missing, I argue, is a transverse classification reflecting the consequences for politics in terms of democracy. An asymmetrical solution may prove to be sustainable or unsustainable in terms of the stability pact. In a comparable way, it may be one or the other in terms of democracy as well. The problem can be visualized more clearly if, instead of three economic policy outcomes, we imagine four possible outcomes. That fourfold scheme follows from distinguishing between the sustainability of democracy on the one hand and the sustainability of the stability pact on the other.

Stability Pact:

		Sustainable	Unsustainable
Democracy:	Sustainable	Complete success	Fiscal federalism
	Unsustainable	Authoritarianism	Complete failure

Figure 5.2 Four possible outcomes when considering democracy as important as the Stability Pact

Each of these four political possibilities is worth considering in some depth. For the sake of the analysis I first concentrate on them one by one. At the end of the chapter I will then return to the question of what basic conditions might lead to success rather than failure.

Complete Success

According to the alternative complete success, democracy in the member states proves to be resilient. The stability pact succeeds by providing the foundation that makes it possible for a common currency to operate unaccompanied by a fiscal union. The constitutional structure of the Union therefore need not, it is assumed, develop in the same fashion as it did in the United States, in Canada, or in Germany. The federal budget, in these latter countries, accounts for upwards of half of all public spending.

A glance at the established federal states would thus lead one to expect a corresponding development in the case of the European Union. Here, however, the stability pact creates a barrier to fiscal federalism. There is no publicly expressed demand for a federal fiscal policy for Europe – no central right of taxation, no democratic pressure for the suprastate. No fiscal union, accordingly, will be established. Such was the basic idea of the 1990 settlement between Germany and France.

Since its inception, moreover, this settlement has never been seriously questioned – only regarded as a fact. Substantive objections have been waved away, on the grounds that they are academic. The analytical method projected by the European leaders may be characterized as conscious political institution-building (Lepsius, 1995: 400 ff). Their primary focus is not perceived to be the economy, but rather the political system. There are forces working, to be sure, in the direction of a fiscal union. But, it is thought, that it is the task of the participating governments to hold said forces in check. And this they can do by pledging not to seek a Union-wide system of redistribution corresponding to that operating within each member state.

Reasoning of this kind is well-known in the realm of international politics. Conflict and war may be a 'natural' condition in the intercourse of states. But this counts not *against* but rather *for* the conscious creation and maintenance of obligations that serve to hinder the 'natural' course of events from taking place. By cooperating with each other, nations can civilize themselves to the point that war is no longer seen as an acceptable alternative. A shared interest in peace is believed capable of moving mountains. Citing the experiences of history, and moved by a conviction that the interest in peace is a common one, champions of the institutionalist approach remind us that events on the international level can be prevented from taking their 'natural' course. It is for this reason that functional systems of reciprocal and universal obligations are created and maintained.

As applied in international politics, this approach tells us that we can move mountains by political means – meaning that we can subdue the 'natural' tendency of states to make war upon each other. In the case of a monetary union without a fiscal union, however, it is another 'natural' force that needs to be checked. By means of the asymmetrical structure mentioned earlier, the institutionalist idea is applied to domestic politics. The purpose here is to reduce the space for a fiscal policy that, in 'all too great' a measure, is open to influence by electorates, interest groups, and public opinion.

Put in cooking terms, one could say that a monetary union without a fiscal union is designed to work as a kind of pressure cooker without any safety valve. The purpose of the stability pact is to force through rapid changes in the member states. The 'problem' is that these are democracies. Their social and political life is marked by the prevalence of citizen rights and freedoms, of universal and equal suffrage, of parliamentary or presidential rule, and of far-reaching rights of expression and association. And the last of these features involves, most crucially, the existence of active interest groups endowed with the statutory right to take industrial action on the labor market.

The governments that have pooled their sovereignties understand, to be sure, that the member states are democracies offering their citizens far-reaching rights to associate, to strike, and the like. Yet notwithstanding this, the governments propose to move the 'mountain' consisting of parliamentarism, public opinion, freedom of association, the right to strike, and the right to vote. The risk is that these rights and freedoms will be used to influence policy in the direction of fiscal union. But supporters believe it should be possible to check any developments in this direction – if the governments involved really wish to do so. If only their convictions are strong enough, they should be able to prevent any fiscal union from arising reminiscent of those found in the United States, Canada, or Germany.

The interesting question here is whether this application of the institutionalist concept is sustainable (wholly irrespective of whether it is desirable). Is it possible by political means to counteract such a strong 'natural' tendency as that in question here? Once a common currency is in operation, citizens will have only two alternatives with which to adapt to unfavorable economic changes: relocation from their home region or by lowering their standard of living. Past methods, such as allowing the value of the national currency to fluctuate, are no longer available. Under such conditions, money has the same value for all persons living and working throughout the Union.

If different areas of the Union are affected by economic developments unevenly, policy responses to the consequent problems will be regulated by the stability pact. By the terms of the pact, each individual country is obliged to handle any such problems purely within the means of its own budget. The country in question cannot solve the problem by printing money, by borrowing, or by relying on federal solidarity in the form of tax monies allocated by the center. The only solidarity offered by the other member states is the guarantee that no other member state will be assisted by its neighbors either.

The assumption is, therefore, that in such countries as Sweden and Finland (where it is not considered legitimate for living standards to vary too greatly across the national territory), the citizens residing in southern and central areas will be willing and able to bear increased burdens arising in connection with asymmetrical economic shocks which tend to strike northern and inland areas in particular. Just like the Germans and the French, the Swedes and the Finns will not be able to count on material assistance from other member states. For the scale of the federal budget in the system will be no larger than that obtaining today. The meager resources of the present system amount to just 1.27 per cent of the gross product of the Union. This figure should be compared, for the sake of perspective, with the tax quotient of roughly 50 per cent obtaining within each of the member states.

It appears that one result of a successful adherence to a monetary union without a fiscal union would be enhanced national cohesion. However, counter-intuitive as this may seem, it is reasonable to treat my definition of success as almost virtually true. If the participating countries have accomplished the apparently impossible, then they will certainly have succeeded in vitalizing their democratic structures. The need to keep their own fiscal houses in order – once the currency has been Europeanized without any supporting fiscal union – forces politicians to appeal to the solidarity of their countrymen. For this is the only possible way to cope with the strains on the economies of different regions and social strata will arise from the arrangements adopted on the European level.

Such an outcome may be considered a variation on the theme favored by General de Gaulle, a Europe consisting of democratic nations, *l'Europe des patries*. In this vision of Europe constitutional patriotism is not ethnically based but is instead based on a system of different languages and collective memories. With tax bases remaining overwhelmingly under national control, the successful erection of a monetary union unpaired with any fiscal counterpart will make for constitutional patriotism and majority rule *inside* each country. Such is the result if *both* the stability pact and democracy withstand the strain. The party system, the interest groups, and public opinion will prove themselves to be robust under adversity. National cohesion will be enhanced, and democratic government will be infused with new vigor.

The degree of cohesion exhibited by nations in defending and developing their own tax bases will determine how well they will be able to live up to their obligations under the stability pact. The countries have foresworn, of course, any power over the market or the currency. But where social legislation and fiscal policy are concerned, they will have acquired for themselves even greater control. Prospects for the centralization of power over social legislation and tax monies actually diminish. The reason for this is the success of the stability pact's ban on relief. The parties, the interests groups and the public – all emerge strengthened from their trial by fire.

This conclusion – where the impact of the complete success alternative on democracy is concerned – may appear somewhat paradoxical. Yet a brief reflection on the matter – in the light of the accounts offered by Alan Milward and Andrew Moravcsik – is enough to dispel the apparent contradiction. It becomes hard, on the contrary, to see how it could be any other way. Why should we believe, after all, that the governments of the member states are not doing what they believe to be best for protecting their democracies and tax bases?

Fiscal Federalism

The complete success alternative presumes a virtuous circle for both democracy and the stability pact. But not even an incorrigible optimist can ignore the possibility that events will *not* proceed in the desired direction. When, furthermore, the method employed is so bold, as in the present case, one should be prepared for the eventuality that the project will develop in a manner and in a direction less pleasant to contemplate. The 'problem' here is the form of government applied within the member states. These are democracies, and they hold elections at regular intervals.

Through the instrumentality of parliamentarism or of presidential rule, the policies applied within democratic states can be influenced by the manner in which citizens exercise their right of free expression, their right of association, and their right to strike. The practice of holding leaders accountable has consequences. In addition, unemployment and social exclusion afflict the member countries unevenly and at varying levels of intensity. The principle of comparative advantage does just obtain theoretically; it is also applied in practice. Labor markets vary in structure, both within and between the countries. This means the ensuing strains will affect the various regions and countries of the Union differently. And once the possibility of exchange rate variation has disappeared, individual countries will possess no monetary policy instruments with which to parry the blows.

In a system characterized by monetary union but not fiscal union, the capacity of different regions and countries to adapt to economic changes will still be inhibited by a number of factors, such as: (a) a lingering application of solidaristic wage policies; (b) an insufficient mastery of foreign languages on the part of citizens (which prevents them from developing the requisite mobility); and (c) other instances of inadequate flexibility arising from deeply rooted social and cultural values. All of these factors point to the need for costly regional and labor-market policies operating across national borders.

It may happen, then, that the parties, the interest groups, and public opinion cannot 'deliver' the necessary resistance to a fiscal union, or to inflationary fiscal policies. It is not altogether clear that governments, opposition representatives, regional politicians, and national trade-union leaders will be able to handle the strains of the proposed arrangement in the manner assumed in the complete success scenario. The rights of free expression and association may instead be used to express discontent to such an extent that the debate among parties, the interest groups, and the public cannot play the equalizing and stabilizing role envisioned for it.

The stability pact will be put to the test when regional and social interests start demanding that 'Brussels' compensate them for the distress which has 'unfairly' struck country W, or region X, or social group Y in country Z. The member state in question will have vowed, it is true, to abide by the provisions of the stability pact. But the consequences of so doing have proved 'unexpectedly' serious. Both government and opposition leaders within the country feel themselves bound, for 'the sake of social and political stability', to request a relaxation of the pact's strict rules in this particular case. The temptation arises, in other words, to open up a safety valve in the 'pressure cooker'. The European Union will continuously have to live with the political dilemma of centralization versus fragmentation in order to cope with the predicaments created through a monetary union without a fiscal union.

In the *fiscal federalist* alternative, the member states cannot withstand the strain, and are thus forced into a fiscal union and to the democratization of the suprastate. The stability pact is breached. The collective exploitation of tax bases is commenced. The asymmetry between a centralized currency and decentralized public finances cannot be sustained. A recalcitrant public, a failing party system, and strong interest groups have their effect. Citing extraordinary conditions, the Council of Ministers gives its consent to 'temporary' and 'one-time' departures from the pact's ban on relief.

A populist party in one of the participating countries, for example, may be rapidly gathering strength by stoking the fires of discontent. Such a party may be similar to those, which already today are successfully exploiting discontent in such countries as Austria, Belgium, Denmark, France, and Italy. If severe economic conditions unevenly strike such a country, it may appear that the party in question will be able to paralyze politics in the unhappy state. In the worst case, said party may be on its way to conquering governmental power. The political establishment of the afflicted country then appeals to its partners, imploring them to stretch out a helping hand – in the form of fiscal transfers on a large scale – to save the embattled democracy.

The first time this happens, it may be possible to justify it on the grounds that one time is no time at all. It may work on the second occasion as well. But in the third instance it starts getting hard. Once such practices have been established, they feed the cycle of one concession after the other. The missions of the fire brigade soon become so many, and so large in scale, that it becomes necessary to coordinate these 'exceptions' and to give them a constitutional form. At that point, the Union organs feel called upon to propose changes in the treaties. The right of the European Parliament to collect taxes is soon recognized, as is its power to decide over the use of the monies thus raised.

As a federal fiscal policy takes form, the question of the Union's constitutional character comes to the fore. Should not the European Commission be made democratically accountable? Should it not therefore assume the powers of government in a manner corresponding to those exercised by the federal government in Germany, or the American president and his administration? How can an order of things be justified wherein the European authorities undertake fiscal redistribution, but cannot be held to account for their actions in general elections?

It is a simple thing for a theoretician to declare that a suprastate of this character should be democratic. For democratically accountable politicians, however, a certain problem still remains. How can they persuade their citizens to accept the outcome of majority decisions relating to a federal disposition of national tax bases? The problem of practical politics is that a constitutionally delineated European *demos* ought first to exist, before the suprastatal authorities assume the right of taxation. Otherwise the tensions may become untenable. Growing antagonisms, advancing disintegration, and the like must be deemed precisely as likely as a scenario in which fiscally redistributive policies based on majority decision meet with widespread acceptance. There is cause on this point in particular to warn against wishful thinking.

The problem arises in the degree to which the governments of the member states allow themselves to be pressured into a fiscal union *before* they have succeeded in making the suprastate responsible to the European Parliament. Experiences from the history of the member states suggest it may be difficult to levy taxes upon a people when they are not able to directly take part in determining the uses to which the resulting monies are put. This necessitates the existence of a functioning system – of the sort indicated by Riker and McKay – in which political parties are active on all the various levels of government.

Authoritarianism

The *authoritarian* alternative stands out, for those who hold democratic values dear, as the most unattractive of possible outcomes. In this case, a common currency unpaired with a fiscal union is successfully instituted. But this is accomplished at the price of democracy. The governments are driven to authoritarian measures.

In this scenario, democracy is jettisoned due to the refusal of the member state government to prioritize between fighting unemployment or fighting inflation and their inability to garner popular support for their policies. They choose to defend both the independent standing of the central bank and the stability pact's ban on relief. The asymmetrical structure withstands the strain. But democracy cannot be preserved the member-state in question. The parties, the interest groups and the public debate do not function in the cohesion-creating manner envisioned. Populist parties, strike waves, and an aggressive climate of debate drive politicians to take desperate measures.

Demands are then made on politicians to seek relief from other countries, or to borrow on a large scale in order to safeguard employment levels. No heed is paid to the prohibition against adopting such policies, or to the sanctions laid down for infractions of the rules of the stability pact. But the leading member state politicians refuse to yield to these pressures. Rather than giving in to the wrath of the people, they decide to change the rules of the game. Instead, they will choose to reduce the role of the popular will in the formulation of domestic policy. They argue that the popular objections are not expressive of the 'true' will of the people. Criticisms emanating from the public do not reflect the public interest – only 'special interests'. Such things are averred already under normal conditions. Now, such notions are filled with an outright authoritarian content.

The legal limits for how far a government can go in disciplining a recalcitrant populace are laid down in the European Convention for Protection of Human Rights and Fundamental Freedoms from 1950. 'Everyone has the right to freedom of peaceful assembly and to freedom of association with others, including the right to form and to join trade unions for the protection of his interests' (Article 11). Rough-and-tumble methods of the sort employed in union-busting in the United States are accordingly forbidden. The Convention does not say, on the other hand, that the suffrage must be universal and equal, or that electoral outcomes must be converted into public policy via parliamentarism.

Aside, then, from where rights of expression and association are concerned (in regard to which the hands of the member states are tied by international law), there is room for restrictions on parliamentarism, on job security, on the right to strike, and on the right to vote. How far these restrictions extend in practice, however, is decided not by international undertakings, but by political and cultural factors within each country. It is here that the public debate – or what McKay calls legitimacy – makes itself felt. How far parliament and government dare to go depends on the extent to which a reduction in democracy meets with public acceptance.

Complete Failure

The alternative *complete failure*, finally, means that the member states abandon both the stability pact and democracy. The idea is to let inflation loose and thus to make the euro a soft currency. This calls forth, to begin with, great vitality and inventiveness in the media, in interest groups, and in electoral contests. The short-term effect seems to be a land of milk and honey, in which 'everything' is possible. A political intoxication of this kind is not likely, however, to be of the abiding sort. Catastrophe impends when the European Central Bank loses control over the value of Euro, while at the same time the political conditions necessary for a fiscal union at the European level prove to be absent.

Neither the stability pact nor democracy in the member states is able to withstand the strain in this fourth alternative. The political experiences of Europe during the 1970s and early 1980s give an indication of how this vicious circle is constituted. The combination of being able *neither* to control the value of money *nor* to hold down unemployment undermines faith in democracy (Scharpf, 1987: 294ff; Merkel 1993: 21ff, 363ff).

For psychological and historical reasons the attempt to solve economic problems once and for all – by means of the asymmetrical structure examined in this chapter – leaves little or no room for failure. If the stability pact is thrown over, even while no fiscal union as in the federal alternative is erected, then the policies of the 1970s will not be easily repeated. Thwarted expectations result in deep disappointment. In this case too, authoritarian remedies would be a tempting solution. Extraordinary methods may appear – under certain conditions – to offer the only chance for breaking out of a vicious circle comprised of galloping inflation, rising unemployment, and growing popular contempt for politicians.

The problem lies in the relation between the short and the long term. Democracy is endangered over the long run by a combination of unemployment and inflation. This is precisely the outcome that would occur if neither the member governments nor the Union organs were able to do anything to curb the crippling stagflation. As a result of the single currency, monetary sovereignty was irreversibly surrendered. The member states have lost, in practice, any prospects for influencing monetary policy. At the same time, the governments are unable to win popular support within their respective countries for a union-wide redistributive fiscal policy.

The member states can only amend the relevant treaties with the utmost difficulty. This is the crucial difference between this system as opposed to one in an ordinary state where the monetary prerogatives are reversibly delegated to a central bank. In the latter system, the democratic organs of the state in question are independently empowered to alter the constitution. From a political and 'realistic' standpoint, this can be hard enough. Changing the provisions of the treaty regulating the status of the European Central Bank is at least fifteen times harder. Especially, this is the case if a treaty revision has to be made rapidly in the midst of an international monetary crisis.

Legitimacy is Not Enough

If we apply the categories of 'sustainable' and 'unsustainable' equally to the stability pact and to democracy, we distinguish four instead of three possible outcomes. More can certainly be said about each of these. But I shall refrain. My main object here is to argue that David McKay is reaching only halfway in his admirable attempt to clarify and answer the question of the political, as opposed to the economic, implications of a monetary union without a fiscal union.

In my view, asking only about the legitimacy of the possibilities of monetary discipline, loose money, and fiscal centralization does not clearly capture what is political as opposed to what is economic. Used the way McKay does, legitimacy is a *sociological* term. It denotes the extent to which public opinion accepts a monetary union without a fiscal union. It does not say anything about whether this acceptance occurs inside a framework of citizen rights, universal suffrage, and accountable government. An opinion poll taken in Germany immediately before the outbreak of the second world war might have shown that the Nazi regime was legitimate in a sociological sense. However, from a constitutional point of view it was not.

An asymmetrical solution to the present problem will not work, McKay avers, unless the electorates of the member states give it their active support. I could not agree more. Yet merely pointing out the need for legitimacy is to beg the question, as I see it. The more interesting and important task we are faced with, in my view, is to seek out a solution to the problem in terms of rational political argument *in addition to* those of sociology. *Why* is it that European citizens should consider a monetary union without a fiscal union a trustworthy idea? What *reasons* are there for believing an asymmetrical solution would be sustainable?

Assuming intellectual honesty is their ultimate criterion, citizens and politicians will need to know why the iron law of fiscal centralization can and should be rendered, through a deliberate act of self-binding, inoperative in favour of a new type of political order. Why should the suprastatal element in the European Union be prevented from developing into a democratic structure? Why should we wish to irreversibly surrender monetary powers to an independent federal bank? And why in particular, should we want do that without simultaneously creating an appropriate system of revenue sharing and fiscal redistribution comparable to that found in historically established federations that are democracies as well as welfare states?

Assuming that politics is not only a problem of social legitimacy, a democratic component has to be added as a relevant criterion. If we want to solve the political sustainability problem we should look for a *combination*. Democracy is not enough; it must also be legitimate in order to work properly. Likewise, legitimacy is not enough; it must also be democratic in order to be defensible. A dictatorship might be legitimate in a sociological sense (cf. Kelstrup in this book). Therefore, I argue in this chapter, that a fourfold division – where the sustainability of democracy and the stability pact are both taken into account – is better suited to clarify the sustainability problem in a normatively satisfactory way.

Enlightened Understanding

Picking up the gauntlet thrown at us by the economists we should not dismiss in advance the new up-to-here-but-no-further demarcation line against further political integration chosen by the Christian and Social Democrats. A monetary union without a fiscal union is not unrealistic by any sort of 'necessity'. Neither theoretical (by definition) nor empirical (it has never been experienced) concerns should be considered sufficient. Whether the solution chosen in the Maastricht Treaty will be sustainable remains to be seen.

Given the benefit of the doubt, European leaders should be looked upon as if they were aiming to preserve not only the stability pact but also democratic rule in the member countries. That comparative federalism has not yet uncovered a functioning monetary union in the absence of a fiscal one is hard to dispute (McKay, 2001: 127ff). But how weighty is this as an objection to relocating the up-to-here-but-no-further line of defense against further political integration?

Someone has to be the first, Helmut Kohl and François Mitterrand would presumably have said, had they condescended to discuss the matter with a political scientist. The sustainability of the arrangement we have chosen, they would probably have said, is determined not by the lessons of political experience, but by the specific features of this particular case. Indeed, they might even have admonished, truly great statecraft is characterized precisely by a lack of reliance on comparison and experience. Decisions of this order are distinguished, rather, by their one-time character and their reliance on intuition.

Had I found myself in the company of these two statesmen in the spring of 1990, I would have advised them against behaving so arrogantly. The fact that their plan had never before been attempted did not free them, in my view, from thinking the matter through more thoroughly, or from giving a fuller account of their reasoning. Politicians cannot, of course, devote all their time to research. No decisions would in that case be made. As thoroughly as possible is the critical rider. The norm of enlightened understanding enjoins leaders to base their decisions on the best information available. The fact that a given leader must ultimately reach a decision does not entitle him or her to disregard expert knowledge or tested experience.

Comparing the European with the German Unification

On the basis of a study of German social democracy at the turn of the former century, Robert Michels formulated what he called the 'iron law of oligarchy'. Wherever human beings organize themselves, the result is the rule of the few. What I have described here as the 'natural' tendency of a monetary union – a tendency that the settlement of 1990 flew in the face of – is a kindred notion of 'iron' law. Wherever a common currency is introduced, a fiscal union and a democratic suprastate arise as well. Not just unitary states, such as Denmark, France, and Sweden, but federal states like the United States, Canada, and Germany as well, have learned that a monetary union leads sooner or later to a common exploitation of the available tax bases.

A good recent illustration may be seen in German developments during the 1990s. As a result of the centralization of power over the currency, the federal German budget transfers vast sums of money from its Western to its Eastern parts within the reunited country. Similar examples can be found throughout the world. In all such cases fiscal redistribution takes place, in the form of targeted state programs and other measures designed to equalize conditions between richer and poorer parts of the country. How can a corresponding drive towards territorial redistribution and revenue sharing be prevented, once the EU has established a monetary union in the absence of its fiscal counterpart?

The asymmetry problem scrutinized here emerges with still greater clarity if we consult the developments that took place within Germany during the same crucial period ten years ago. A monetary union *without* a fiscal union was launched as the solution for the European Union at the very same time that the opposite policy – a monetary union *with* a fiscal union – became the formula for unifying Germany. The task for the politicians, it may be said, was to explain the difference.

The theory of a 'natural' drive for fiscal and hence constitutional centralization was used, in the course of these two parallel events, both to *justify* a fiscal union (in the case of Germany), and to *prevent* such a development (in the case of Europe). An 'iron law' of the need to centralize power over taxes and expenditures was seen as obvious in the case of Germany. Where Europe was concerned, on the other hand, it was viewed as important that this same 'natural' development be combated.

In the stability pact, the member state governments pledged not to lay claims upon one another's tax bases. This pledge testified to a great faith in the institutionalist method. The governments judged it possible to prevent 'natural' appeals to solidarity from being heeded. Through a special doctrine devised for the purpose at hand – the ban on relief enunciated in the stability pact – they thought they could prevent the iron law of fiscal centralization from operating in this case.

The two processes of unification – the German and the European – were handled in diametrically opposite ways. The German policy was framed to enhance and stabilize suprastatal democracy. When it came to European unification, on the other hand, governments all across the continent sought to obstruct any comparable development.

Three Conditions for Success

Having thus clarified the problem, I now turn to its resolution. What are the political prerequisites for turning a monetary union without a fiscal union into a success and thus avoiding not only federalism but also authoritarian measures and a complete failure?

It must be judged as a high-risk project, especially against the background given in this chapter, to attempt to hinder the further growth of the supra-state while at the same time trying to preserve and develop democratic rule inside the member states. Taking such a risk can only be justified, I would argue, if three conditions are met and broadly understood. These three conditions (Gustavsson 1997, 1998, 2000) deserve special attention when trying to avoid a political disaster.

Suprastatism Must Remain Provisional

The first condition concerns the way the suprastatal but non-accountable first pillar, which regulates the centralized powers over the market and currency. How can suprastatism and democratic accountability be reconciled? By suprastatism I mean the particular combination of majority voting, direct effect and precedence for federal law that distinguishes a federal form of government from a confederate one. By democratic accountability I refer to a system in which it is possible to replace the holders of political office through general elections founded on universal suffrage and civil rights, and to achieve an alternative set of policies thereby.

All federal elements in a political structure face the problem of how to reconcile suprastatism and democratic accountability. How can decision-making be carried out on a suprastatal basis while maintaining the accountability of office-holders, i.e., ensuring that leaders can be replaced and policies changed through elections?

The most common solution to the problem is to strike a balance between the one-state-one-vote principle, on the one hand, and the one-citizen-one-vote principle, on the other. This is accomplished through a two-chamber system, in which the states are equally represented in the one chamber and the citizens equally represented in the other. Not only Canada and the US have overcome opposition in this way, but also Austria, Germany, Spain, and Switzerland.

A great and interesting exception to this general rule is the European Union. Its member states are democracies. Governance within the first pillar, however, diverges from the usual pattern by which suprastatism and accountability are combined. Within the framework of the first pillar, decision-making is suprastatal in character, while at the same time it is beyond the reach of collective judgement and review.

The argument most frequently used in defense of the EU's constitutional asymmetry is the one set forth in the 1993 verdict (*BVerfGE*, 17: 155-213) of the German Constitutional Court. The question facing the Court was whether the Law of Accession to the Treaty on European Union – which the Bundestag had passed by a large majority in December 1992 – could be reconciled with the demands for democratic accountability enshrined in the German Basic Law. Not until the Court had answered that question in the affirmative could the Maastricht Treaty be ratified.

The Court argued as follows: the suprastatism established in the first pillar of the Union Treaty is provisional. Sovereignties are delegated rather than surrendered. Such a delegation of sovereignties is acceptable, according to the Court, as long as the criteria of the Basic Law are upheld. According to these criteria, the use of common competencies must be *marginal* in relation to the functioning of German democracy as a whole, and the uses to which these competencies are put at the European level must be *predictable*. The delegation of sovereignty must also be *revocable*; that is, the German authorities must retain the prerogative to re-assume the powers delegated if the criteria of marginality and predictability are not met.

The German Constitutional Court deemed these three criteria to have been met, and so concluded that the ratification of the Treaty was consistent with the demands for democratic accountability laid down in the Basic Law.

The German Constitutional Court's position has in fact been widely embraced - as indeed it should - in order to rescue the idea of a monetary union without a fiscal union. One of the most elaborated versions of this position can be found in the work of Fritz Scharpf (1994: pp. 131 ff). He calls for an overall European arrangement which is compatible *both* with the demands for autonomy put by the member states *and* with the advantages associated with collective action arising from the principle of provisional suprastatism.

As a reformist and piecemeal constitutional engineer, Scharpf argues that we should attempt to achieve as much democracy as possible. If our purpose is to defend the principle of democratic governance in Europe, we must proceed on the basis of a realistic picture of the political options facing us in view of the completed internal market and a monetary union without a fiscal union. In practice, this means that technocratic rhetoric, rule, and practices make it easier to let first pillar issues remain submerged from political view. This way many sensitive issues that are democratically provocative, such as family related legislation and demands for fiscal redistribution via Brussels, could be deliberately avoided (Scharpf, 1999: 29 ff).

Offensive Intergovernmentalism Must Prevail

As a corollary to this first idea a corresponding condition is important. When it comes to the second (foreign policy), third (justice and home affairs), and – as I name it – fourth (social policy) pillars the handling of these issues need to remain openly and explicitly grounded in the legitimacy of each individual member-state electorate. These issues should be handled as far *above* the threshold of political visibility as possible. This should be done because the method of coordination, as opposed to suprastatism, is the only proper method of avoiding the centralization of additional legal and fiscal powers without seeing any possibility of a corresponding centralization of responsibilities.

By the - still informal - fourth pillar of the European Union I am referring to *offensive intergovernmentalism*. This is said in contrast to the more defensive safeguarding of external and internal sovereignty in defense and police matters.

To adapt words taken from the Presidency Conclusions from the Lisbon European Council in March 2000, offensive intergovernmentalism can be described as 'a new open method of coordination' that has been applied to reducing unemployment levels. It does not come about through suprastatism, as in the first pillar, but through coordination in the new, informal fourth pillar. This new form coordination is created by concerted action, comparison, and benchmarking in order to become 'to become the most competitive and dynamic knowledge-based economy in the world, capable of sustainable economic growth with more and better jobs and greater social cohesion' (Lisbon European Council, 23 and 24 March 2000, Presidency Conclusions, para. 5).

- Implementation of the strategic goal [of employment, economic reform and social cohesion] will be facilitated by applying a new open method of co-ordination as the means of spreading best practice and achieving greater convergence towards the main EU goals. This method, which is designed to help Member States to progressively develop their own policies, involves:

- fixing guidelines for the Union combined with specific timetables for achieving the goals which they set in the short, medium and long terms;

- establishing, where appropriate, quantitative and qualitative indicators and benchmarks against the best in the world and tailored to the needs of different Member States and sectors as a means of comparing best practice;

What Makes a European Monetary Union... 115

- translating these European guidelines into national and regional policies by setting specific targets and adopting measures, taking into account national and regional differences;

- periodic monitoring and peer review organised as mutual learning processes. (Lisbon European Council, 23 and 24 March 2000, Presidency Conclusions, para. 37.)

Offensive intergovernmentalism is meant to strengthen the Euro-zone by policy convergence through 'benchmarking, policy transfer and lesson-drawing' (Dyson, 2000: 260). Policy failure should not only be defined in relation to inflation, budget deficits and public debt. As important in the perspective of democratic accountability and visibility is job creation, a stable public sector infrastructure with good schools, good day-care, family allowances and pensions in order to improve labor-market flexibility and to avoid social exclusion.

National Democracies should be Vitalized rather than Apathized

Accepting the restrictions formulated by the German Constitutional Court as marginality, predictability and revocability there does not seem to remain any better alternative than sticking to democratic accountability and visibility within each single country.

However, concentrating on democratic accountability and visibility within each single member state will have a practical consequence. If the member-states are to surrender national powers to a democratically unreachable monetary union it should – as a counterbalance – *vitalize rather than apathize* the system of nation-wide political parties, interest groups, and open government.

Otherwise the national political life inside a monetary union without a fiscal union – in periods and areas of recession and deflation – would have to face a very hard choice. A breakdown of nation-wide political parties and trade unions would force the member states to choose between taking the step up to a fiscal union or giving up political rights and free elections in order to prevent social unrest and populist political parties from gaining influence. In order to make the stability pact work, while avoiding a fiscal union and maintaining basic human rights the member states will need *more* rather than *less* national democracy.

National political parties, popular movements, and public opinion will have to stress the importance of the second, third, and fourth pillar issues. These are *not* marginal in the meaning of the German Constitutional Court. Conversely, it is because of their democratic marginality that the powers regulating a unified market and unified currency have been centralized without a corresponding growth in democratic accountability at the European level. For the stability pact to work in practice, the citizens must know that the bulk of powers are still within democratic reach inside each member state.

Let us assume that we succeed in persuading ourselves that first pillar issues are relatively unimportant. Assuming that this can be done, it does not seem totally unrealistic that national democracies could be vitalized to such an extent that we would be able to manage a system of a monetary union without a fiscal union.

However, this demands far more enlightened understanding and reformist insight than has hitherto characterized the agitation in favor of further European suprastatism and political coordination. Over the last decade this has all too often been presented in the simple-minded format of 'informing' reluctant and misinformed fellow-citizens about the historical necessity of yielding to the inevitable.

In the terminology introduced by Kenneth Dyson, this tendency to inform downwards rather than to discuss at an equal footing calls for a 'Kantian' instead of a neo-liberal 'Hobbesian' or 'Lockean' political culture. 'The Euro-zone is a Kantian culture to the extent that moral defensibility by reference to general principles is accorded a high value by its actors, they [should] see each other as partners or friends rather than enemies or rivals, and they [should] base their relations on the principle of mutual aid rather than egoistic self-interest' (Dyson, 2000: 8).

As isolated principles, provisional suprastatism and offensive intergovernmentalism are not going to contribute much to the political sustainability of monetary union without fiscal union. Those two principles will have to be accompanied by – and embedded in – a democratic culture fostering politics in the 'Abraham Lincoln' sense of government not only *for* and *by* the people but also *through* the people.

It is a common mistake to underestimate public opinion. Especially, I think it is important to avoid making that error in deliberating the political sustainability of a monetary union without a fiscal union. Unlike what neo-liberals are ideologically inclined to believe, citizens ever since the French revolution have been taught to emphasize the importance of free will, choice and – which is especially important in this context – learning from experience and rational argument.

Supposedly, intellectual freedom will remain and prosper. In that case widespread public concern about critical rationalism and enlightened understanding will keep reminding the neo-liberals, inspired by Hobbes and Locke, that the absence of these core elements renders the idea of democracy meaningless. If there is no choice, why should governments be accountable to national electorates?

Note

1   Broader accounts are given by Dyson (1994, 1999, 2000); Dyson and Featherstone (2000); McKay (1996, 1999, 2001); Scharpf (1994, 1999, 2000, 2001); McNamara (1998); Moravcsik (1998); Tondl (2000); Verdun (2000); Verdun and Christiansen (2000); Weiler (1999); Marcussen (2000); Karlsson (2001).

References

Allégret, J. et al (1999): *La zone euro et les enjeux de la politique budgétaire*, Grenoble: Presses Universitaires de Grenoble.
BverfGE [Entscheidungen des Bundesverfassungsgerichts] (1993): 89, 17, 155-213.
Dyson, K. (1994): *Elusive Union: The Process of Monetary and Economic Union in Europe*, London: Longman.
Dyson, K. (1999): 'Economic and Monetary Union in Europe', in B. Kohler-Koch and R. Eising, (eds): *The Transformation of Governance in the European Union*, London: Routledge, pp. 98-118.
Dyson, K. (2000): *The Politics of the Euro-Zone. Stability or Breakdown?*, Oxford: Oxford University Press.
Dyson, K. and K. Featherstone (2000): *The Road to Maastricht. Negotiating Economic and Monetary Union*, Oxford: Oxford University Press.
European Convention for Protection of Human Rights and Fundamental Freedoms, Rome, 4, XI, 1950, [http://www.coe.fr/eng/legaltxt/5e.htm].
Feldstein, M. (1997): 'The Political Economy of the European Economic and Monetary Union: Political Sources of an Economic Liability', *Journal of Economic Perspectives*, vol. 11, no. 4, pp. 23-42.
Gustavsson, S. (1997): 'Double Asymmetry as Normative Challenge', in A. Føllesdal and P. Koslowski, (eds): *Democracy and the European Union*, Berlin: Springer, pp. 108-131.
Gustavsson, S. (1998): 'Defending the Democratic Deficit', in A. Weale and M. Nentwich, (eds): *Political Theory and the European Union. Legitimacy, Constitutional Choice and Citizenship*, London: Routledge, pp. 63-79.
Gustavsson, S. (2000): 'Reconciling Suprastatism and Democratic Accountability', in C. Hoskyns and M. Newman (eds): *Democratizing the European Union. Issues for the Twenty-first Century*, Manchester: Manchester University Press, pp. 39-64.
Karlsson, C. (2001): *Democracy, Legitimacy and the European Union*, Uppsala: Acta Universitatis Upsaliensis (= Skrifter utgivna av statsvetenskapliga föreningen i Uppsala, 146.).
Lepsius, R. M. (1995): 'Institutionenanalyse und Institutionenpolitik,', in B. Nedelmann, (Hrsg): *Politische Institutionen im Wandel*, Opladen: Westdeutscher Verlag (= Kölner Zeitschrift für Soziologie und Sozialpsychologie, Sonderheft 35), pp. 392-403.
Lisbon European Council 23 and 24 March 2000. Presidency Conclusions. [http, pp.//ue.eu.int/]
Marcussen, M. (2000): *Ideas and Elites. The Social Construction of Economic and Monetary Union*, Aalborg: Aalborg University Press.
McKay, D. (1996): *Rush to Union. Understanding the European Federal Bargain*, Oxford: Clarendon Press [Second edition as *Federalism and European Union*, Oxford University Press, Oxford 1999].
McKay, D. (1999): 'The Political Sustainability of European Monetary Union', *British Journal of Political Science*, vol. 29, no. 3, pp. 463-485.

McKay, D. (2001): *Designing Europe. Comparative Lessons from the Federal Experience*, Oxford: Oxford University Press.
McNamara, K. R. (1998): *The Currency of Ideas. Monetary Politics in the European Union*, Ithaca N.Y.: Cornell University Press.
Merkel, W. (1993): *Ende der Sozialdemokratie? Machtressourcen und Regierungspolitik im westeuropäischen Vergleich*, Frankfurt am Main: Campus Verlag.
Michels, R. (1911): *Zur Soziologie des Parteiwesens in der modernen Demokratie*, Leipzig: Klinkhardt.
Milward, A. S. (1992): *The European Rescue of the Nation-State*, London: Routledge.
Moravcsik, A. (1998): *The Choice for Europe. Social Purpose and State Power from Messina to Maastricht*, Ithaca N.Y.: Cornell University Press.
Mundell, R. A. (1961): 'A Theory of Optimum Currency Areas', *American Economic Review*, vol. 51, pp. 657-664.
Riker, W. H. (1975): 'Federalism', in F.I. Greenstein & N.W. Polsby (eds): *Handbook of Political Science*. vol. 5, Reading, Mass.: Addison Wesley, pp. 93-172.
Scharpf, F. W. (1987): *Sozialdemokratische Krisenpolitik in Europa*, Frankfurt am Main: Campus Verlag.
Scharpf, F. W. (1994): *Optionen des Föderalismus in Deutschland und Europa*, Frankfurt am Main: Campus Verlag.
Scharpf, F. W. (1999): *Regieren in Europa: Effektiv und demokratisch?* Frankfurt am Main: Campus Verlag.
Scharpf, F. W. (2000): 'Economic Changes, Vulnerabilities, and Institutional Capabilities', in F.W. Scharpf and V.A. Schmidt (eds): *Welfare and Work in the Open Economy. From Vulnerability to Competitiveness*, Oxford: Oxford University Press, vol. 2, pp. 21-124.
Scharpf, F. W. (2001): 'Notes Toward a Theory of Multilevel Governing in Europe', in *Scandinavian Political Studies*, vol. 24, no. 1, pp. 1-26.
Tondl, G. (2000): 'Fiscal Federalism and the Reality of the European Union Budget', in C. Crouch (ed.): *After the Euro. Shaping Institutions for the Governance in the Wake of European Monetary Union*, Oxford: Oxford University Press, pp. 227-256.
Verdun, A. (2000): *European Responses to Globalization and Financial Market Integration. Perceptions of Economic and Monetary Union in Britain, France and Germany*, London: Macmillan.
Verdun, A. and T. Christiansen (2000): 'Policies, Institutions, and the Euro: Dilemmas of Legitimacy', in C. Crouch (ed.): *After the Euro. Shaping Institutions for the Governance in the Wake of European Monetary Union*, Oxford: Oxford University Press, pp. 162-178.
Weiler, J. H. H. (1999): *The Constitution of Europe*, Cambridge: Cambridge University Press.

Part III

EMU, EU and Democracy

6 Democracy, EU and the EMU
MORTEN KELSTRUP

The purpose of this chapter is to discuss the relationship between democracy, the EU, and the EMU. The chapter is in some aspects about democracy in the EU in general, but its specific purpose is to discuss democratic aspects of the EMU, in particular the Euro-cooperation. The problem is not only to look at the institutional structure of the EMU but also to reflect on how the development of the EMU might influence democracy in Europe.[1]

Of course, one of the major problems in regard to the EU has to do with EU's relationship to democracy. The discussion of this topic is difficult in many aspects. One difficulty is that in discussing democracy, one has to recognize that there are many views on democracy, many 'models', and that rather basic normative views are related to the different interpretations of democracy.[2] Another difficulty is that in the EU very many actors have views on democracy, and if the debate on democracy in the EU has to be – in itself – democratic, the debate has to take the view of others into consideration.

Linking this discussion to the EMU – or more concretely to the Euro-cooperation – is even more difficult. Here one of the difficulties is that we, in all fairness, have to admit that we do not know exactly how the EMU is to develop. In addition, the EMU-cooperation is a new institutional construction in the European context. It is dynamic and its future development depends on many unforeseeable factors. Thus, we have to base our discussion on assumptions about the future development of the EMU.

One of the points made below is that the discussion about the EMU cannot be isolated to the economic sphere. In an international context this will seem rather self-evident. Yet, in the Danish debate this view – that we were to discuss not only economics but also EU's political structure – was in itself controversial. Seen in the light of the development since the Danish referendum, it seems very strange that one could have the view that the Euro-development is only economic.

On Democracy and Democratic Legitimacy in the EU

Democracy and Understandings of Democracy

Fundamentally, democracy is about people's self-government.[3] The concept includes aspects of autonomy and control. Democracy implies that 'people' – whether this is perceived individually or collectively – have/has influence upon the collective decisions that affects themselves. One might claim that democracy implies: 1) that people have the possibility of participating in the collective decisions which have a bearing upon their own lives (*the participatory aspect*), 2) that in the political process there are alternatives and a choice in regard to representatives as well as in regard to policies, i.e. competition between persons and policies within structures for responsibility and control (*the competition aspect*), and 3) that there are limits in regard to how much the collective decisions can intervene in the fundamental rights of the individual (*the protection aspect*). It is, of course, possible to formulate the fundamental principles in democracy differently and to stress other nuances. Depending on whether one puts the main emphasis upon participation, competition or protection, you might talk, respectively, of participatory democracy, competitive democracy or protective democracy. They can all be seen as variations of a fundamentally liberal conception of democracy.

Democracy has a specific political aspect and a broader societal aspect. By *political democracy* one can understand a political system that is institutionalized in such a way that it: 1) includes widespread participation in the political decision making processes based on the principle of political equality, 2) involves competition between different views and actors in the political decision making process, including mechanisms which keep the leaders responsible and gives a possibility to remove them, and 3) puts limitations to the exercise of political authority, i.e. includes the protection of the basic rights of individuals. By *societal democracy* one can understand societies in which there: 1) is a widespread acceptance of the equal right to political participation, 2) exists a free public debate and possibilities of creation of a public opinion, and 3) is a widespread respect for other individuals and their fundamental rights (see Gustavsson in this book).

Societal democracy in this sense implies the existence of a '*civil society*', understood as the existence of a multitude of actors who accept fundamental human rights and fundamentally equal political rights as well as respect for the possibilities of individual persons for acting and communicating without control from political authorities. In a simplified way, one could say that societal democracy is the same as the existence of a *'democratic culture'*.

It is not the purpose of this chapter to go in depth in regard to the different perceptions or models of democracy or the many different ways in which democracy can be institutionalized. In present debates on democracy it is important to understand that we, in particular, have institutionalized democracy as democracies in states. We have democratic structures locally and *in* the states, but there is hardly any equivalent thinking about the question what democracy entails in the international system or world society. We have only very few attempts to institutionalize democratic features at a level beyond the nation state. The international system has essentially been viewed as a power-based anarchy characterized by conflict and cooperation among states. The most recent literature on democracy and parts of the literature on international relations calls for developing understandings of democracy which cover the nation states all right, but also extends beyond these. This problem is important in our understanding of the relationship between the nation states and the processes we sometimes describe as globalization. It is also important in our understanding of democracy in relation to the European Union which actually is one of the few attempts to further democracy in relation to supranational governance. Thus, this general debate also constitutes a significant basis for a discussion about democracy in relation to the EMU.

National Democracies are Challenged by Globalization

An important point in understanding the problems which modern national democracies face, is that we experience a widespread globalization which puts the nation states and the national democracies under pressure. I shall not here go into the huge debate about different meanings of the term globalization, but only briefly understand *globalization* as more than economic globalization, i.e. as the creation of social systems across national (state) borders of such a strength or coherence that the states cannot control the social systems in question. We have already for a long time had a far-reaching economic globalization through the creation of the international economy, the international capitalism if you will. In our historical period we are experiencing an intensified economic globalization, not least due to the opening of the international financial markets. Simultaneously, we are experiencing a rapidly expanding globalization in other fields, for instance in relation to media, technology, research, different cultural systems and – partly – also politically.

One might say that the modern states have passed through a

development which in many respects has consolidated them as the most important political units, but that they are now under pressure, especially from the processes of globalization. In brief, it can be claimed that the states have developed from being '*administration states*' and '*taxing states*' into being '*constitution and law states*'. Some states became '*nation states*'.[4] Especially in the 19th century the European states opened themselves for democratic forms of legitimacy, a development later followed by other waves of 'democratizing waves'. In some privileged regions some nation states could further (especially after World War II) develop into '*welfare states*'. Here, I understand a welfare state as a state with a high degree of internal solidarity between the citizens which based on this foundation and via the state budget secures social benefits for the underprivileged. The Nordic states have led the way in this development.

To formulate it heavy-handedly, the national democracies are challenged by the economic globalization. The economic relations – in regard to trade, labor, capital and services – are contesting the existence of national economies and gives added weight to an international economy and international competition. This casts doubt upon the abilities of the states to regulate. Some believe that globalization exerts special pressures on the welfare states.[5] The economic globalization entails that it becomes harder to preserve or re-establish the 'chains of governance' which ensure that the persons depending on the political decisions can also influence them within the framework of the nation states. The basic regulation in the democratic nation states is the so-called '*democratic chain of governance*' or chain of delegation. Within a constitutional state, the basic chain of delegation encompasses: 1) a people which, in the society in question, elects a representation, which 2) elects a government, which 3) control the single ministers and the administration, and 4) which produces the results which then are evaluated by the people. The respect for the people as being 'sovereign' and the parliamentarian chain of delegation must be considered central to a state-based understanding of democracy. But the processes of globalization are challenging these features. It becomes *more difficult to ensure one basic democratic chain of governance.*[6]

On Democracy and Democratization in Relation to the EU

The EU might on the one hand be perceived as a change in the political and economic organization of Europe which contribute to an increased globalization, economically as well as in other ways. The opening for the free movement of goods, capital, persons and services (the EU's 'four freedoms') entails, of course, increased competition and also encompasses far reaching processes of harmonization across the former state boundaries. The formation of the EMU can be seen as a part of this liberalization. On the other hand the EU might *also* be seen as a political and judicial association which establishes common regulations supranationally and transnationally, and which also – through common external policies – establishes the EU as an 'actor' which can influence the conditions for globalization. Thus, the EU can be part of the formation of international regulations ('regimes'). One might say that the EU's institutional and political part constitutes an new political system, and that this gives special possibilities of governance at the supranational level. The EMU can be perceived as part of this but also as part of regional regulation and as an expansion of that system.

One might debate which of the two perspectives on the EU is the most important one. Partly, at least, this is the well-known debate about the question whether the EU is to be seen as a liberal or a social democratic project. The best interpretation seems to be that the EU includes increased liberalization *as well as* increased supranational and transnational regulation, that *the EU is a battleground between different strategies of regulation*, and that one of these battles is about the degree to which the EU should further economic liberalization and the degree to which the EU should regulate liberalization and globalization.

The 'Democracy Dilemma' in Relation to the EU

EU is different from almost all other international organizations and associations because it has some democratic elements. For instance, the EU is based on the rule of law and has a self-understanding (identity) which includes democratic values and principles. EU also attempts to develop its democratic character and to establish and strengthen its democratic legitimacy. The direct democratic legitimacy in the EU is mainly acquired through direct elections to the European Parliament and through the development of policies which gives the EU a 'democratic face'. Also the recognition that the rules of the EU are directly applicable to the individual citizens is part of this picture. Thus, the EU has a certain direct legitimacy. The most important pattern of legitimacy for the EU is, though, indirect. The EU bases the greater part of its legitimacy on the democratic legitimacy of the individual states.

There are limits in regard to the degree of democracy in the EU's political system itself. It is commonly recognized that the EU has a 'democratic deficit'. Sometimes, it is even claimed that if the EU had been a state, the EU would not itself be able to fulfil the criteria which should be fulfilled in order to join the EU!

Is it then a good idea to promote the 'abolishment of the democratic deficit' in the EU? The question is in fact rather difficult. In a basic way, we face what might be called a *'democracy dilemma'* in regard to the EU. This view can be explained in the following way. If we think democracy as liked to state forms, the dilemma consists of a choice between two positions both of which are problematic. On the one hand, it is possible to choose that the EU should be made more democratic by a strategy which locate and keep democracy in the EU at the level of the nation states. The problem with this understanding is that by opting for state based democracies, a long series of regulatory policies within the EU falls *outside* the boundaries of democratic control. On the other hand, one might claim the EU can only become a 'real' democracy, if the EU also develops a state form and acquires the 'normal' democratic attributes that goes with a democratic state. This point of view implies that the EU shall become a democratic state, possibly a federation. It will almost unavoidably lead to a weakening of the democracy in the member states. It might challenge many of the 'democratic advances' which have taken place within the European states. The fear for this last-mentioned development has led some to defend the *preservation* of the democratic deficit in the EU! The thought behind this view is that the demand to abolish the democratic deficit in the EU will lead to an European state building and undermine the established democratic nation states.

The common but problematic view that democracy has to be linked with state forms of government seems to lie very deeply in public discourses. For example, is it characteristic for a large part of the Danish EU-debate (or the Danish 'EU-discourses', if that term is preferable), that these portray a competition between the EU and the nation-state based democracies. Views might be different as to whether it is preferable to: 1) promote an expansion of the democratic sides of the EU, or 2) defend the national democracy against the threat from the EU. But the discourses share what in my perspective is a false premise.

The view here is that one should get away from the close connection between democracy and the concept of the state. This is not easy. But in a debate about democracy and the EU – and democracy in relation to the deepening of the EU-cooperation with the Euro-cooperation – it is important to avoid the two simple and insufficient positions: *either* to see globalization, the EU as well as the EMU as an undermining of the national democracies – with the consequence that the most important thing to defend is national democracies, *or* to believe that the solution to the problems is to create a European state, without taking into consideration that this move might imply a serious de-democratization of the participating nation states and an important loss of the achievements for democracy reached in the nation states. My conclusion from these reflections is that it is necessary to think in categories of democracy that goes beyond a narrow linkage to the nation states, but at the same time, respect the central aspects of the already established democracies.

But how is it possible to do so? How is it possible to develop more democratic structures in regard to policy processes which go beyond the nation states? How is it possible to do so without giving up (too much of) the democratic achievements in the nation states? The answer to that question leads to discussions about different political forms in the EU. Here, I will, in particular, suggest that more focus should be placed upon the *democratic legitimacy* of the EU. My view is that it is important for *all* institutions with political power to have legitimacy, and that processes of democratization are closely linked to the formation of demands for democratic legitimacy, also at others levels than the state. The EU *can* be developed into a more solid democratic legitimacy. The general thought is that much can be done to democratize international and supranational institutions, and also the EU, and that this is possible in Europe without creating a European state. In the following, I sketch a perspective on democratic legitimacy. Afterwards, I shall briefly use this perspective in a more concrete understanding of democratic legitimacy for the EU and the EMU.

On Democratic Legitimacy

Collective decisions which are not based on violence or threats, must – if they shall be accepted – base their authority upon legitimacy. They should be seen as justified by the people to whom the decisions are directed, i.e. by the governed. There are many forms of legitimacy. What can be accepted as legitimate in a society, depends on the existing norm in that society. More specified one might claim that there are *five different dimensions* of democratic legitimacy. They are all relevant for the discussion of legitimacy. Each has an influence on the acceptance of the collective decisions in question.[7]

1) One dimension deals with the *legality* of the decision. This implies that the decisions must be taken in accordance with the different rules which formally have been accepted within the social system in question. Typically, concrete decisions must be in accordance with articles in a constitution, an existing law, or with a treaty.

2) A second dimension deals with the criteria for participation/non-participation in the relevant decision-making processes, i.e. *criteria for*

identity, membership and participation. The prevailing criteria must be understood and justified. It adds to the democratic legitimacy of a certain political system if it is clear for all who belong – and who do not belong – to the system, who have the right to participate, and who do not have this right. Basically, a criteria for democracy is that those affected by decisions should have the right to take part in the decisions (the principle of congruency).

3) A third dimension is that the structures for *representation, responsibility and control* must be justified. It depends on the political culture in question, which demands a concrete political system should fulfil in regard to representative structures, responsibility and control. But an important part of democratic legitimacy is that such institutionalized rules exists, are accepted and adhered to.

4) A fourth dimension is that the *decisions and outcome* of the political system should be justified in regard to the prevailing norms of the societies in question. The idea is that if a political system produces acceptable outputs, this will add to its legitimacy, while the lack of output or output which is not seen as very positive, can detract from the legitimacy of the system.

5) The fifth dimension is that the legitimacy of a decision-making system depends on the de facto acceptance of the system. Support to a system has to be shown. Thus, acts of *legitimation* are necessary. Typically, election results can be acts of legitimation. An important distinction exist between direct and indirect legitimisation.[8] If a political system has legitimation from the individuals which belong to the system, for instance through direct elections, we talk of direct legitimacy. If a system has legitimation from other legitimate collective actors, we see the legitimation as indirect. Typically, an international organization will – if its legitimacy is based on the acceptance of states – have an indirect legitimation. We might see the EU as having, basically, an indirect legitimation, but as developing more direct legitimation, for instance through the direct election to the European Parliament.

Much might be said about these five different dimensions of legitimacy and about the ways in which they interrelate. The perspective entails that there are many different dimensions in which a decision-making system, for example an organization, can achieve legitimacy. In parallel, there are many dimensions in which a *legitimacy deficit* might arise. In addition, the different dimensions of legitimacy might be competing. It is, for instance, typical for some elites to regard the dimension related to output efficiency as very important and to regard this as being hampered by too developed democratic participatory structures. Thus, much emphasis on participation might lead to less legitimacy.

Some Points of View on Democracy and Democratization in the EU

These views leads to a certain ambivalence in regard to democracy in the EU. In one perspective the EU is a very positive contribution to more democracy in the relationship between European states, in particular compared to the anarchy that has dominated and could otherwise dominate Europe. For some of the states in Europe, the membership of the EU promotes and strengthens democratic norms *within* the states. The international political system in its classic sense, understood as a system where it either is the 'right of the strong and mighty' or war that dominates, is one of the most undemocratic systems we can imagine. The EU is in this perspective a progress in civilization. We meet this perspective in many ways, also related to the argument that the EU is a peace project. This is true, also in the sense that the EU has changed the way of problem solving between the European states from power-relations and war to negotiations and regulated decision making.

In a different perspective the EU has problems in regard to democracy. This is clearly so in the perspective in which we compare the EU to democracy in a state. As mentioned, this perspective leads to important problems related to the 'democracy dilemma'. The dilemmas of the EU are also great if we analyze EU's relation to democratic legitimacy. If we briefly look upon EU in the light of the five dimension of democratic legitimacy mentioned above, the conclusion is that there are problems in the EU in relation to all of these. Yet, in another perspective, they all represent *important areas in which the EU can be democratized*. This shall briefly be described:

1) The EU's actions can, generally speaking, be said to follow the principles of the rule of law. But the practices of the EU can increase in their legality. This was, in particular, clear in the problematic practices which lead to the fall of the Santer Commission. Most people that know the cooperation within the EU will probably agree that the administrative culture in the EU needs improvements.

2) In the EU there are some problems in regard to the dimension of identity and belonging. One problem is whether one can define a European identity as the basis for EU's political system, and how one is to

conceive of this. Further, if we cannot identify a common European identity, is it then possible to foresee a possible construction thereof? Another problem is related to the question of an European 'demos'. The major picture seems to be that EU's political system rests on the people of EU's member states, but not on an European demos. This has for some lead to the so-called 'no-demos thesis': the view that – because the EU lacks a 'demos' – it cannot become a democracy. This is a too fast conclusion to draw. One might consider whether a European demos could develop (be socially constructed). Since the demos in states are historical constructions, one cannot *a priori* exclude that this could also happen for the European construction. Another relevant view is that the EU could reach some democratic legitimacy, even if it would not score high on the identity dimension.

3) The *representative structures* and the *structures of responsibility* in the EU can hardly be characterized as satisfying in the perspective of democratic legitimacy. The EU has a 'double' system of representation. The people of the member states are represented through their national governments, in particular in the European Council and the Council of Ministers. In addition, the entire EU-electorate is represented through the election of representatives in the European Parliament. Furthermore, there are some other representative structures, for instance, in the Committee of Regions. They do not have much power. Basically, it makes it easier for one of the important actors *without* a clear democratic mandate, the Commission, to operate. The Commission has an indirect legitimacy (as being appointed by the member countries), but lack direct legitimacy. It might be seen as an improvement in the representative structure that the EU Parliament has gained in power, also increased possibilities to control and eventually dismiss the Commission. One critical comments to the 'structures of responsibility' in the EU is that it is not possible for EU's electorate to remove EU's Councils of Ministers. A second problem is that there are some areas in EU's complex decision-making structure in which there are unclear criteria for representation and control. This is in particular true in relation to EU's committee system, also the part which sometimes is called the 'commitology'. In general, the representative structure needs reforms in many ways.

4) The fourth dimension of legitimacy, the production of important and effective output, has always played an important role in the legitimization of the EC/EU. A basic justification for the powers given to the institutions of the Community has for long been that the special

system of negotiations and decisions should promote *'efficient' solutions* to transnational problems. A central discussion in the evaluation of the EU is of course whether the EU actually produces such solutions. Important discussion are concerned with the questions whether the present system permits sufficient 'leadership', and how the structures can be adapted so that an EU with a much larger number of member states can act efficiently. Clearly, EU's performance in regard to output and efficiency can be improved.

5) Finally, it is important whether the EU has a strong legitimation. It is one of the problems for the EU that the support for the project is rather low. The EU has for long worked to get closer to the citizens and get more popular support but not with impressive results. The relative low turnout to the direct elections for the European Parliament is a very important measure in this perspective. The EU is not so vulnerable to a relative low direct legitimation, because it mainly rests on the indirect legitimation from member states. Yet, the EU could have problems also in regard to this kind of legitimation, for instance when member states – as Denmark – have reservations in regard to major developments of the EU. Situations in which some states refuse to participate in some policies or in which they do not implement EU's decisions undermines this aspect of EU's legitimacy.

An important problem in the discussion of EU's relationship to democracy concerns EU's influence on national democracies. Basically, the democratic chains of representation and control in the states *are* affected by the emergence of EU's decision making. One might argue that these chains are not by any *necessity* weakened, and that national systems might adapt to the EU. But it is probably true that the EU only to a small degree has strengthened established democracies, while it, on the contrary, has contributed to a *de-democratization of the national democracies* in many areas. The analysis of the relation between the EU and the national democracies is difficult, because one cannot just compare the present situation with an ideal situation in which the national democracies are in complete control. As discussed above, the economic globalization results, to a large extent, in a weakening of national democracies. Thus, it might be wrong to blame the EU for the difficulties which are experienced in regard to the classical chains of parliamentary control in the national democracies.

A special aspect of the debate on democracy in regard to the EU has to do with the constitutional debate within the EU. It is still contested whether EU's treaty base is to be considered as a constitution or just as a treaty which is applied in accordance with international law. The debate will have increased importance after the decisions at the intergovernmental conference in Nice. Some will claim that the EU is based on a cooperation between sovereign states and basically is founded in international law. In accordance with this view, the EU is only exercising the authority which the member states have delegated and 'pooled' on the basis of their own constitutions and own sovereignty. This is also the official Danish understanding.[9] Others will claim that the EU already *has* a constitution and already, through this constitution, *has* established basic rules for EU's own internal judicial and political life. This view create uncertainties in regard to the exact relationship between EU's 'constitution' and the constitutions of the states.[10] This uncertainty is likely to weaken the status of the constitutions of the nation states. The lack of clarification has the effect that we see a competitive relationship between the democracy in the EU and in the nation states. It might be more fruitful if the democratic endeavors within the two, overlapping political systems, through more clarity could supplement each other.

These are some aspects of the debate on democracy in relation to the EU. This will now be used in a more specialized discussion of democracy in relation to the EMU and the Euro-cooperation. The main view is that the EU in general has an important, but somewhat contradictory and also unfinished relationship to democracy. As indirectly indicated, the EMU is here seen as part of the expansion of the EU, and a discussion of democracy in relation to the EMU has accordingly to be closely related to a discussion about democracy and democratic legitimacy in the EU in general.

The EMU as a Part of the EU-system

The very early understanding of economic integration in the European Economic Community included that the integration of markets should be extended to – or would lead to – an economic and monetary union. In the early 1970s the EC developed and accepted far-reaching plans for the realization of an economic and monetary union before 1980, the so-called Werner plan. This part of the integration projects was hampered by the oil crises and the monetary instabilities in the 1970s, and it was not before the end of the 1970s that the much weaker cooperation in the European Monetary System (EMS) was established. Renewed interest in an economic and monetary union emerged in the mid 1980s related to the plans for the EC's Single Market, and more concrete plans for an Economic and Monetary Union were accepted in the late 1980s, partly on the basis of the report from the so-called Delors Commission. The Single Market and not least the introduction of the free movement on capital at the end of the 1980s created a pressure for further institutional steps to regulate monetary matters. At the same time there was some disagreement about the strategy, for example whether the economic convergence between the EU-countries should precede fixed exchange rates, or vice versa, or whether the economic convergence and the steps towards a common currency should – run in parallel. Another major issue was whether an economic and monetary union should have a political parallel. A complicated negotiation game after 1988 and around the process of unification of Germany in 1989-90 lead to the two intergovernmental conferences in 1991. This again resulted in the Treaty of the European Union (the Maastricht agreement) which included a schedule for the EMU, including also a schedule for the third phase for the establishment of the EMU, the initiation of the Euro-cooperation.[11]

In this perspective, Euro-cooperation is only one, although an important, step within European integration. It is based on long development and much preliminary work. In this area as in so many other problem areas within the EU we have seen an incremental development in which one – step by step – has constructed a new set of institutions and regulations. In light of the uncertainties which have dominated the whole debate whether it would be possible to realize an economic and monetary union, it is in many ways surprising that the plans have materialized. When the plans have been successful in spite of the odds against, is it not least because of the special relationship between France and Germany and, in particular, the way in which the two states reacted in the process of German unification (see e.g. Hoffmeyer and Dyson in this book).

The EMU was to a large extent institutionalized on the basis of German ideas of how this new bank, the European Central Bank (ECB), could be institutionalized in a way which would make it independent and bind it to follow an anti-inflationary policy. As a contrasting view, the French wanted a more political institution, an 'economic government', which would have political power in regard to the EMU. The result of the negotiations was an institutionalization of the EMU which made it rather independent of the EU's other political structures. Yet, in the period after the ratification of the Maastricht Treaty there has been a development which has strengthened – political cooperation around the EMU.[12] This can be interpreted as a gradual, political institutionalization which has changed the institutional system in the direction of the French line. Part of this development has been concentrated around the establishment of a special group of ministers of finance from the participating countries. It is to a large extent this body which operates together with the Council of Ministers of Finance – which represents the political counterpart at the EU-level to the European Central

Bank. The German view on the institutionalization of the EMU was, on the other hand, underscored by the so-called Stability and Growth Pact which came into force simultaneously with the start of the Euro-cooperation at the beginning of 1999. Yet, the European Council was in the same period preoccupied with EMU-related subjects. The overall evaluation should most likely be that irrespective of the institutionalization of the ECB as a formally very independent body, there is a development within the EU which goes in the direction of more political attention to EMU-problems. It is still an open question to which degree the EU will develop an institutionalized 'political answer' to the ECB, *how strong* this answer will be, and exactly *which position* this will have within EU's overall framework. The perspective here is that the EMU – and also its institutions – is to be viewed as a part of the entire EU-system. The EMU is, with the ECB as its central institution, a rather independent institution with a clear commitment to a rather narrow target: price stability. But it should be expected that the interplay between the ECB and the other political institutions in the EU will develop further. This also leads to the expectation that the other institutions of the EU will develop in a dynamic way.

On the EMU's Democratic Legitimacy

Since the EMU is part of the entire EU-construction, the democratic aspects of the EMU should also be evaluated as part of the overall discussion of democracy in the EU. This does not, however, prevent a more narrow focus on the EMU-construction in itself.

Is the Present Institutionalization of the EMU Democratic?

Central decisions about monetary policy in the entire Euro-area is placed in the hands of the Governing Council of the ECB. Clearly, the possibility for the people as voters to get influence on these decisions is very limited. The voters in the participating states might get some, albeit limited, influence in the European Parliament, but this will not give them influence on the ECB. And if they get influence on the policies of their national government, this will not either give them much, if any, influence on the ECB.

But it is only on the basis of a very simplified view of participatory democracy, that this limit in influence seems undemocratic. Within constitutional democracies it is rather frequently that special tasks are isolated and delegated to independent institutions with special functions.

These institutions have an indirect legitimacy and cannot – and should not – be controlled in their specific tasks by politicians. The purpose of such constructions can be to ensure that the tasks can be undertaken without interference from day-to-day politics or, more generally, from political authorities. This consideration is fundamental when we argue for the independence of the judiciary. But it is also important in regard to other institutions, for instance for research councils. In fact, most national central banks are secured a high degree of independence. This is, in particular, true in Germany, but it is also true in Denmark. One might add that we also find other ways in which special institutions are protected against changing majorities. This is basic in any constitutional democracy, and the rules which make constitutions hard to change have exactly this function (see Plaschke in this book).

In spite of these considerations, there are some democratic problems in regard to the EMU-construction. One problem is that the decisive guidelines for the European Central Bank can only be changed at an intergovernmental conference through an amendment of the treaty. This will require unanimity. An intergovernmental conference only has indirect legitimacy. Some might argue that this is not a democratic problem. It might be added that the competence which a state by accepting to join the Euro-cooperation delegate to the European Central Bank can be taken back, formally, by the state in question. Viewed from the point of view of international law which see the states as sovereign, this is true. As mentioned, there is no agreement on this interpretation of the constitutional part of the EU-construction. But even if this view is accepted, it should be taken into consideration that it is not realistic in practice that a state leaves the Euro-cooperation. This implies that the possibility which a state has for changing the guidelines of its national bank – either by law or by changes of its constitution – does not have a parallel in the EU. In some ways the ECB is even more independent than a central bank in a constitutional state. The institutionalization of the EMU has thus in some aspects made the power to control monetary policy more distant from the people and representative bodies than within constitutional states.

It has been raised in the Danish discussion of the ECB whether the fact that the ECB is bound to follow the objective of anti-inflation should be judged as undemocratic. In my opinion the answer is that, basically, there is no single policy-goal which can be considered undemocratic as such. If there is a problem with the goals of the ECB, it is related to the freezing of this goal. The problem is that one cannot point to procedures through which the citizens of individual counties have a possibility – through specified procedures – to changes in the objectives of the ECB, except for the possibility of change in the treaty itself. One might say that there are many large formal obstacles blocking the possible participation in decisions which can influence the decisions in the ECB. The freezing of the guidelines is so strong, I think, that there is a problem in regard to respect for democratic procedures. Yet, I am still hesitant to label the institutional structure around the ECB as undemocratic. As mentioned, it is not exceptional within democracies to find areas which are put aside from 'normal' procedures. And one might also argue that the EU is such a fluid and dynamic institutional system that one should not exclude changes in the institutionalization around the ECB. Thus, my conclusion is that the institutional structure of the EMU is 'somewhat undemocratic'. Yet, the most important issues related to the democratic legitimacy of the EMU are not the formal construction around the ECB.

What are the Perspectives for the Democratic Legitimacy of the EMU?

We might ask the more general question, what are the perspectives for the democratic legitimacy of the EMU? This question can be discussed in many different ways. Here I will briefly discuss it from the five different aspect of democratic legitimacy which I presented above. The discussion is rather inconclusive, but it might serve to show a perspective. It might make us aware of the dimensions which are important in this concrete case for the legitimacy of the EMU.

One question concerns the *legality* in the management of the EMU. There is no reason to mistrust the ECB and other managers involved in advance. On the contrary: the fact that the ECB has so strong an independent status and has a clearly defined task will help to ensure that the administration is taking place in accordance with the rules. On the other hand is it clear that there might arise problems of legality in relation to a number of issues. In particular, many politically sensitive judgements must be made concerning the way in which individual states comply or do not comply to the criteria of convergence, also the criteria included in the Stability and Growth Pact. The question about legality is not just a technical question. And how it is handled, will most likely be decisive for one important dimension of the legitimacy of the EMU.

Another question is whether the *criteria for membership* of the EMU will be seen as justified. It is not least in regard to EU's enlargement that one has to decide whether new states will be accepted as members or not. Is it possible to find criteria that will be accepted as objective and reasonable? Some states might be acknowledged as members, while others might well be very dependent of the euro, but still placed outside it. Is it possible to treat this problem in a way which makes it an acceptable structure? Or are dependency structures in reality established without corresponding influence? How judgement is made in regard to these matters, might be decisive for an important aspect of the legitimacy of the EMU.

A third aspect of legitimacy is whether the EMU's structures of representation, responsibility and control appear as just. I have already pointed out that the existing EMU construction has problems in regard to this dimension of legitimacy. Most likely, the institutional structure within the EU will develop further. One could argue that the legitimacy of the EMU could be increased if they allocated more influence to bodies with direct democratic mandates (in particular representative bodies) and established clearer structures for responsibility. Yet, the effect of strong political bodies in the EU in regard to the EMU (for instance an 'economic government') might prevent the ECB in fulfilling its overall function, perhaps with the consequence that it will loose legitimacy in regard to some other dimension (in particular the efficiency-dimension).

The fourth – and perhaps most decisive – aspect of legitimacy is concerned with the *results* of the EMU. Are the effects of the EMU of a sort which contributes to its justification? This question has, in particular, two aspects. First, it is important that the EMU becomes a stable and strong currency. If this is not the case (if for example the euro falls much more than it has done so far in relation to the dollar), the loss of legitimacy will at some point be very serious, and the acceptance of the euro could be threatened. Another question is whether the effects of the EMU are *fairly distributed*. Is there some kind of protection against 'asymmetric shocks' which possibly could affect the EMU? It is important whether EU's economic system with the EMU will lead to a fairly equal pattern of growth, or whether the development will lead to the arise of new inequalities. Very uneven developments can easily contribute to the loss of legitimacy for the EMU in certain states or regions. An additional problem is that for most people it will be impossible to distinguish between the effects of the euro and other causes for negative economic development. A negative scenario for the EMU would be that the EU with the euro experience large economic inequalities. This might lead to important adaptation in the states or areas which are hit most severely. Because of the competition (which is supposed to be harder when the euro is fully implemented) these basically national adaptation programs might be very hard. This might in the affected regions undermine the support of the EMU and, possibly, more generally contribute to a critical attitude to the EU. Thus, the EMU and the EU could in such a situation lose part of its legitimacy.

The fifth dimension of democratic legitimacy is concerned with the degree to which legitimate actors in practice gives the EMU *legitimation* by supporting it. The legitimation of the EMU is to a large extent indirect, that is based on the support from the states. But it is possible to imagine this indirect support extended with different forms of *de facto* consent from the markets as well as the populations. Argued in another way: it is possible to imagine a crisis for the EMU-system if central actors for various reasons (for example due to domestic political developments in the central individual countries) withdraw their support to the EMU and attempts to withdraw from the EMU system.

These remarks about the different dimensions of democratic legitimacy show that it is *far too soon to state whether the EMU will succeed in achieving a high degree of democratic legitimacy or not*. The future for the EMU must be considered as very open. My best judgement is that in particular two elements will be the most decisive for the EMU's ability to win democratic legitimacy. Firstly, it will be very important whether the euro is becoming a stable, accepted and fairly strong currency. Secondly, it will be important whether the EMU – or the EU-economy with the euro – can avoid significant disparities which might provoke withdrawal of support in individual states or regions. The latter possibly might provoke an '*evil spiral of de-legitimation*': a development in which the lack of success leads to a further undermining of the conditions for achieving success. It is nearly too easy to imagine situations in which local or national politicians in times of prosperity take the credit for successes, while the same politicians in times of crises might blame the EMU and more generally the EU for all the problems. If adjustment programs are called for, this could lead to escalating political problems. There is a certain risk that some politicians are only pro integration in times of prosperity but hostile towards integration in times of difficulties. If this is true, a negative development might easily become self-propelling and contribute to loss of legitimacy of the EU.

On the EMU and Democracy in Europe

A Double Perspective on the EMU

Naturally, one might also discuss the democratic aspects of the EMU in a wider perspective. Very briefly I shall discuss the possible impacts of the EMU on democracy in Europe. Let us take the point of departure in the debate about EU's relationship to globalization. As mentioned, on the one hand, the EU can be said to promote economic globalization. On the other hand, the EU can be seen as an important political project for the establishment of governance not only in its own region, but also with influence in the global system. Maybe the EU is the best organized region in the world with the best possibilities for avoiding the negative aspects of economic globalization.

Because the EMU is part of the EU project, the EMU can be seen in the same double perspective. On the one hand, the EMU can be seen as increasing the free movement of factors of production, increasing the competition, the mobility etc. in Europe. One of the effects of the common currency, the euro, is most likely rising competition and increased mobility. Such a development will lead to benefits for the most competitive companies, while others might be squeezed out of the market. If the common currency is followed by further harmonization, for example in relation to tax policy, labor market regulations and social policies, this might increase competition further. On the other hand, the EMU might be seen as an arrangement to secure the European economy, not least as a mechanism to prevent monetary crises, inflation and policies which are to the disadvantage of ones neighboring states.

This double perspective is also relevant in relation to the EMU's influence on the enlargement of the EU. On the one hand, a significant contribution from the EU – as for the EMU – to democracy in Europe is that the EU and the EMU can contribute to the stabilization of the Central and Eastern European countries and their economies within a greater European framework. A smoothly functioning Euro-cooperation might in this context become a significant factor, not least because the states in Central and Eastern Europe in the first phases after the transformation to market economies have relatively poorly institutionalized economic systems. On the other hand, the demands to adjust to the EMU might be so strong and the resulting effect of participating under sharpened competitive conditions be so problematic, that it might create serious problems for the Central and Eastern European countries. These difficulties are of course increased if particular crises arise. The 'evil spiral of de-legitimation' which I mentioned above, might not least be relevant for the Central and Eastern European societies.

More generally, the EMU has a double impact on the national democracies in the European states. One effect is that economic matters most likely will be stabilized. Another effect is that the national democratic authorities most likely will be weakened. The immediate effect of the Euro-cooperation is that the participating state loses a political instrument, the ability to pursue a monetary policy. It is contested whether this really matters when the state in question already is bound by EU's rules and regulations and in addition vulnerable to the effects of globalization. If the *de facto* alternative to participation in an economic and monetary union is currency turmoil or the domination – via the market – by one currency, earlier the German Mark, now the euro, then it is not the worst alternative to be tied up within the EMU. It is probably more important how the political structures in the EU develop in general and maybe as a reaction to the effects of the first phases of the Euro-cooperation.

The conclusion of these considerations is that the consequences of the EMU for democracy in Europe depends on developments yet unknown (for the following scenarios, see also Gustavsson in this book) One scenario – which I basically will term *'the positive EMU-scenario'* (even though it might be discussed if it really is so positive in all aspects) is that a cooperative, democratic Europe develops with an economic framework stabilized through the EMU. In such a Europe there might – due to a positive and stable economic development – also be room for democratization in societies and the political systems at all levels. One can imagine a development of widespread respect for basic democratic norms in Europe and increased social and political possibilities. If we get greater participation, competition in the political processes and protection of human rights and values, this will mean a process of democratization in Europe. The EMU could in such a positive vision be a part of a civilizing and democratic vision for the future of Europe.

On the other hand is it very easy to conceive a *series of negative EMU-scenarios*. One negative scenario might be that central EU-institutions are overloaded with problems while they at the same time might only have a low degree of legitimacy. This might be the case if the EU does not deliver sufficient answers to the many wishes for reforms. Another negative scenario might be triggered if the enlargement process is not fulfilled and a feeling of abandonment arises in the applicant countries. An equally problematic situation might arise if the new countries are forced to excessive adjustments without getting enough in return. A further negative scenario might be that an unbalanced development within the EU (or possibly within an enlarged EU) hits large regions with a very negative development, for instance caused by 'asymmetric economic shocks'. Some areas might experiences economic stagnation and massive social and political problems. How far such negative scenarios might be allowed to develop will depend on the policy in the EU and of the states. A decisive point will probably be whether the EU can contribute with solutions to the crises. Is this possible for the EU in situations in which the economies are in crises and the local and national politicians are so pressed that they cannot live up to the adjustments called for. Will the EU in such a situation be willing and strong enough to intervene with structural policies and policies of reallocation?

The negative scenarios are multiplied, if political, in a number of the applicant countries to the EU, especially in Central and Eastern Europe, aspects, as for instance the 'evil spiral of de-legitimation', are included. It is not an aim in itself to create scary scenarios. But it is important to also consider very problematic possibilities. One scary development is that the enforced neo-liberal globalization leads to social and political 'reaction' which gets a dynamic development of its own.[13] In general, we have far too little understanding of the processes which trigger or feeds 'reactionary' developments. It is not to be excluded that increased competition in the EU – combined with increased demands for adjustments – will further 'reactionary' political forces in Europe. In parallel to the reactions to globalization, it is conceivable that the liberalization and openness which is cemented by the EMU will provoke some political forces to turn against the 'undermining of traditions' which also is an effect of enforced liberalization. It is perhaps possible, as in the debate on globalization, to distinguish between 'black', 'red' and 'green' reactionary forces, tied to the defense of national values, social values and ecological values, respectively. If we argue as the devil's advocate, we might imagine that enforced competition in Europe will push many people affiliated with old values into the defensive. A really negative vision would be that we get the 'Europe of 1000 Haiders': a Europe in which very many different groups, some national and some with other identities and programs, turn against the overall European project and try to sabotage it in different ways. The local and national democracy in such a context can even become the mediator for such forces and can give them formal bastions of power. Thus, it is a possibility that democratic structures might pave the way for undemocratic movements.

It is not difficult to point at problems which might lead to negative developments. But such scenarios shall in all fairness be compared to situations as they would look if no EMU-cooperation existed at all. We might add that we do not exactly know whether it will be the positive or the negative scenarios which will dominate. The formation of the EMU is in many ways a daring project with many unknown possibilities. And it is so within a European project which already is a daring experiment!

Increased 'Politization' and its Influence on EU's Institutional Development

The most likely development will probably be that the EMU gets into some kinds of crises, but that the states and the EU attempts to solve these (see Hoffmeyer in this book). It is very important whether the political systems at the various levels, also the EU-level, are responsive to the problems which arise. In many ways the general democracy in the EU will be tested: is it able to produce practical answers to the problems? Can it be avoided that the rather centralized power structure of the EU develops with too great a distance to (the) people's real problems?

We should expect to experience a *'politicization'* in the EU. By 'politicization' we mean that a question becomes controversial in the sense that it is debated between important actors. One might also say that it becomes an issue in a political system. We can expect more issues in EU's political system and also questions which call for negotiations and action. Probably, major issues can be expected for instance in relation to the structural and redistributive policies of the EU. Demands for stronger or different redistributive policies in the EU might trigger new problems and affect the balances between the EU member states. Politicization will most likely take place within the EU and in the different societies, leading to greater cleavages between groups.

The increased political controversies will probably influence EU's institutional development. An important perspective is that if the EU is to become a more efficient political system, it has to develop institutions which – even better than now – are able to deal with controversial issues on a permanent basis. It is an interesting question how politicized problems related to the EMU are to be treated in EU's institutional system? As it is today, the strong political structure that could match the ECB is lacking. Some changes have happened in the direction of stronger political structures, but further changes must be expected. EU's institutional structure cannot be seen as being inflexible. Rather, we are dealing with a dynamic system, and in some ways the EU is a political battle-ground for competition between different strategies.

Now, it is already part of the EU debate that the institutional structure of the union should be changed. The intergovernmental conference in Nice decided on some changes and initiated a new debate which is to lead to major changes on a new conference in 2004. Probably, it will be very difficult to distinguish between the institutional changes which will stem from the EMU and the changes which might have other causes. The EU already has a dilemma in regard to enlargement and changing decision structures. On the one hand, an enlargement of the EU without significant changes in the institutional structure will probably water out EU's decision-making system. On the other hand, if the wish for deeper integration is accepted of some countries, it will be necessary with increased 'flexibility'. And this implies an internal split within the EU in which the member states in reality are ascribed different status. One of the central questions regarding the EU's institutional development is whether a simultaneous enlargement of the EU and a closer integration of *'Kerneuropa'*, the core of

Democracy, EU and the EMU 143

Europe, will happen. If such a development is coming, adherence to the Euro-cooperation might well have important influence on the position of the state in question, Denmark, for example. Of course it is a highly relevant question where in a more differentiated EU each single country will locate itself.

Conclusions

This contribution has dealt with democracy, the EU, and the EMU. On the basis of a broad and multidimensional, liberal understanding of democracy this article has first discussed democracy in relation to the EU. It has been argued that if democracy is only thought of as related to a national framework, we end up having a 'democracy dilemma'. A major perspective is that it is necessary to demand democratic legitimacy which goes beyond the nation state while simultaneously trying to keep, strengthen, and adapt the established national democracies. It has been pointed out that the debate on the EU and democracy is far from over, and that many concrete possibilities for increasing the EU's democratic legitimacy exist. It has also been pointed out that the EU in some fields has a de-democratizing effect on the national democracies.

The EMU has been described as an economic and political construction placed in extension of the existing EU-cooperation. The interpretation presented here is that the EMU contains elements which are only very marginally democratic, but that it is wrong to view these in isolation. It is very decisive for the contribution of the EMU to democracy in Europe how the *de facto* EMU-cooperation develops. It has been pointed out that important uncertainties exist as to whether the EMU will contribute to increasing stability in Europe or not. The expectations are that large political problems will arise when the EMU is developed further, and that these will result in increased politicization of EU- and EMU-questions. It is very important whether EU's overall political system is responsive to these problems. In this sense democracy in all of the EU is challenged.

Notes

1   The chapter is based on a article in Danish which was an input to the Danish debate in the year 2000 on Denmark's participation in the Euro-cooperation. The purpose was not to support either a yes or a no, but to analyse some of the perspectives related to democratic aspects of the decision.
2   For a closer discussion of the concept of democracy and democratic theory, see

Jakobsen and Kelstrup (1999).
3 The ambiguous formulation is made on purpose. It is contested whether the view on democracy should have a collective or individualistic understanding of the concept 'people' ('demos'). My use of the term covers the understanding that one does not by necessity have to choose a collective understanding (that builds on the 'people' is a collective unit with a common identity) or an individualistic understanding (that builds on the people as being a group of individuals). One might define democracy in a way which holds both possibilities open.
4 For a more thorough description see i.e. Habermas (1999); see also Kelstrup (1999).
5 The question is however contested. Some indicators point towards that the welfare state, because amongst other facts its massive investments in education and steps taken against social conflicts, it is like the bumblebee: 'it can fly despite all predictions to the contrary'.
6 The challenge from globalisation might be formulated as the development through which *globalisation breaks with 'the congruity principle'*. By the latter I mean the principle which secure a 'congruence' between the rulers and the people being ruled.
7 The following discussion on democratic legitimacy builds to a large extent on the analysis in Beetham and Lord (1998b); cf. also Kelstrup (2000).
8 In parallel, we might talk about direct and indirect legitimacy. It is not all kinds of legitimacy which can be seen as either direct or indirect.
9 One of the problems for Denmark in relation to the EU is – as all observers of the development will know – the existence of some unclear elements in the constitutional situation. One element hereof is that in principle Denmark adheres to a 'dualism' which recognises that international agreements – also in the case of the EU – have to be transformed into Danish legislation, but in reality one tends to follow a 'monism' in which, for instance, Danish courts base their rulings directly on EU rules and regulations, cf. Rasmussen and Basse (1999).
10 See for example Weiler (1999).
11 For a detailed description see DUPI (2000, chapter 2).
12 For a very detailed description, see DUPI (2000, chapter 2).
13 See for example Ulrich Beck's criticism of the neo-liberal ideology of globalisation and his identification of different forms of reactions, Beck (1998: 195 ff.).

References

Beck, Ulrich (1998): *Was ist Globalisierung?* Frankfurt am Main: Suhrkamp.
Beetham, David and C. Lord (1998a): 'Legitimacy and the European Union', Chapter 2 in Weale and Nentwich (eds. 1998), pp. 15-33.
Beetham, David and C. Lord (1998b): *Legitimacy and the European Union*, London and New York: Longman.
DUPI (2000): *Udviklingen i EU siden 1992 på de områder der er omfattet af de danske forbehold*, Copenhagen: DUPI.
Føllesdal, A. and P. Koslowski (eds.) (1998): *Democracy and the European Union*, Berlin-Heidelberg: Springer.
Friis, Lykke (1999): 'EU og demokrati – den dobbelte nødvendighed', in Andersen et al. (red.): *Den demokratiske udfordring*. Magtudredningen, Hans Ritzels Forlag, pp. 280-299.
Friis, Lykke (1999): *Europa-Parlamentet før valget. Mod en ny forfatningskamp*, Dansk

Udenrigspolitisk Institut, Fokus-papir nr. 2, 1999.
Gustavsson, Sverker (1996): 'Preserve or Abolish the Democratic Deficit', in Eivind Smith (ed.): *National Parliaments as Cornerstones of European Integration*, London: Kluwer Law International, pp. 100-23.
Gustavsson, Sverker (1998): 'Defending the democratic deficit', in A. Weale and M. Nentwich (eds. 1998): *Political Theory and the European Union. Legitimacy, constitutional choice and citizenship*, London: Routledge, pp. 63-79.
Habermas, Jürgen (1998): 'Jenseits des Nationalstaats? Bemerkungen zu Folgeproblemen der wirtschaftlichen Globalisierung', in U. Beck (Hrsg.) (1998): *Politik der Globalisierung*, Frankfurt am Main: Suhrkamp, pp. 67-84.
Hix, Simon (1999): *The Political System of the European Union*, London: Macmillan.
Jachtenfuchs, Markus: (1998): 'Democracy and Governance in the European Union', in A. Føllesdal and P. Koslowski (eds.) (1998) *Democracy and the European Union*, Berlin-Heidelberg: Springer, pp. 37-64.
Jakobsen, Uffe and M. Kelstrup (red.) (1999): *Demokrati og demokratisering: Begreber og teorier*, København: Forlaget Politiske Studier.
Kelstrup, Morten (1992a): 'European Integration and Political Theory', in Kelstrup (ed.) (1992): *European Integration and Denmark's Participation*, Institute of Political Science, UC, Denmark, Copenhagen Political Studies Press, pp. 13-58.
Kelstrup, Morten (1993): 'EF's politiske system', *Politica*, 1993/3, pp. 253-268.
Kelstrup, Morten (1998a): 'Integration Theories: History, Competing Approaches and New Perspectives', in A. Wivel (ed.) (1998): *Explaining European Integration*, Copenhagen: Political Studies Press, pp. 15-55.
Kelstrup, Morten (1998b): 'Om det danske demokrati og den europæiske integration', in Kelstrup og Versterdorf (1998), pp. 9-43.
Kelstrup, Morten (1999): 'Demokrati, politiske systemer og globalisering', in Jakobsen and Kelstrup (eds.) (1999), pp. 82-137.
Kelstrup, Morten (2000): 'Legitimacy, Democracy and the European Union: Perspectives in the normative discussion of EU's future political structure', Copenhagen: Institute of Political Science: CORE working paper 2000/2.
Kelstrup, Morten and Peter L. Vesterdorf (1998): *Et Demokratisk EU?* Rådet for Europæiske Politik, Århus: Systime.
Lord, Christopher (1998): *Democracy in the European Union*, Sheffield: Sheffield Academic Press.
Rasmussen, Hjalte and Ellen Margrethe Basse (1999): 'Danmarks deltagelse i EU-samarbejdet og i andet internationalt samarbejde', Folketingets rapport fra *Konference om behovet for en grundlovsrevision*, 1999.
Skjalm, Karsten (1998): *ØMU Baggrund og perspektiver*. DUPI fokus, 1998/6.
Weale, Albert and Michael Nentwich (eds. 1998): *Political Theory and the European Union. Legitimacy, constitutional choice and citizenship*, London: Routledge.
Weiler, J. H. H. (1996): 'Legitimacy and Democracy in Union Governance: The 1996 Intergovernmental Conference and Beyond', *ARENA Working Paper* no. 22/96.
Weiler, J. H. H. (1999): *The Constitution of Europe. 'Do the new clothes have an emperor?'* Cambridge: Cambridge University Press.

7 Will Monetary Unification Make it Easier or More Difficult to Democratize the European Union?

PHILIPPE C. SCHMITTER

This chapter attempts to place the advent of EMU in the context of both 'Euro-democracy' and 'domestic democracy', i.e. in terms of its impact upon supra-national and national politics. It begins with the notion of a 'double-bind' that is affecting both levels of aggregation. The EU is undermining domestic democracy without replacing this decline in accountability to citizens by a higher level of democratic representation and decision-making. The EMU can only make this worse, but it may also trigger a large-scale process of politicization across national boundaries. The chapter, therefore, concludes that EMU makes the eventual democratization of the EU both more problematic and more urgent.

No one can answer this question with any degree of certainty. The process of European integration is sufficiently unprecedented so that it is virtually impossible to draw even tentative answers from previous instances in Europe in which the creation of a national currency and the formation of a national political regime occurred within roughly the same timeframe. When this happened – for example, in Germany and Italy in the Nineteenth Century – the process was overshadowed by the threat of force by the hegemonic unifying power and/or by the outcome of violent international conflict.

If nothing else, the complex of institutions that we now call the European Union (EU) is the product of voluntary choice by actors that expect to retain their independent existence as national states and agree to pursue common policies by peaceful means. And no one expects that to change in the future, regardless of the preferences of its (*de facto*) hegemonies, Germany and France.[1]

Hence, whatever its effects upon the eventual democratization of these institutions, the contemporary monetary unification of Europe will be the outcome of protracted negotiation and compromise among 'consenting adult-states' that will retain both their entry and exit options. Provided it is willing to pay the economic, social and/or political costs of 'non-membership', no country is going to have to join and no country will be prevented from leaving the EMU. Which is not say that its national institutions, including its 'domestic democracy', will not suffer the consequences of what the others decide to do. Denmark may choose to 'free-ride' with its own independent currency, but that does not mean that the Danes will not be 'sucked into line' or 'caught in the turbulence' of those who are pedaling together.

Before turning to the generic problems involved in democratizing the EU, it is important to observe that, as is the case with joining monetary unification, there is no *a priori* reason why its institutions have to be made more democratic – least of all, in the near future. In *retrospect*, virtually all Europeans would agree that transforming their initially autocratic national polities into liberal representative democracies was a good thing, even if there was little consensus (and, in many cases, a great deal of violent resistance) at the time this was accomplished. In *prospect*, however, the case for democratization is much less compelling at the supra-national level. Not only are there serious impediments of size and scope involved in creating such an accountable Euro-polity, but there is also very little evidence that individual citizens of Europe presently want such a thing. They still identify overwhelming more with their national (or, in some case, sub-national) units and place much greater confidence in the capacity of their 'co-nationals' to respect their freedoms and govern them in a legitimate fashion. Even those who are most insistent in decrying the 'democracy deficit' of the EU do not necessarily draw the conclusion that the answer lies primarily in changing its institutions. It is at least as plausible to conclude that what is needed are major reforms in the way that national institutions process the decisions made in Brussels and make them transparent and responsive to individual citizens and their representative institutions.

In short, even if it could be demonstrated the EMU will make the democratization of the EU less, rather than more likely, this might not be a valid argument against merging one's national currency with the euro and accepting the authority of the European Central Bank. Those who argue (and, I gather, many of them are Scandinavian) that their 'domestic' political institutions and practices will remain, for the foreseeable future, much better at protecting their rights (and, especially, their entitlements) as citizens than any conceivable set of supra-national ones, might very well welcome EMU – if they were convinced that it would postpone or even make impossible the creation of an eventual Euro-democracy.

Contemplating Euro-Democracy

In a book entitled 'How to Democratize the European Union ... and Why Bother?'[2] I argue that there are two good reasons why it may be timely to begin this experiment with supra-national democracy sooner rather than later:

1) There is considerable evidence that rules and practices of democracy at the national level have become increasingly contested by citizens. This has not (yet) taken the form of rebellious or even 'unconventional' behavior, but of what Gramsci once called 'symptoms of morbidity' such as greater electoral abstention, decline in party identification, more frequent turnover in office and rejection of the party in power, lower prestige of politicians and higher unpopularity of chief executives, increased tax evasion and higher rates of litigation against authorities, skyrocketing accusations of official corruption and, most generally, a widespread impression that contemporary European democracies are simply not working well to protect their citizens. It would be overly dramatic to label this 'a general crisis of legitimacy', but something is not going well – and most national politicians know it.

2) There is even more compelling evidence that individuals and groups within the European Union have become aware of how much its regulations and directives are affecting their daily lives, and that they consider these decisions to have been taken in a remote, secretive, unintelligible and unaccountable fashion. Whatever comfort it may have given them in the past that 'unwarranted interference' by the Eurocrats in Brussels could have been vetoed by their respective sovereign national governments, this has been dissipated by the advent of qualified majority voting. Europeans feel themselves, rightly or wrongly, at the mercy of a process of integration that they do not understand and certainly do not control – however much they may enjoy its material benefits. Again, it would be over-dramatizing the issue to call this 'a crisis of legitimacy' but the 'permissive consensus' of that accompanied European integration in the past is much less reliable – and supranational officials know it.

These two trends are probably related causally – and together they create a potentially serious '*double bind*' for the future of democracy in Europe.[3] If the shift of functions to and the increase in supra-national authority of the EU have been contributing to decline in the legitimacy of 'domestic democracy' by calling into question whether national officials are still capable of responding to the demands of their citizenry, and if the institutions of the EU have yet to acquire a reputation for accountability to these very same citizens when aggregated at the supra-national level, then, democracy as such in this part of the world could be in jeopardy. Admittedly, the grip of this double bind is still loose, but tightening. The national 'morbidity symptoms' show no sign of abating; the supra-national 'permissive consensus' shows abundant signs of waning. Between the two, there is still space for the introduction of democratic reforms, but who will be willing (and able) to take advantage of the rather unusual political opportunity space formed by monetary unification and eastern enlargement (not to mention, the increasingly skewed outcome of Euro-elections) is by no means clear. The potentiality exists for acting pre-emptively before the situation reaches a crisis stage and before the compulsion to do something becomes so strong that politicians may overreact, but will it be exploited?

In this work, I also argue that it is neither feasible nor desirable to try to democratize the Euro-polity *tutto e sùbito* – completely and immediately. Not only would we not know how to do it, but there is also no compelling evidence that Europeans want it. Nothing could be more dangerous for the future of Euro-democracy than to have it thrust upon a citizenry that is not prepared to exercise it and that continues to believe its interests and passions are best defended by *national* not *supranational* democracy.

What I propose in some detail are a number of specific but modest reforms in the norms of citizenship, the channels of representation and the rules of decision-making within the European Union. I chose not to offer a comprehensive vision of what the end-product will look like – only to suggest incremental steps that could be taken to supplement (and not supplant) the mechanisms of accountability to citizens that presently exist within the member states. My basic assumption from the start was that, precisely because the EU is neither a state nor a nation (and may never become either *in strictu sensu*), the practices of an eventual Euro-democracy will have to be quite different from those existing at the national level. It is, therefore, all the more imperative that Europeans act cautiously when experimenting with political arrangements whose configuration will be unprecedented and whose consequences may prove to be unexpected – even, unfortunate.

My second assumption was that the so-called 'Monnet Method' for promoting European integration has exhausted its potential. This strategy guided the process from its beginnings and involved exploiting the interdependence between preferred issues of economic policy and those that arose subsequently. Cooperation between the Eurocrats in the

Commission and representatives of European-level interests (especially, those of business and the professions) ensured a steady supply of 'spillover' proposals that were intended to expand the scope of activity and level of authority of EU institutions. Many of these met with the initial resistance of national government representatives, but gradually, fitfully and almost unobtrusively these efforts contributed to transforming the calculation of national interests. Countries found themselves subsequently agreeing to pool their sovereignty in areas that were not initially contemplated or only vaguely referenced in treaty provisions. In addition, the day-to-day operations of so-called *comitologie* laid the foundation for literally hundreds of lower level agreements that became part of the *acquis communautaire*. From this perspective, the decision on monetary unification in the Treaty of Maastricht could well be described as 'the mother of all spillovers'.

For reasons that I will discuss later in this chapter, I am not convinced that EMU will re-kindle the neo-functionalist logic of spill-over and provide the integration process with a renewal of the momentum it so obviously lost since the difficult ratification of that treaty and the disappointing results of the subsequent Treaty of Amsterdam. The reason for this is that citizens are now far more aware of how widely and deeply their lives are being affected by the EU. The politicization of these issues has become both the cause and the consequence of partisan mobilization for and against further extensions of the scope and level of EU authority. While, in my opinion, this is a healthy (and long overdue) development, it does pose some serious difficulties for the immediate future. Switching from the deliberately 'apolitical' strategy that predominated during the early years of the integration process to an overtly 'political' one based on democratization might help to regain momentum, but it is a much riskier enterprise. My 'modest proposals for reform' are self-consciously intended to exploit the same logic of indirection and gradualism that Monnet used initially, except that this time the result may not be so foreseeable or controllable. Euro-democratization, especially under such unprecedented circumstances and for such a large-scale polity, is bound to activate unexpected linkages, to involve less predicable publics and to generate less limited expectations.

Avoiding Some Temptations

If we have learned one thing from recent research on democratization, it is that there have been (and still are) many different sequences involved in institutionalizing the relation between citizenship, representation and decision-making. And these, in turn, have produced rather substantial differences in both the pace at which democracy was consolidated and the type of democracy that was eventually established.

Therefore, one should be wary of reifying the experiences of previous democratizers, especially the experience of a single sequence of nation building, state formation and regime consolidation. It is very tempting to assert that, because the EU does not have the necessary and sufficient elements that produced democracy in country 'X', it cannot possible be democratized until it acquires them. For reasons that are obscure to me, this seems especially characteristic of German scholars who postulate a 'universalistic' sequence whereby an *ethnos* must precede a *demos* and, the latter can only be created by an explicit constitutional act whereby this *demos* or people 'submits itself to a political order of its own invention'.[4] Perhaps, it is because Germany was one of the few European states where 'a belief in communality' (*Gemeinsamkeitsglauben*) preceded the formation of its national state, or because legal-formalism is such a strong component in its juridical tradition (*Verrechtligung*), or both. Elsewhere in Europe, the state was often established long before a 'feeling of belonging to a (single) community' existed among its subjects and, indeed, played a significant role in bringing about such a feeling. Moreover, in one major case, there was no single-formal constitutional 'act of will', just a lengthy accumulation of precedents (Great Britain). In others (France, Spain, Portugal), there have been so many constitutions and major constitutional revisions that it seems absurd to claim that any of them provided an exclusive foundation for political order.

My hunch is that the moment for a dramatic act of 'self-constitutionalization' has long since passed in the EU and that the *ethnos-demos-politeia* sequence is going to have to be inverted – or, it will not lead to a stable democratic regime for all of contemporary Europe.

It has, therefore, been my presumption that the EU at this stage in its development neither needs nor is prepared for full-scale constitutionalization. The timing is simply wrong. In the absence of revolution, *coup d'etat*, liberation from foreign occupation, defeat or victory in international war, armed conflict between domestic opponents, sustained mobilization of urban populations against the *ancien régime* and/or major economic collapse, virtually none of its member states have been able to find the 'political opportunity space' for a major overhaul of their ruling institutions.[5] The fact that they all (with one exception) have written constitutions and that this is a presumptive *sine qua non* for enduring democracy indicates that at some time this issue will have to be tackled if the EU is ever to be democratized definitively – but not now!

Which is not to say that nothing can or should be done in the near future. Many different drafts of a potential Euro-constitution have been produced, circulated and promoted. The reason, however, that these efforts have had so little effect may be due less to the quality of the politico-legal talent that went into assembling these impressive documents than to the way in which they were discussed and drafted.

The reigning assumption seems to have been that anything as important as constitutionalizing Europe must be treated as a momentous and concentrated *event* – not a gradual and fitful *process*. Above all, it must be accomplished by experts (constitutional lawyers, for the most part) and protected from the pleading of special interests and the scrutiny of mass publics. Only these specialists can be trusted to produce a coherent and consistent draft that will not reflect the self-serving aims of politicians and their surrounding clienteles.[6]

In my view, this *au-dessus-de-la-melée* strategy may have worked relatively well under past circumstances when some type of national emergency or founding moment provided the context for deliberation and choice. It will not produce the same beneficial result in the case of the EU where there is no foreseeable emergency and the founding moment has occurred more than forty years ago. What is needed is an entirely new strategy that adopts a much longer timeframe and seeks deliberately to involve special interests and mass publics at various stages of the process. Only by deliberately politicizing the issues involved at the level of Europe as a whole and by gradually building up expectations concerning a more definitive set of rules with regard to citizenship, representation and decision-making can one imagine a successful constitutionalization of the EU. Admittedly, this is not the way most of the member-states went about accomplishing this task, but as we have already seen above the EU is not a mere repetition of previous nation, state and regime-building processes and it may well be leading to an outcome that is unprecedented.[7]

As we shall now see, this is where monetary unification may enter the picture since it is likely to provide one of the issues around which different expectations will focus. Controversies revolving around the distribution of its costs and benefits across and within countries could provide the raw material that will determine, not only whether the eventual Euro-polity will become a state, but also whether its regime will be democratic.

Introducing EMU as a Possible Motive for Urgency

Monetary integration is one possible motive for having to deal with Eurodemocracy sooner rather than later. Unfortunately, for our analytical purposes, it is not the only factor that is likely to affect the choice of decision-making rules in the immediate future. The enlargement of EU membership to include an (as yet) indeterminate number of Central and Eastern European countries is much more salient. For example, the agenda of the Nice Intergovernmental Conference was much more driven by worries about the impact of these small, over-represented and underdeveloped countries on existing balances between member states in both procedures (voting weights and seats) and policies (agricultural subsidies and regional funds) than it was by anticipations of how these countries were going to react to EMU – if and when they ever get into it. One could even speculate that 'lesser' items such as drafting and implementing a common foreign and defense policy or resolving the serious implementation gaps that persist in certain substantive policy arenas will take up so much attention that monetary integration will simply be forgotten. Most probably, the conflicts provoked by a common exchange policy and interest rate will be assigned to the virtually invisible machinations of a highly specialized and very secretive group of decision-makers, i.e. to the European Central Bank or to the even less transparent deliberations of the Council of Economics and Finance Ministers (ECOFIN).

Whatever visibility the common monetary policy attains if and when the citizens of the twelve member states that joined the EMU have its bills in their wallets and its transparency of wages and prices in their minds, I am convinced that Europeanization of this policy area will not provide the integration process with a renewed dynamic of spill-over into functionally related matters. EMU institutions are much more 'segmented' in their operation than was the case for trade negotiations, the Common Agricultural Program, Structural and Regional Funds or any of the other policies previously pursued by the EU.[8] By design, the directors of the European Central Bank seem to be prohibited from speaking to anyone except each other, and from taking into consideration any data other than those on monetary mass, fiscal balances and rates of inflation. Moreover, instead of producing decisions that are readily observable, discretely distributed and temporally specific – such as a price level for mutton, a permit to merge with another firm, or a definition of what a cucumber is – those of the ECB are more difficult to measure in terms of their economic effect, diffuse in their social impact, and take a much longer time to register on political institutions. And, even when they are registered by the affected groups, their differential effects will be much more difficult to translate into demands for compensation or expansion in related domains.

So, my suspicion is that monetary unification alone will not produce much further integration *via* functional spill-over. It is much more likely to generate diffuse reactions within large clusters of public opinion than focused responses by circumscribed groups of beneficiaries and victims. The latter furnishes raw material to interest associations, especially those representing class, sectoral and professional categories; the former typically has provided the fodder for 'catch-all' political parties and 'broad-band' social movements. The latter has proven useful for furthering integration, despite the sharp controversies they sometimes provoked; the former triggers a politicization of issues that is much less predictable and could just as well increase as decrease resistance to further devolution of authority to EU institutions.

Which brings me to the likely political consequences of monetary unification, since that is increasingly the terrain upon which its longer-term contribution to European integration is going to be experienced.

Let us begin by distinguishing two broad categories of political effects: (1) those *directly* involving the differential responses to the policies set by the Council of Ministers and implemented by the European Central Bank; (2) those *indirectly* affecting the probability of the eventual political integration of Europe. Both could contribute to making the eventual democratization of the EU more or less difficult.

Tracking the Direct Effects

The direct effects are, needless to say, a bit easier to predict – even if they remain difficult to sort out from other challenges and controversies that are bound to assail the EU in the coming months and years.

First and foremost is the expectation that a common exchange and interest rate policy will have a differential impact across the participating member states and across the sub-national units within these member states. How this will be distributed will depend on initial factor endowments and the extent to which national institutions are capable of adjusting to the loss of autonomy in these policy areas. The usual assumption (often illustrated historically by reference to post-Risorgimento Italy) is that the gap between rich and poor countries/regions will widen and, therefore, demands for redistributive policy measures will increase. To the extent that the losers are becoming increasingly capable of forging alliances across national borders, this raises the specter of a polarization into pro- and anti-integration clusters of public opinion that may not correspond to long-standing lines of domestic cleavage. It goes without saying that those who are negatively affected will be more vociferous in their opposition than will be those who are benefited in their support. In the worst scenario, this could be sufficient to fragment national party systems without providing enough fodder for their transposition into a viable European party system. To paraphrase Marx and Engels, the old (national) order will have been destroyed before the new (European) one is ready to emerge! More optimistically, one could imagine that EMU will produce such a strong net balance of winners over losers that the inevitable complaints of the latter can be encapsulated within insignificant fringe parties of the extreme right or left whose Europe-wide expression will be marginal (and, in all likelihood, undermined by fierce nationalistic disputes).

As plausible as this 'polarization' hypothesis seems, it is confounded by a simple empirical observation: support for EMU (as far as we can judge it from surveys of mass public opinion) seems to be significantly stronger in the less-developed 'Southern' member states than in the more-developed 'Northern' ones. Those who are supposed to be initially disadvantaged and who have had to make the greatest changes in national policies and institutions to meet the convergence criteria for EMU are the most favorable – despite the fact that they are predicted to be the relative losers! Those who have been practicing 'sound monetary economics' in their respective national compartments for some time are more sceptical about doing the same thing at the level of Europe as a whole. Of course, this distribution of opinion could reverse itself as the effects of EMU begin to accumulate, but it should give us some pause.

A *second* direct impact is likely to come from the sheer visibility of differentials in income and prices across the member states. It is one thing to 'know' that Germans are better paid than Portuguese, or that French wine can be cheaper in Spain; it is another thing to have this expressed in the same units of currency on an everyday basis. My hunch is that this transparency is going to generate new forms of interaction among occupational and, especially, consumer groups. In addition to the obvious competitive pressure this will put on firms, it will also mean a quantum leap in political collective action across national borders – much of which is probably going to focus on demands for national-level responses to disparities in taxation, monopolistic or oligopolistic pricing, wage setting mechanisms, levels of collective bargaining and systems of welfare provision – but some of which is going to find its way into the corridors of

Brussels. Tax harmonization is one obvious issue that will become more salient (and it is still a matter that requires the unanimous approval of all EU members) (see Gustavsson in this book). Trade unions may find it increasingly difficult to explain to their members why their salaries and benefits are so much less than in a neighboring country, and it will become easier to envisage Europe-wide collective bargaining, at least for certain relatively privileged and more mobile professions. One is tempted to predict a diminution in the more corporatist forms of national interest concertation, especially at the macro-level, and a greater tendency for more flexible and specialized, i.e. pluralistic, modes of pressure politics, if it were not for the factor of individual country's having to meet rather strict fiscal and budgetary constraints contained in the Stability and Growth Pact. As I have argued elsewhere, this has proven to be a powerful incentive for the revival of macro-corporatist practices in several member countries.[9] (Incidentally, as is often the case, even those EU members that are not formally bound by such an agreement and whose relative prices, wages and benefits are not so transparent will still be affected by the common policies adopted by those that are.)

And this new transparency in prices, wages and benefits is closely connected to the *third* direct effect that is likely to emerge – namely, the growing disparity in political influence between capital and labor. Any form of liberalization within a market economy will tend to enhance the relative value of that factor of production that is most mobile and, hence, capable of reacting to the enlarged opportunities with the lowest adjustment costs. Globalization, in the sense of a lowering of barriers to the flow of capital, technology and managerial skills across national borders, has already had a quite considerable effect on this 'balance of class forces' and will continue to do so with or without EMU. Most workers and many employees simply do not have the 'cosmopolitan skills' in language and life style that allow them to move easily across these borders. Moreover, their mobility is further restricted by a variety of non-transferable entitlements to national systems of unemployment insurance, welfare payments, public housing, retirement, education, etc.

Monetary unification exaggerates this intrinsic disparity and adds to it an even greater burden – namely, the loss of two national policy instruments that helped this very large segment of the population adjust to exogenous shocks or shifts in relative productivity: currency devaluation and deficit spending (see Plaschke in this book). Once EMU and its 'Stability and Growth Pact' are in place, all that is left at the national level are policies that are aimed at improving competitiveness by lowering the cost of labor. The accepted slogan for this effort is 'flexibility', although that can include an absolute as well as relative decline in various social entitlements.

In defense of EMU, one should observe that this shift in the burden of adjustment will take place in any case (and, liberal economists argue, should have taken place long ago). The existence of the euro and the EU policy mechanisms surrounding it do open up the possibility for negotiating collective agreements that could 'Europeanize' certain measures of social policy and protect some particularly exposed groups from the even more brutal and disruptive impact that unrestricted globalization could produce. They also provide a compelling argument that national politicians can use to introduce changes in welfare systems and collective bargaining that their economies can no longer afford – it, at the same time, allows them to pass on the political responsibility for these measures to those remote and faceless bureaucrats in Brussels and, now, Frankfurt.

A *final* direct effect was predicted, but has not yet been observed – as far as I can judge: namely, the probability that the authorities of the new European Central Bank would be overzealous in their efforts to promote price stability in order to enhance their originally weak credibility and, thereby, generate more austerity and less growth than would otherwise have been the case. Again, according to this scenario of 'over-austerity', those members that had been more inflation-prone in the past should have found themselves much worse off in relative, if not absolute, terms. We have seen periodic conflict over interest rates and the ECB has quite publicly resisted following the momentary demands of even its most powerful member, Germany, for their reduction. What we have not seen (yet) is the translation of these demands for different policies into a clear set of national (or sub-national) winners and losers. One can always claim that, thanks to certain accidents of timing, Europe has been able to avoid such a zero-sum conflict (and even to preside over a virtually monotonic decline in the euro vis-à-vis the dollar). To the surprise of most observers (I think), neither the interest rate setting mechanism nor the decline in value has produced a marked rise in the intensity of conflict between EMU member states – least of all, a polarized confrontation between those that previously had 'hard' and 'soft' currencies. My hunch is that all of their economies have become so diversified and interdependent that the lines of cleavage on these topics tend to be just as salient within each of them as they are between them. Under such conditions, it becomes virtually impossible to speak of a 'national interest' in a specific rate of exchange, much less to produce sufficient 'national unity' to make such a demand effective.

Groping for the Indirect Effects

The *indirect political effects* of EMU are even more difficult to pin down. They are going to be 'contaminated' by a host of other simultaneous developments at both the supra- and the national levels and who knows how long their 'incubation period' will be. Nevertheless, there is one notion that permeates almost all thinking about the secondary consequences of EMU: namely, the proposition that it will transform European integration from an economic into a political process. One frequently encounters the assumption (usually by economists) that, since the EU does not presently constitute an 'optimum currency area', it will have to acquire the characteristics of one – or it will fail. From this follows the notion that the participants will have to adopt a series of 'flanking policies' in order to promote the mobility of factors of production and symmetry of reaction to external shocks that such an optimal area is said to require. Since these policies, especially harmonization of fiscal policies and elimination of barriers to the flexible deployment of labor, are bound to be controversial, the EU will have to come up with a continuously revised set of rules for making binding political decisions that will permit it to overcome the resistance of individual member states and affected social groups. Driven by these 'functional imperatives', all that would remain to make the EU into a full-fledged federal state would be the drafting and ratifying of an eventual constitution.

Above, I have suggested several reasons why the EMU may not have such a strong 'spill-over effect' – least of all, one that would be powerful enough to produce both a state and a regime at the level of Europe as a whole. I can imagine a number of 'policy equilibria' that would fall far short of both for the indefinite future. Mostly, these solutions involve allegedly 'technical' corrections in related areas that would be presented to the general public (*ex post*) as inevitable and in their own interest. If and when 'asymmetric' pressures do assert themselves upon the member states, there will most certainly be a great deal of controversy surrounding their political resolution. However, I suspect that the EU institutional response will be both 'flexible' and 'forgiving' leaving a range of options for individual countries to 'opt-in' and 'opt-out'. Economists (and political scientists who think like economists) seem to have forgotten that common currency areas such as the Scandinavian Monetary Union and the Belgium-Luxembourg Economic Union have lasted for some time without generating any appreciable momentum for political unification. One could even consider the pre-World War One Gold Standard as an analogous transnational arrangement and it was insufficient to prevent war between its members, much less to entice them into closer political cooperation! The 'trick' has been to so segment and de-politicize the setting of exchange and interest rates as to convince the population that politically targeted intervention was either technically unfeasible or potentially counter-productive.

Which is not to say that EMU is not going to have an impact upon the practice of both national and supra-national politics. Elsewhere, I have argued that European integration has already shown signs of producing significant changes in 'domestic democracy' through its mechanisms of differential empowerment:[10]

1) It has increased the relative power of executive over legislative institutions.
2) It has increased the relative power of national (i.e. central) territorial authority over that of sub-national units.
3) It has increased the relative power of national judiciaries to the extent that they have been able to use the supremacy and direct effect of EU law to enhance their power of constitutional review.
4) It has promoted the influence of economic and monetary authorities at the expense of ministries and para-state organizations dealing with social, cultural and other matters.
5) It has increased the relative influence of interest associations over that of political parties.
6) It has increased the relative influence of business and professional associations at the expense of trade unions and social organizations.
7) It has increased the influence of more specialized 'sectoral' forms of associability at the expense of broader, 'inter-sectoral' or class-based ones.

None of these changes have been conclusively proven – least of all, across all member countries. They remain, however, 'plausible working hypotheses' for research. In each case, one can cite some evidence of contrary trends. For example, sub-national political units have mobilized more-and-more against central national governments and they have frequently turned toward Brussels for support. Consumer and environmental lobbies have risen to contest the hegemony of business and the professions and many have found the corridors of the Commission or the European Parliament more accessible and sympathetic to their causes than national ones. Resistance to the 'juridical imperialism' of the European Court of Justice is increasing and national politicians have become more and more uneasy about the limits that its decisions have placed on their policy options. In short, the EU's impact upon domestic democracy is still evolving and subject to the usual dialectical forces of challenge and response.

If I were to venture a guess about the probable impact of EMU, I would say that it will strengthen all of the above trends – with some subtle variations. For example, not only will those public institutions dealing with economic and monetary affairs gain even more influence at the expense of other ministries, but central bankers aggregated at the level of Europe as a whole will find it easier to assert their monetarist priorities at the expense of those national officials more concerned with economic expansion and employment levels. Political parties and social movements will find themselves more excluded from critical aspects of decision-making (and forced to adjust their programs accordingly), but even those specialized units of organized interest that had previously gained such privileged access to EU *comitologie* will find themselves more and more on the outside looking in on the hermetically sealed operations of the ECB. National executives, of course, will have lost one of their major instruments of power, i.e. the ability to print more money and loan it to themselves and their friends, but they may be able to use this 'transposition' to the level of Europe as a convenient excuse not to make decisions (and to pass on the responsibility to those in Frankfurt and Brussels).

Trying to Reach a Conclusion

All of these trends pose a serious challenge to 'domestic democracy' – especially in those smaller, more culturally homogenous European countries where its practice has long been associated with what I believe the Danes call *nærhedsprincippet* ('nearness' in English and 'subsidiarity' in Euro-speak), and with high levels of public redistribution of income, provision of services and protection against economic and social risks. For the national citizens of these countries should have no illusions about an eventual Euro-democracy. If and when it comes, it will have to be re-invented and, whatever the institutions that are eventually chosen, they are not going to resemble those already in use in their member states. Euro-democracy will have to be a much larger-scale, more remote and multi-layered regime that will depend heavily on opaque mechanisms of representation and take decisions by complex 'weighted' formulae. At least for the foreseeable future, it will not provide its citizens with an overarching political identity or a substantially improved set of rights or entitlements, and it will not extract great sums of money and devote them to equalizing opportunity or even to compensating for differences in risk and accomplishment.

Which is not to say that even those who are used to the familiarity and intimacy of small-scale democracy will not come to appreciate this unavoidably cumbersome thing. I am convinced that the democratization of the European Union is a desirable objective and that EMU makes it all the more urgent. I am also convinced that all of its member states – especially, incidentally, its smaller ones – will be better off within its embrace rather than outside it. Some countries may be temporarily comforted by the illusion that they can continue practicing 'domestic democracy' as before with all its national peculiarities, but they will soon discover that their elected representatives will be less and less capable of monitoring and intervening effectively in the process of making decisions for Europe as a whole. If they decide to leave the EU (or not to join it in the first place), they will discover even more quickly that these politicians cannot deliver what their citizens want and need purely on a national scale. And, whatever they choose to do, they will continue to suffer the consequences of decisions made by those who do participate in its complex and obscure processes.

So, I am convinced that EMU makes Euro-democracy more necessary, but does it make it easier? There, I confess, my response is much more ambiguous. Many features of this policy area make it unusually difficult for citizens and their political parties, interest associations, and social movements to grasp its impact and to mobilize citizens to demand that rulers pay more attention to their interests and passions. One can virtually forget about the prospects for ensuring *ex ante* consent given the necessary secrecy and the technical nature of the issues involved. The best one can expect is some modicum of *ex post* accountability – and even that has not proven easy to accomplish at the national level. For central banks and central bankers (along with general staffs and generals) belong to a species of institution that democratic theory and practice has tended to ignore. These agencies act as 'guardians' or 'custodians' providing certain public goods that are necessary for a democracy to function well, but they cannot themselves be organized democratically or even controlled democratically – or, they would fail to perform adequately (see Kelstrup and Plaschke in this book). Theorists of democracy do not like to admit that such nondemocratic agents are necessary. They are even less likely to concede that the role of some of these guardians/custodians has increased considerably in recent decades, precisely because of the expanded agenda of regulation that is demanded by a more mobilized citizenry trying to cope with more liberalized markets and interdependent polities.

Fortunately, however, monetary unification is not the only new policy area on the a horizon of the European Union. It is only when one combines the uneven effects its decisions are bound to have upon member states with different endowments and social groups with different capacities to respond to the opportunities and threats of globalization/Europeanization with other issues such as enlargement to include the countries of Central and Eastern Europe, enhanced cooperation in internal security affairs and the formation of a common external security policy that the prospect for Euro-democratization begins to look more promising – and imperative.

Notes

1 This excludes the (hysterical) suggestion by a distinguished American economist, Martin Feldstein (1997), that monetary unification will lead to war between the members of the European Union. In general, both political scientists and economists from the United States adopt a so-called 'realist' position with regard to EMU and the EU in general. They tend to favor both, but only if neither results in any substantial change in benefits for the USA or the 'world order' under its hegemony. In the unlikely event that the euro does have a negative impact on the use of the dollar as the world currency and the privileges of seigniorage this entails, they strongly oppose EMU and are prepared to predict the direst of consequences for it.
2 Philippe C. Schmitter (2000): *How to Democratize the European Union ... and Why Bother?* Lanham, MD: Rowman & Littlefield.
3 Presumably, something like this double bind is what Fritz Scharpf had in mind when he wrote: 'Since ...Europe is part of the problem (of democratic legitimacy), European policies can also help alleviate it', 'Governing in Europe: Effective and Democratic', unpublished paper, Max Planck Institute for the Study of Societies, Cologne, no date, p. 8.
4 The quote is from Claus Offe, 'The Democratic Welfare State: A European Regime Under the Strain of European Integration', (Humboldt University, unpublished essay, 1999), but it seems reflective of a broader strand of German thinking that goes back to Jellinek, Weber, Habermas, and the contemporary Supreme Court Judge, Dieter Grimm – all of whom are cited approvingly in the above article.
5 I can only think of one clear case: Switzerland in the early 1870s. It would be interesting to explore this exception, although the fact that this country had a 'one-party-dominant-system' (Freisinnige/Radical) at the time must have been an important factor – and, not one that can be repeated at the EU-level.
6 The fact that several of these constitutional drafts have come out of the European Parliament and that one of their most manifest objectives was to increase the powers of that very same institution suggests that 'institutional' – if not 'personal' – self-interest cannot be ruled out of the process.
7 In other words, I emphatically disagree with the conclusion of Fritz Scharpf that 'the

(EU's) democracy deficit cannot be reformed away', 'Democratic Policy in Europe' in Hesse and Toonen (1995). In my view, it can only be reformed away and any effort to resolve it in the near future by full-scale constitutionalization will only be counter-productive.

8   For a particularly clear and convincing exposition of the reasons why the making of monetary policy in the EU will be different from the usual 'network' mode of governance, see Dyson (1999).

9   (with Jürgen Grote), 'The Renaissance of National Corporatism: Unintended Side-Effect of EMU or Calculated Response to the Absence of European Social Policy?', *Transfer. European Review of Labour and Research*, vol. 5, nos. 1-2, Spring-Summer 1999, pp. 34-63.

10 'Reflections on the Impact of the European Union upon 'Domestic Democracy' in its Member States', in M. Egeberg and P. Laegreid (eds.): *Organizing Political Institutions*, Oslo: Scandinavian University Press, 1999, pp. 289-300.

References

Dyson, Kenneth (1999): 'Economic and Monetary Union in Europe', in B. Kohler-Koch & R. Eisling (eds.) (1999): *The Transformation of Governance in the European Union*, London: Routledge, pp. 98-118.

Feldstein, Martin (1997): 'EMU and International Conflict', *Foreign Affairs*, 76, November-December, pp. 60-73.

Hesse, H. H. and T. A. J. Toonen (eds.) (1995): The European Yearbook of Comparative Government and Public Adminstration, vol II, p. 91.

Schmitter, Philippe C. (1999): 'Reflections on the Impact of the European Union upon 'Domestic Democracy' in its Member States', in M. Egeberg and P. Laegreid (eds.): *Organizing Political Institutions*, Oslo: Scandinavian University Press, 1999, pp. 289-300.

Schmitter, Philippe C. (2000): *How to Democratize the European Union ... and Why Bother?*, Lanham, MD: Rowman & Littlefield.

Schmitter, P. C. and J. Grote (1999): 'The Renaissance of National Corporatism: Unintended Side-Effect of EMU or Calculated Response to the Absence of European Social Policy?', *Transfer. European Review of Labour and Research*, vol. 5, nos. 1-2, Spring-Summer 1999, pp. 34-63.

8 The European Central Bank and Democracy: the Political Framework of Economic Policy in the EMU
HENRIK PLASCHKE

Introduction

The basic issue to be discussed in this contribution relates to the principles governing economic policies in the framework of the EMU. In this context, the European Central Bank plays a crucial role as a powerful political and economic actor. The ECB, however, is also interacting with other important actors, including governments, other EU institutions, actors on the international financial markets and other private and public economic and political actors. Understanding the framework of economic policies requires an understanding of this interaction. Political choices to be made regarding the role and position of the EMU will exercise an important influence on the future of European societies in crucial fields. Who is to make these choices? In which fora? According to which criteria? With what sort of interest representation? Departing from the question of the degree of democratic steering of economic policies these questions shall be addressed. The contrast between the potentials of the EMU and the lacking willingness to use these potentials coupled with the built-in grey zones and contradictions of the political and institutional structure of the EMU is, however, likely to give rise to tensions and politicization. Countries and social groups feeling unevenly and unfairly treated by the mode of functioning of the EMU are likely to seek to modify it. It is thus rather improbable that the present institutional set-up of the EMU will be maintained. One may therefore point to the need for continued discussion and analysis – not only of the form and content of the EMU but also of its politico-cultural foundations.

The steering of economic policies constitutes an important element in the development of *societal democracy*. As emphasized elsewhere in the present volume (Kelstrup, 2002) societal democracy presupposes the existence of a '*democratic culture*'. It may be added that *a societal democracy also presupposes a certain societal control over the economic system* implying, among other things, a certain autonomy of the political system with respect to the distribution of economic power. The latter tends to be unevenly distributed. In the absence of such autonomy the political system would simply have to adapt itself to the balances of economic power. In the Western democratic systems this problem has to a certain extent been managed via a compromise between economic ('one mint = one vote') and political ('one man = one vote') power. The latter has *imposed* a set of binding constraints on the former. Therefore not everything can be bought for money.

Economic policies have played an important role in the formation of an economic foundation of societal democracy. Therefore, the formation of economic policy is a matter of politics rather than a matter of techniques. In the domain of politics *choice* exists and economic policies reflect, among other things, political priorities and power interests. As economic policies constitute a crucial element of economic steering they tend to be contested and to be an arena for political and ideological interests.

Monetary policy is an important element of economic policy and hence it is also an important element in the fulfillment of societal and economic goals such as full employment. The 'technicalization' of monetary policy, however, hampers the development of adequate democratic instruments for its steering. Thus, for many citizens monetary policy appears to be a sort of 'black box' more related to technicalities than to politics. Monetary policy may therefore safely and with no further forms of democratic control be left to the 'experts' of politically independent Central Banks and to the financial markets. This depoliticization of monetary policies tends to be reinforced by the current fashion in economic thinking with its fallacious emphasis on the ineffectiveness of economic policy and its simplistic understanding of inflation, budgetary deficits and 'structural problems' as the sources of contemporary economic difficulties.

A further constraint on monetary policy derives from contemporary developments in the global economy – particularly related to global finance. The degree of political regulation of the global economy is weak compared to that of the national economies. Hence the possibilities of compromises between economic and political power is weakened. International capital movements play a crucial role in this respect: a high degree of international capital mobility implies that the *exit* option (Hirschman, 1970) is available to economic power holders. Via capital flight capital owners may act internationally and hence avoid making compromises with a territorially bounded form of political power. The crisis of the 1930s provides a series of examples of territorially bounded forms of political power being undermined by internationalized economic power.

In the post-war period this dilemma was to some extent solved by the compromise of *embedded liberalism* (Ruggie, 1972). A particular combination of liberalization, especially in the area of international trade and regulations and controls in particular with regard to international capital movements implied a certain sheltering of national economies and economic policies with regard to international economic power. Similarly the development of the Western welfare states during the second half of the 20th Century was founded on a compromise between economic and political power. This combination of liberalization and regulations worked well for several decades and it was probably one of the permissive conditions for several decades of strong economic growth, material progress and consolidation of national political democracies. However, recent years have witnessed increased challenges to the political steering of economic policies due, among other things, to the globalization of financial markets and the comparatively high degree of international capital mobility. In particular the potential of monetary policies appears to be challenged by increased international capital mobility.

The European Economic and Monetary Union (EMU) plays a double-edged role in this context. On *the one hand*, it is part of a global process of liberalization and deregulation implying a weakening of the political control of economic policies via the establishment of independent central banks and the locking of monetary policies to the aim of price stability. But on *the other hand*, the EMU may also be seen as a sort of response to global processes of liberalization; a response which may contribute to and facilitate new forms of political regulation of the international political economy. The international role and position of the EMU is likely to interact with and to some extent depend on other fundamental dimensions of the EU, including the political and institutional developments of the EU as well as developments in the interdependence of monetary and financial issues and labor markets and the public sector. Capital owners – the actors of the international financial markets – are likely to play an important role as power holders in this respect. However, different strategies towards fund holders – from a passive adaptation to an active steering – are feasible.

The basic issue to be discussed in the present contribution relates to the principles governing economic policies in the framework of the EMU. In this context the European Central Bank (ECB) plays a crucial role as a powerful political and economic actor. The ECB, however, is also interacting with other important actors, including the governments of the

EU countries, other EU institutions, actors on the international financial markets and other private and public economic and political actors. Understanding the framework of economic policies requires an understanding of this interaction.

Political choices to be made regarding the role and position of the EMU will exercise an important influence on the future of European societies in crucial fields. Who is to make these choices? In which fora? According to which criteria? With what sort of interest representation? Departing from the question of the degree of democratic steering of economic policies these questions shall be addressed in the following text.

General issues related to the notion(s) of democracy and to the more or less democratic character of the EU shall not be addressed in the present text. Similarly, I shall only briefly touch upon the general developments in the relationship between EMU and the ECB and the political system of the EU. These questions are, however, addressed elsewhere in the present volume (Kelstrup, 2002). I shall start by briefly surveying the main characteristics of European economic policies within the framework of the EMU. Departing from a more general discussion of the phenomenon and concept of independent institutions in democratic political systems I shall then proceed with a discussion of various characteristics of the ECB as an agent of *political* power in the formation of European *economic* policies. In the conclusion it will be pointed out that the establishment of the EMU in its current shape institutionalizes a constraint on the democratic steering of economic policies. The EMU, however, at least potentially also constitutes an instrument for reinforcing the political regulation and steering of the global economy. The realization of this potential is, however, far from automatic, and it is difficult to catch sight of any sort of political willingness to realize such a potential in the present European politico-cultural conjuncture. In view of the highly asymmetrical international economic power relations prevailing in the absence of international and/or regional regulatory institutions such as the EMU it would, however, be delicate to claim that the absence of the EMU would in any sense imply a reinforced potential for democratic steering of the economy. The EMU therefore cannot be claimed *per se* to lead to a weakening of the democratic steering mechanisms of the EU.

In the eyes of the present writer it is in any case rather improbable that the institutional set-up of the EMU will be maintained in its present form. One may therefore point to the need for continued discussion and analysis – not only of the form and content of the EMU but also of its politico-cultural foundations.[1]

The New Framework of European Economic Policies

The establishment of the EMU implies rather drastic changes in the conditioning framework for European economic policies. These changes are complex and touch upon numerous aspects. The most important changes may be summarized in the following manner:

Centralization and Decentralization of Economic Policies

The creation of the single currency and the establishment of the European Central Bank imply a *centralization* of monetary policies as the task of formulating and implementing these have been granted to a common European institution (the ECB). Furthermore, this institution has been given a status of being independent of national governments. Other forms of economic policy, such as fiscal policies, taxation and labor market policies, to a large extent, rest *decentralized*. Such policies remain the domain of national governments and hence they stay under national control. Even if a certain coordination of such policies takes place at the EU-level, the forms of coordination are non-binding and the existence of common norms or rules remains the exception rather than the rule. The coexistence of centralized and decentralized economic policies implies the possibility of tensions among different areas of economic policies. I shall return to this point below.

The *external* dimension of EU's monetary policies has a particular status with respect to centralization/decentralization since issues relating to the exchange rate of the euro with regard to other currencies (particularly the $) are to be handled by ECOFIN (the Council of Finance Ministers), i.e. by governments acting jointly. On the other hand the ECB has made it rather clear that it does not intend to leave this area to the discretion of ECOFIN, and it has thus opposed possible plans of creating zones of fixed exchange rates between the major international currencies. As the external exchange rate may influence the internal rate of inflation, the external and the internal dimensions of monetary policies are not mutually independent, and therefore a sort of grey zone exists with respect to monetary policies. With the exception of two former French and German Ministers of Finance, national governments have not shown much interest in adapting a more activist stance in this area so far.

Autonomy of Fiscal Policies?

In principle, the existence of a common currency and monetary policy implies a *greater* national autonomy for other forms of economic policies, in particular fiscal policies. Thus, expansive policies for individual countries will be facilitated: the dangers of speculation against such a policy will be diminished, the relatively closed character of the economy of the EU area implies the absence of external balance problems. Balance of payments between member states disappear (although they may reappear via country credit risks), and the risks of financial and inflationary crowding out (i.e. expansionary fiscal policies leading to higher inflation and interest rates) will be lowered. In the present shape of the EMU this potentially increased autonomy is, however, likely to be diminished by the so-called Growth and Stability Pact. It may also be constrained by insufficient tax resources due to unregulated tax competition between member states and the lack of common norms and/or rules regarding minimal rates of taxation. Abstracting from this latter (important!) aspect a common currency does not imply fiscal constraints on member states, and it seems likely that the politically imposed constraints (the Stability Pact) on national fiscal policies are likely to lead to conflicts between countries and in a somewhat longer time perspective to a more or less overt modification or change of these constraints (Soskice, 1999). A real testing of the stability of the Stability Pact, however, is likely to require some sort of a recession implying increasing budget deficits.[2]

The potentials for conflict are reinforced by the fact that common fiscal policies are so weak at the European level. The common EU-budget is rather insignificant (less than 1.5 per cent of the EU's common GDP) and even very marginal increases in the size of the budget have until now proven extraordinarily difficult to achieve. Taking this fact into account, it appears far from self-evident that significant increases in the common budget are to be expected. Perhaps increased national budgetary activism and creative thinking would be a more likely trend even if it may to some extent vary between member states.

Political Regulation versus Financial Market Agents

The shaping of the EMU has led to a modified balance of power between, on the one hand, an institutional and political regulation of the economy and, on the other hand, the so-called market forces, i.e. in reality the operators on the international capital markets, in favor of the latter. The establishment of The Single Market in the mid and late 1980s included the removal of restrictions on short-run international capital movements, and similarly the first stage of the EMU implied the removal of possible remaining restrictions.

Free capital movements imply an important power resource to the operators on the international capital markets with regard to national governments: the *exit* option. Following a standard result of international economics, the following three elements are intimately connected: (1) free international capital movements; (2) autonomous monetary policies, and (3) fixed exchange rates. If you start by choosing one of the three, you have to choose between the other two. You cannot have both. On the other hand, any two out of the three may be combined.

If one, for instance, starts by restraining international capital flows, the combination of fixed exchange rates and autonomous monetary policies may be realized. This sort of combination dominated the international economy in the first decades after the end of the second World War when the US accepted a certain role for restrictions on international capital flows as an instrument for the reconstruction and subsequent growth of Western Europe (Ruggie, 1982).

If one instead starts by liberalizing international capital movements, as was increasingly the case in the 1980s and 90s (Helleiner, 1994), a choice between autonomous monetary policies and fixed exchange rates becomes inevitable. Setting the rate of interest based on domestic priorities (e.g. full employment) implies floating exchange rates in order to avoid capital flight. This combination was used extensively during the 70s, and the US has again utilized it in recent years.

If one would rather start by combining free capital movements and a fixed exchange rate, the rate of interest has to be set according to external priorities (balancing capital flows). This combination has dominated the latter half of the 80s and the 90s with the subordination of growth and employment to the constraints of monetary stability and subsequent high real interest rates (i.e. rate of interest − inflation). This combination also seems to be underlying the (vanishing?) *rhetoric* of a strong Euro and the official aims and goals of the EMU. Whether it has also been underlying the practices of monetary policies in the EMU is less evident: the first years of the euro seemed rather marked by an uncertain and probably involuntary combination of adjustments to the international environment and a limited and hesitating maintenance of monetary autonomy.

In this context, it is necessary to bear in mind that a large and almost closed and self-contained economy as the European economy is much less vulnerable to fluctuations in exchange rates than are the individual European states and their currencies. The economic impact of a floating exchange rate is rather limited for the EU area, and the potential for maintaining independent monetary policies is therefore also correspondingly larger. Similarly, the inflationary impact of a falling exchange rate is after all relatively insignificant. It may also be emphasized that the actual instruments available to the ECB in controlling the exchange rate seem rather powerless. Whenever the ECB has attempted to strengthen the euro via increases in the rate of interest, results have been modest or counterproductive. Perhaps a firm strengthening of the euro exchange rate would require a highly restrictive interest rate policy incompatible with other economic and political considerations and goals. Or perhaps it is impossible to localize an equilibrium rate of interest: if increasing interest rates are *interpreted* as signs of weakness, falling rather than rising demand for the financial active in question may follow. In such a case, it would seem difficult to equilibrate demand and supply only via manipulating the interest rate.

The increased monetary autonomy that could follow from the single currency goes beyond choosing between fixed exchange rates and monetary autonomy. The real potential force of the single currency is to be found in the fact that it could facilitate the development of new instruments suitable for controlling and steering international capital movements. The potential for easy speculative gains and short-run financial considerations have in recent years led to the abandoning of such control instruments. However, the single currency could facilitate a modification of the balance of power between an institutional and political regulation of the economy and the so-called market forces – but this time in favor of the former.

Balances of Power Between Member States

The establishment of the EMU implies a certain modification of the balances of power between the member states. Before the EMU, the formally independent national monetary policies had, to a large extent, to adapt to developments in German monetary policies. This asymmetry was the consequence of the dominant position of the German economy, free capital movements and the quest for exchange rate stability. In the framework of the EMU, the ECB is obliged to formulate its policies following common European interests. National central banks are represented within the ECB but they are supposed not to represent national interests. Monetary policies have been Europeanized.

It is difficult and perhaps somewhat too early to see to which extent this formal Europeanization is real compared to the earlier period of real (but not formal) *Bundesbank* dominance. On the one hand, viewpoints and priorities closely affiliated with those of the *Bundesbank* are not only represented by the German representatives within the ECB, but e.g. also by the Dutch President of the ECB. If, on the other hand, one tries to compare the policy reactions of the ECB with what could have expected from a European version of the *Bundesbank*, things are not particularly clear. What could we have expected from a European *Bundesbank*? Any interpretation of this question depends on how one interprets the logic of previous

Bundesbank priorities. A standard interpretation of the *Bundesbank* as being entirely focused on price stability is too simplistic. In reality, the *Bundesbank* has always to some extent taken broader economic considerations (developments in the German economy, problems of handling capital flows etc.) into account even if it is not legally bound to do so. In some way, the ECB is likely to do the same but it remains to be seen in which way. The experience of the first two and a half years of the ECB seems to point to a combination of persistent orthodoxy and a certain level of confusion and uncertainty. The ECB is perhaps best seen as still being in a rather uncertain search and learning period in which: 1) available policy instruments seemingly do not work very well; 2) the potential and limits of central bank independence is to be established and tested, and 3) policy divergences are likely to persist even at the top level of the ECB.[3]

Independent Central Banks and Defensive Governments

The establishment of the EMU has been accompanied by important modifications of the national institutional frameworks of economic policy formation. In all the member states, the central banks have been granted an independent status if this was not already the case beforehand. The exact meaning of independence is rarely specified. Independence of what? No political institution such as the ECB can be independent in any absolute sense of the word. Central bank independence refers to independence with regard to the national democratic political institutions such as governments and parliaments. This, in no way implies that central banks could be independent of politics! So if central banks may be independent of democratically elected governments what *do* they depend on? Among other things possibly on financial interests and the international capital markets and their actors although dependence on other actors cannot *a priori* be excluded. Why emphasize dependence on capital markets? As a consequence of the liberalization of capital movements actors on capital markets hold a strategic power position with regard to governments and central banks. This position is furthered by the fashionable ideology of attributing the task of assessing the 'soundness' of economic policies to the financial markets.

Central bank independence of governments and dependence on financial markets have been reinforced by the relatively defensive attitude taken by governments towards the ECB. *Firstly*, the Maastricht Treaty has defined the primary goal of the ECB as that of maintaining price stability. The notion of price stability, however, is indeed far from being a rigorous and precisely defined notion, and the task of operationalizing the notion has been attributed to the ECB who has adopted an unnecessarily restrictive definition, i.e. an inflation rate between 0 and 2 per cent (Buiter, 1999). *Secondly*, while the Maastricht Treaty in a rather vague and unspecified way has formulated various secondary goals for the ECB, its formulations have been so imprecise and vague that the ECB has been able to develop its own interpretation of these goals which is *exclusively* focused on price stability: possible secondary aims have been ignored (De Grauwe, 2000). *Thirdly*, a kind of asymmetric relationship has developed between the ECB and governments: using central bank independence as a pretext, governments have been relatively passive in discussing and assessing the ECB and its policy choices while the ECB has been much more activist regarding governments' policies. In other words: the ECB is in charge of EU's monetary policies without interference from any sort of political counterpart while it is also interfering in governments' affairs via its recommendations, statements, publications etc.[4] Governments seemingly accept this outside interference without any claim of reciprocity: the ECB is left to itself (cf. Dosenrode (chapter 3) in this book). The consequence is that the ECB is able to manifest itself with only limited political response. This again is a consequence of the way the previously mentioned grey zone is handled politically. It reflects a political choice.

A Political Counterpart to the ECB?

The ECB does, however, face a certain political counterpart in the form of the so-called Eurogroup which is an informal council comprising the ministers of finance participating in the euro. As mentioned above, the construction of the EMU implies a potential tension between common monetary policies and national fiscal and other economic policies. The Eurogroup group derives from a French initiative aiming at creating an institutionalized political counterpart to the independent ECB, so as to limit the power position of the latter when facing governments. Very limited public knowledge is available regarding the actual mode of functioning of this council. Seemingly, however, contradictions between particularly Germany and France tend to hamper developments of common economic policies. Thus, according to France the Eurogroup handling of economic policies should start from the premises of the common economic situation of the Euro-zone in the same way as the ECB is supposed to work from common EU premises with no consideration of individual countries. On the other hand Germany seems to argue that the Eurogroup should start from the premises of individual national situations rather than from the common situation of the whole Euro-zone (Moatti, 2000).

The difference between these two viewpoints should not be underestimated. If we are to follow the first viewpoint, common monetary policies should lead to a fiscal solidarity at the EU-level implying that all the member states should in some way be jointly responsible for economic imbalances within single countries. Were we rather to follow the second viewpoint, common monetary policies should not lead to any further developments in common economic policies and the responsibility for coping with national imbalances should therefore be national and not common. In other words, the second viewpoint seeks to limit possible spillover effects from the single currency to single economic and fiscal policies. The classical conflicts regarding strategies of economic policies between 'North European' views represented particularly by the Germans and the Dutch and 'South European' views represented particularly by the French and the Italians hence seem to reappear within the Eurogroup. This is perhaps not so surprising and similarly there is no reason to expect the 'North-South' conflict within the EU to disappear.[5]

The weak and/or falling euro can be expected to influence the balance of power between these two viewpoints. 'Southern' views may utilize the weak euro to argue for a stronger political counterpart to the ECB. In any case, the legitimacy of the single currency is negatively influenced by the weakness of the euro – not so much for economic reasons but more due to the ideological conception of the euro as a strong and stable currency. This conception has obviously been frustrated by the persistently low exchange rate of the single currency. Since nobody knows the precise reasons for this, the floor is open for more or less qualified guessing and this guessing may present a certain political interest. Competing interpretations of the weak euro flourish and the interplay between competing interpretations and connected political strategies may obviously influence the future institutional framework of European monetary and other policies.

The institutional structure of the EMU and the predominant forms of political and economic thinking among the European governments tend to push monetary policies towards a relatively passive form of adaptation to the global financial system. Governments have attributed a central role to the ECB in defining the general orientations of economic policies and the ECB has willingly accepted this role. At the European level, governments play a relatively passive role due to disagreements, among other things. At the national level governments and other social actors (including labor market organizations) to a varying degree compensate for the ensuing consequences and tensions. In economic terms, this is likely to be conducive to divergence rather than convergence. There is no reason to expect the general framework of economic policy formation to remain at its present level. In a long-term perspective several rather different developments may be envisaged (e.g. Soskice, 1999; Commissariat Général du Plan, 1999). I shall, however, not pursue this point any further. Instead, I shall focus on the political basis of the present EMU construction – and in particular on the question of its democratic foundations.

Some Considerations on Independent Institutions in Democratic Political Systems

The fundamental political role of the ECB in the formation of economic policies in the EU has been discussed above. As emphasized above, the key role of the ECB has been *assigned* to the ECB by the governments. This in no way precludes that the ECB has willingly accepted this powerful position – and perhaps even tried to reinforce and strengthen its own role. However, in view of the passivist attitudes of governments, it is hardly surprising that the ECB has attempted to fill the void.

However, as alluded to above, the underlying notion of central bank independence is somewhat unclear. The notion of independent institutions or agencies is familiar from elsewhere in democratic systems, and a brief discussion of the position of central banks in comparison to other forms of independent institutions might seem relevant. Furthermore, even a politically independent institution like the ECB will interact with other parts of the political system, and it would therefore seem obvious to ask whether and in which way independence is likely to influence the conditions of this interaction. In this context it is also important to take into consideration the theoretical basis of the idea of central bank independence.

The presence of independent agencies is a well-known and accepted factor in democratic political systems (cf. Schmitter and Kelstrup in this book). The potentials and limits of independence may be illustrated by a brief comparison of: 1) the legal systems and the role of the courts and 2) the role of the military in democratic political systems. The courts in a democratic political system are independent of the other parts of the political system in the sense that they are to make their decisions (sentences) within a framework defined by legitimate government and parliament (the executive and the legislative powers). These latter define the framework but are not to interfere in the filling out of the framework which is the *exclusive* task of the courts. In their exercise of power (making sentences), these are to be entirely independent of other social interests – be they political, businesslike or other. Even if representatives of the executive and/or legislative powers may every now and then have problems in trying not to influence the courts, the principle of separating the three levels of powers listed (and hence also the independence of the courts) is accepted by all major political players in democratic systems as a matter of principle. It may furthermore be added that democratic political systems also tend to be characterized by a system of *checks and balances* assuring a certain equilibrium between the different levels of the political system. This takes a particular importance, e.g. in the case that executive power tries to interfere in the domain of the courts.

If the independence of courts constitutes a generally accepted principle in democratic political systems, the position of the armed forces is rather different. On the one hand it is obvious that the military in order to function in a satisfactory manner needs a certain operational independence – even if the precise delimitation of this latter may prove delicate. On the other hand, it is equally obvious that no democratic system can accept a politically independent military. It is e.g. clear that it would be unacceptable if the armed forces started defining their own tasks independently of an authoritative political system or if they started making their own balancing and choosing between different political priorities and aims. In such case, the armed forces would constitute a unit of power that could challenge the authoritative democratic exercise of power. The armed forces may have their own interests to promote, and furthermore the armed forces are unlikely to be neutral with regard to other social and political interests. It is unlikely that a strong and independent military could function as an impartial and neutral holder of political power.

The Independent Central Bank as a Political Institution

How can one situate the political position of the central bank in light of the remarks regarding the role of the courts and the armed forces? A direct comparison shall not be attempted but it is possible to formulate a series of pertinent questions following the previous discussion. At least the following questions would seem relevant when we are to assess the position of the ECB in the European political landscape:

1) Is any system of checks and balances with regard to the independent central bank defined by the EU system and/or the national political systems?
2) Which kind of political and democratic legitimacy can we attribute to the independence of the central bank?
3) Is the independent agency supposed to make not only technical but also political decisions?
4) Is the independent central bank neutral with regard to social and political interests?

5) Is the division of labor between the independent institution and the rest of the political system clearly delimited or are there important grey zones with an unclear distribution of competencies?

Let us try to discuss these questions one by one.

1) Checks and balances

The system of checks and balances must be characterized as weak. As pointed out earlier, the ECB does not face a political counterpart at the level of the European polity (a part from the relatively insignificant Euro-group which is too weak to be considered a counterpart). The ECB is in principle accountable to the European Parliament but the latter has no legal power towards the ECB. This rule can only be changed by a change of Treaty, which is obviously highly prohibitive. Furthermore, the ECB does not need to publish minutes of its Governing Council meetings. Before the creation of the ECB, a number of more or less independent national central banks faced their respective national political systems as counterparts. These latter, however, tend to be more unified and less fragmented than the political system of the EU. The relative degree of independence of the ECB must therefore be characterized as being higher than that of the national central banks. If we compare the ECB to the American Federal Reserve we may note important differences. In the American case minutes and voting records are published, and more importantly the Congress may change the legal status of the Fed by simple majority voting. As noted by De Grauwe (2000) the position of the ECB is remarkable in a democratic political context: *any* political institution, including a central bank, must in the last instance be accountable to the people/the public, and it would therefore seem obvious that a high degree of independence should be accompanied by a correspondingly high degree of accountability towards the representatives of the public, i.e. the political system. The position of the ECB, however, is based on a rather different logic: an extraordinarily high degree of independence is accompanied by a rather low degree of accountability![6]

2) Legitimacy

The formal political legitimacy of the ECB is clear: it derives from the Maastricht Treaty. The democratic legitimacy, however, is somewhat more questionable. Firstly, because of the particular combination of high independence and low accountability as discussed above, and secondly because of the general problems of democratic legitimacy in the EU system. I cannot here discuss the issue of democratic legitimacy but it is worthwhile emphasizing that an important aspect of this issue relates to the connections between the development of the EU polity and the strengthening of the executive power (governments) relative to national parliaments and domestic societies (Moravcsik, 1994). The EMU mainly results from negotiations at the level of the executive powers (Dyson and Featherstone, 1999), and the democratic legitimacy of the ECB may therefore be qualified as indirect. And perhaps also as insufficient in view of the rather weak connection between on the one hand, parliaments and domestic societies and the executive power, on the other hand.

3) Technical versus political decisions

As a matter of principle, independent institutions should only deal with technical matters while politically accountable institutions should handle matters involving trade-offs between political, social and cultural values.

As mentioned previously the ECB has been assigned a task (the maintenance of price stability) whose precise delimitation and operationalization has been left to the ECB to define. As a consequence a very narrow definition of price stability has been adapted and other possible secondary goals for the ECB (mentioned in the Maastricht Treaty) have been ignored.[7] Should the operationalization and fulfillment of the goal(s) of the Maastricht Treaty be considered a technical or a political matter? To this question the ECB and many politicians would most likely say a *purely* technical matter: price stability is an indivisible advantage for everybody, it does not imply any costs for anybody and therefore it should be above politicization.[8]

Price stability may *all other things equal* be said to be an absolute advantage. One of the problems is that the assumption of *all other things equal* is a convenient and crucial but far from innocent assumption. In reality *all other things are never equal*, and since price stability and other economic goals are mutually connected, price stability may not be an absolute advantage. In some cases, it may, for example, be expected that a moderate inflation like 3-5 per cent could be preferable to, for example, totally stable prices (Akerlof, Dickens and Perry, 1996). Furthermore, the effects of low or zero inflation crucially depends on *how this result is realized*. Price stability realized via a high real rate of interest limiting demand (investment and/or consumption) and employment is likely to have an impact rather different from what could be expected from price stability established via labor market pacts or other forms of consensus based policies. In the context of the ECB the problem is that the Bank only disposes of so few instruments for realizing price stability: first and foremost the rate of interest. This instrument is costly, not very effective and it has important derived secondary effects on demand and employment. Furthermore it is certainly not a particularly appropriate instrument in the case of imported inflation (e.g. due to oil prices) and stagnating demand.

The fact that an instrument of economic policy is not particularly effective does not necessarily imply that it should not be utilized. But it does imply that its utilization may involve delicate political trade-offs where costs and benefits are to be carefully assessed before a decision should be made. Since costs and benefits are usually not evenly distributed among different social and geographical groupings, we are in the last instance facing a political rather than a technical choice. If this choice is to be made by the ECB – and this is the case in the EMU – we may expect a bias in favor of limiting inflation compared to what would be the case if others segments of a population were to make the same choice. Or to put it differently: we may expect central bankers to be willing to pay a relatively high price in terms of e.g. demand and employment for ensuring price stability while other actors equally in favor of stable prices perhaps would be less willing to give the same priority to price stability in view of its costs in terms of demand. Firstly, it is well known that central bankers seem to have a sort of built-in tendency to see inflationary dangers lurking around every corner at every possible moment of time[9] and secondly, the close links that often characterize the relationship between central bank(er)s and the financial sector tend to bias central banks towards price stability and creditors' interests.

4) Political and social neutrality

Central banks have traditionally been closely connected to the financial sector due to the common needs for skilled expertise in finance, among other things. This common need facilitates the circulation of personnel between central banks and the rest of the financial sector. Banking and other forms of financial interests often tend to have a stronger representation within central banks than e.g. union interests although this issue to some extent depends on balances of power within each country. One may expect these asymmetries in terms of interest representation to systematically bias central banks in their deliberations and assessments. Furthermore, central banks have – like the rest of the financial sector – eagerly supported the previously discussed liberalization of international capital movements. One of the effects of this liberalization has been a strengthening of the position of central banks towards governments: in order to be more effective towards unregulated capital flows central banks could use liberalization as an argument for furthering their own independence with regard to governments and the national democratic systems. In a certain sense it may be claimed that central banks have an objective interest in favoring free capital movements: this may serve them in promoting their political interests.

5) Distribution of competencies

As mentioned above the division of labor between the ECB and governments is characterized by certain tensions because of the coexistence of centralized monetary policies and decentralized fiscal policies. One may therefore speak of a grey zone with an unclear distribution of competencies. How do the ECB and governments cope with this?

In many respects, the EMU is distinctively marked by a monetarist conception separating monetary (prices, interest etc.) and real (production, employment etc.) matters. Therefore, we should perhaps also expect the policy recommendations and the general interpretative framework of the ECB to be equally marked by monetarism. But this is far from being the case. Although the 'monetarists' in Frankfurt can hardly be accused of pursuing social democratic policies based on Keynesian principles, they nevertheless seem to have a clear-cut practical understanding of the interdependence of real and monetary aspects. Therefore, they persistently insist on the macroeconomic and social preconditions for price stability and therefore also on the connection to the rest of the economy, including the labor market and the public sector.

In spite of the fact that most European governments in recent years have been social democratic, things look rather differently when seen from the viewpoint of governments. The respect for central bank independence seems to be given priority (in spite of occasional rhetoric outbursts of critique) and national economic policies should be adapted to the priorities of the ECB rather than vice versa. In spite of the obvious interdependence of central bank policies and governmental policies, only rather limited and moderate discussion of the ECB priorities is voiced. As a consequence, general economic policies tend to be subordinated to monetary policies and the priorities of the ECB.

An asymmetry follows: on the one hand, the ECB with a rather clear-cut understanding of economic policy issues – based on its financially orientated political interests – and on the other hand, a series of governments *choosing* a policy of passivity regarding important issues in economic policies formation. The responsibility for formulating the overall framework for economic policies therefore to a large extent falls on the ECB and its definition of monetary policies. Other forms of economic policies may function within this framework.

In other words: to a considerable extent governments seem tacitly to accept that the ECB dominates the grey zone.

Why are governments seemingly willing to assign so much power and responsibility to the ECB? If we are to believe the official explanations the efficiency gains of central bank independence are so important that possible disadvantages must be considered of limited importance. It may here be objected that the possible gains from central bank independence are rather uncertain (e.g. Bassoni and Cartapanis, 1995; Bowles and White, 1994; Forder 1999; Pivetti 1996). However, even if these gains could be justified it is nevertheless necessary to insist on a couple of critical issues regarding the position of the ECB and its underlying political and philosophical foundations. That is to say if we are concerned with issues of democratic principles and not only with economic efficiency.

Firstly, the politically determined assignment of a remarkably powerful political position to the ECB reflects a noteworthy belief in the infallibility of a selected and rather limited number of actors (the leadership of the ECB).[10] Correspondingly, the position of the ECB in the EU polity is characterized by a significant lack of corrective and/or compensatory mechanisms vis-à-vis the ECB (weak accountability, no political counterpart and no system of checks and balances). This belief is indeed remarkable. The general fallibility of human beings is commonly acknowledged, and this point is precisely reflected in the construction of democratic political systems with their emphasis on checks and balances necessary to counterbalance possible infallibilities – even among well-intended human beings!

How can we explain this seemingly strong belief in infallibility? At the level of ideas and ideology it most likely reflects a renewed belief in old neo-liberal economic conceptions brushed up and reformulated in formal language. Following the apparent crisis of Keynesian inspired economic policies in the 1970s these conceptions have gained new momentum. The belief in technical and 'non-political' solutions to issues of political economy is part if this conception. Powerful and well-protected experts (i.e. central bankers) may be singled out as the most qualified experts in this respect.[11] At the level of social mechanisms and power relations part of the explanation of the renaissance of neo-liberal economic conceptions is likely to be found in the modifications in the international political economy following the Anglo-American-led attempts to deregulate the world economy, particularly at the level of finance. New alliances and patterns of political economy interests have resulted from these modifications (Gowan, 1999; Helleiner, 1994).

At a slightly different level the belief in infallibility may also reflect a couple of ideas well known from earlier European history: the belief in '*strong men*' and the belief in the '*correct line*'. The '*strong men*' of today, however, are no longer authoritarian dictators. They are rather supposedly highly qualified 'independent' experts who can take the 'necessary' decisions from a well-protected resort without any unnecessary interference from the outside. Similarly, Lenin and the omniscient Party in possession of the key to ultimate truth no longer define the '*correct line*' but the latter nevertheless survives in a new and surprising disguise. On behalf of democracy it is no longer the *Party* but the capital markets which may reveal historical necessity to us.[12]

This belief in infallible institutions and solutions is highly problematic in a democratic political culture. An important characteristic feature of such a culture must be the acknowledgement of the need for and the space available to competing and coexisting political conceptions and interests. Even at the level of economic policies. This is not a terrain beyond social interests.

Secondly, the creation of the ECB involves a very significant concentration of power – economically and politically. As discussed above, this is one of the consequences of: 1) the institutional position of the central bank; 2) of the lack of a political counterpart: 3) of the low degree of accountability and of the general political structure of the EU. In a US context, the former vice-president of the World Bank Joseph Stiglitz (1997) has raised the question of whether the strong concentration of power within the Federal Reserve is compatible with democratic values. As the power position of the Federal Reserve is normally considered weaker than that of the ECB, the question is equally pertinent in a European context.

The position of the ECB within the political and economic system of the EU adds a new and qualitatively different dimension to the already existing 'democratic deficit' of the EU.[13] This derives, however, less from the acting of the ECB than from the political systems and interests responsible for the institutional architecture of the EU. The responsibility is political and connected to the national governments of the EU. It is further reinforced by the passive attitudes of most EU governments towards the ECB. To this observations it must, however, also be added that the ECB has certainly not contested this excessive concentration of power. In this sense, the ECB shares a part of the responsibility for the lacking democratic foundations of the ECB.[14]

The Dilemmas of the EMU

The EMU implies a number of constraints for the European societies regarding the formation of economic policies. But it also creates new possibilities. With the EMU a new framework is created. But it is not filled out. The questions then are: *how* is this framework to be filled out, and *who* are going to make the decisions in this respect?

I have already touched upon the question of how to fill out the frameworks of economic policies in the discussion above of the dilemma between independent monetary policies, fixed exchange rates and free or regulated capital movements.

In the last instance, one may expect that the question of *how* is going to be settled by the question of *whom*. Forms of interest representation are crucial in this respect. In the grey zone between centralized monetary policies and decentralized fiscal policies the message propagated, amongst others, by the ECB of adaptation to the logic of globalization, competition and financial markets appears to have had a relative strong foothold at least until now. Credibility in the eyes of the financial actors is primordial and needs to be gained at almost any price. So-called structural adjustments in the national economies are fundamental in this context. The consequences of the search for credibility appear e.g. in the area of labor market policies with the persistent claim for more 'flexibility'. Departing from the popular idea of the American labor market as being more flexible than the European markets, the latter need to adapt to the American ideal (easier dismissal of workers, more emphasis on market mechanisms in wage formation, lower unemployment benefits etc.). In reality, the European labor markets have actually been reacting rather far from uniformly to this idea of increased labor flexibility (Regini, 2000) but the mythology of adapting to the US model has not disappeared. Trying to adapt to the US model, however, is like giving an inch to the devil: he will take a yard! How can we possibly expect labor markets dealing with human beings made of flesh and blood to become as flexible as capital markets where capital can be moved with an extraordinarily high degree of speed (press the button!)? In a situation of high capital mobility labor markets are bound to be insufficiently flexible. Trying to impose sufficient flexibility would be an endless screw as long as the financial markets are assigned the task of assessing the soundness of the national economies in practice. The financial markets are not democratically accountable. They are free to behave with a total lack of social responsibility.

The financial instability and creeping stagnation of the global economy may, however, show the fragility of the current model of unregulated globalization. But a change is unlikely to emanate from the ECB or from financial interests. The return of political initiative and audacity from governments, among others, seems indispensable. In such a context, the EMU and the single currency could prove to be interesting and powerful instruments in re-regulating the global economy and particularly global finance. Taxation of international short-run capital flows, for example, in the form of a Tobin tax as a means of stabilizing capital flows, or as means of generating tax revenues could be one possibility but other regulatory steps could also be imagined (other forms of transaction taxes, mandatory deposits, restrictions on inflows etc.). As a relatively small country like Chile has successfully imposed restrictions on short-run flows, a large and powerful unit like the EU should certainly be able to impose more visionary and encompassing reforms at the level of re-regulating global finance.

The political and economic autonomy of the EU in the international system could be reinforced while the power of global financial markets could be weakened by the development of a regulation of international capital movements. This would allow the EU to attach a greater importance to domestic priorities e.g. in economic policies and to pay less attention to the confidence, opinions and interests of the financial operators. In a more or more globalized world increasingly dominated by financial interests, the importance of this point should not be underestimated. Furthermore, as mentioned previously the *independence* of central banks with regard to governments is connected to their increased *dependence* on the international capital markets. A re-regulation of the latter may therefore be expected to decrease the dependence of central banks on capital markets, and therefore also to facilitate dialogue with and perhaps even the re-embedding of central banks within the democratic political processes and institutions. Such developments need not necessarily question the maintaining of the formally independent status of central banks.

In the years to come, the EU system is likely to face a series of important and delicate challenges (enlargement, slow growth, persistent unemployment and social marginalization etc.) which may also in a long-term perspective suggest the need for changes in the basic orientation of economic policy formation in the EU. Such developments may call into question the established power position of the ECB. Furthermore, we should not exclude the possibility of more profound reforms in the political and institutional system of the EU. Such reforms *could* imply a democratization of the EU system and *should* obviously also include a thorough reconsideration of the problematic aspects of the EMU – regarding democratic and other issues. No forecasting of future developments shall be attempted here. But let us try to indicate a number of areas and issues where changes and modifications could seem feasible and realistic.

Let us start by distinguishing between changes that are feasible within the framework of the Maastricht Treaty and changes that would require a modification of the Treaty. As pointed out by Buiter (1999), a number of relatively minor changes are perfectly feasible within the framework of Maastricht. Certain changes (in particular changes related to a greater openness towards the public) could in principle simply be initiated by the ECB. However, this would obviously require changes in the dominant mode of thinking within the ECB.[15] Other changes could be implemented within the Maastricht framework but would require the interplay of several EU-institutions. This would in particular be the case if the ECB should develop a *lender of last resort* function. Presently there are only national lenders of last resort. This would most likely prove rather problematic in case of a financial crisis.

Other changes in the structure of the EMU would, however, most likely require Treaty changes. This is particularly so, if an adequate system of checks and balances involving a strengthening of both the Parliament and the Council is to be developed. In my view, such a change is distinctly necessary since the independent status of the ECB must be considered an obstacle to the democratization of the EU system. But it is also likely to prove difficult and politically delicate since important political and economic interests are at stake. Furthermore, it would also in some sense influence the rest of the EU polity but this point shall not be pursued any further here.[16]

If rather basic changes in the structure of the EMU and the position of the ECB indeed do seem crucial, it must also be emphasized that both the EU system and the national governments may actually have to live with the present EMU construction. Indeed, everybody far from shares my emphasis of the lacking democratic basis of central bank independence. Presently, we can observe a renewed interest in federalist ideas but, on the other hand, it is far from evident whether these enjoy general support within the EU and its member states. Furthermore, the present discussions about federalism seem more concerned with form than with content. Obviously, the persistently low exchange rate of the euro is a source of permanent frustration (and to a lesser degree a source of imported inflation) but, on the other hand, it is perfectly possible for the Euro-zone to continue life with a low and somewhat unstable exchange rate. In many respects, this is probably an advantage although it is slightly unfortunate that so many stories of the virtues of a strong currency have been around in recent years. It is not difficult to demonstrate the economic advantages of increased cooperation e.g. at the level of fiscal policies, taxation and other policies and we certainly cannot exclude that other forms of coordination may develop. However, up to now all attempts of strengthening common policies in these areas has failed due to strong resistance from national and other interests. In particular the failure to develop a common strategy regarding common norms of taxation is significant. It is likely to imply continued market based adjustments and hence the dangers of a shrinking tax base. One may obviously also point to the persistently high unemployment and the rather serious issues of social exclusion and marginalization dominating the scene in most European countries. However, political mobilization against these developments is far from simple and hence rather easy to ignore.

Let us, as a last point, simply recall the fact the EMU has not yet been properly tested when these words are being put to paper (July 2001). In view of the many possible outcomes of a first test, it is hardly advisable to attempt any forecast. The EMU remains an open-ended project. For my own part, I can only *hope* that this fact may be used for the promoting of democratization rather than for its shrinking.

Concluding Remarks

One of the most important roles of democracy is to function as a counter-force to the systematic inequalities generated by a market economy that is not politically regulated. A market without political regulation equals the law of the jungle. The significance of this is obviously not only economic but also political.

In historical terms, the rule of democracy has expanded to encompass more and more fields of social activity: from voting rights for only a part of the population to voting rights for most of the ('indigenous') population, from political rights to social and cultural rights, from the areas of politics and the parliament to the cultural, social and economic areas. The dominating modes of economic and political thought in recent years, however, have to a certain extent blocked this expansion of democratic rule. The application of democratic principles is increasingly being restricted to the political and parliamentary areas while democratic control of the economy is increasingly seen as a principle to be avoided due to its supposedly negative effects (inflation, public debt etc.). The widespread tendency to withdraw important and powerful political agencies such as central banks from the domain of democratic rule is part of this process.

Monetary policies constitute an important element of economic policies. Their importance is further increased by the fact that fiscal policies may, to a certain extent, be subordinated to monetary policies due to the precise form of the EMU. The EMU hence does imply limitations on the extent of democratic rule in the area of political economy. The extent of political and democratic control of the economy is increasingly restricted.

However, as it has also been pointed out above, the absence of the EMU would not necessarily create a situation more propitious to democratic rule due to the uneven international economic power relations (role of financial markets, continued US hegemony etc.) whose role would be reinforced by the absence of the single currency. Therefore, it cannot be claimed that the EMU actually worsens the problems of democracy in Europe. Such a claim cannot be substantiated without knowledge of a known, feasible and democratic alternative. Such an alternative may emerge at some later stage. Presently, it is hardly in sight.

This development may seem paradoxical. In principle, the EMU may both allow for a weakening of the democratic control of the economy and for an extension of the possibilities of democratic control via an extension from the national to the European level. This latter development would increase Europe's global autonomy. The institutional construction of the EMU, however, favors a weakening rather than an extension of the democratic control of the economy. Similarly, the ruling European constellations of power seem to be characterized by political passivity, a defensive attitude to social change, a reluctance to engage in innovative politico-cultural visions and a wish to adapt to globalization rather than to master globalization from the premises of an explicit set of social and cultural values. These points also favor the weakening rather than the extension of democratic control.

It is not difficult to point to factors that could reorient the EMU construction from its present somewhat outdated form to a more up-to-date version. Some of these factors have been discussed above. Solid and well-founded political and economic arguments exist. But there is a fundamental lack of political mobilization. Top-down mobilization usually tends to focus more on instruments and means and less on goals and social values. This is perhaps one of the reasons why they usually do not work very well.

Hence, bottom-up forms of mobilization could be an interesting alternative. This sort of mobilization, however, also faces very difficult handicaps, including the continued fragmentation of the European political space into national spaces. The contrast between the potentials of the EMU and the lacking willingness to use these potentials coupled with the built-in grey zones and contradictions of the political and institutional structure of the EMU is, however, likely to give rise to tensions and politicization. Countries and social groups feeling unevenly and unfairly treated by the mode of functioning of the EMU are likely to seek to modify it.

As responsible scientists it is our task to point to these issues. As responsible citizens we may also attempt to devise solutions and strategies aimed at defining a political framework for Europe where economy and democracy are no more treated as contradictory.

Notes

1 See also Madsen and Plaschke (1998, 1999), Plaschke (1998) and Plaschke and Madsen (2000) for earlier contributions. I am grateful to my colleague Poul Thøis Madsen (Aalborg University) for long-time fruitful collaboration and precious comments on an earlier draft of the present chapter.
2 While waiting for this to come we can console ourselves with the relatively optimistic simulations produced by OECD (1999). As these, however, are based on rather restrictive assumptions (e.g. that demand shocks have no permanent effects on output and on the ratio of government net lending to GDP and that nominal shocks only have permanent effects on the price level while all other variables are unaffected in the long run) they are likely to underestimate the possible tensions deriving from the Stability Pact.
3 In this respect, the reading of an article by Padoa-Schioppa (2000) who is a member of the Executive Board of the ECB is interesting. His words about the 'loneliness of the ECB' seem to be rather far away from the usual orthodoxy of other ECB spokespersons.
4 A simple glance at a randomly chosen ECB publication, i.e. the latest available ECB Monthly Bulletin (August 2001), confirms the political interference of the ECB in governments' affairs not related to monetary policy, such as fiscal policy and structural reforms of goods and services markets of the euro area.
5 The case of Ireland (i.e. a relatively poor 'Southern' country) refusing to subordinate its present expansionary economic policies to those of the other member countries may also be seen as a case of a North-South divergence, even if Ireland in terms of macroeconomic balances diverge somewhat from other 'Southern' countries of the EU.
6 See De Grauwe (2000). The debate between Buiter (1999) and Issing (1999) is also of interest in this context. Issing who is a member of the Executive Board of the ECB provides an inconditional defense of the ECB when faced with Buiter's criticisms.
7 The notion of price stability is far from unambiguous: which goods and services are to be included (e.g. property, financial assets, and the rate of interest), how should we take quality changes into account (e.g. when quality is increasing and prices constant), at which levels (superior, inferior) should we talk about stability etc.? As to the ECB's choice of goals see also Buiter (1999) and De Grauwe (2000).
8 The theoretical foundations of this conception are to be found in so-called new classical macroeconomic theory. As this school of thought starts from the assumption that the monetary system is neutral with regards to the real economy which again is supposed to converge towards equilibrium if undisturbed, it is hardly surprising that it concludes that economic policies (and monetary policies in particular) cannot influence employment apart from in a short-run perspective. As demonstrated by e.g. Hall and Franzese (1998), Iversen (1998) and Skott (1997) a couple of rather marginal but plausible changes in the basic assumptions of the underlying models is enough to see that economic policies may indeed produce durable effects on the real economy under quite reasonable circumstances.
9 See also Luttwak's (1997) humorous and very appropriate analysis of *Central Bankism* as a religious phenomenon.
10 In a number of recent publications George Soros (e.g. 1997) has developed a remarkable analysis of the analytical and political implications of our *necessarily incomplete* knowledge of economic and other social phenomena. Soros' work is among others inspired by the works of Karl Popper. See also Cross and Strachan (1999) for a discussion of Soros' analytical foundations.
11 Marcussen (2000) has traced the birth and growth of neo-liberal ideas in the EMU-process.

12 Such a statement may sound exaggerated. However, the general belief that capital markets reveal the true and objective history of the state of the economies, and that free capital markets are needed so as to avoid the hiding of truth, is indeed very widely spread and easy to come across. One may for instance think of the popular idea that capital markets only punish countries behaving irresponsibly. Hence it is in some sense their own fault. These arguments are both empirically and theoretically very fragile. They are for instance based on the extraordinarily naive assumption that capital market *actors* do not have interests with regard to economic policies. In order words these arguments presuppose that capital owners are objective and impartial observers of economic policies. See e.g. Madsen and Plaschke (1998) fur further developments.

13 It must be added, however, that the absence of an EMU would not necessarily be advantageous seen from a democratic viewpoint. A *de facto Bundesbank* control of European monetary policies, free capital movements and competitive adjustments of interest rates is not necessarily an attractive alternative.

14 The polemic between Buiter (1999) who is a member of the Monetary Policy Committee of the Bank of England and Issing (1999) who is a member of the Executive Board of the ECB is interesting in this regard. None of the constructive and well-founded criticism and suggestions advanced by Buiter is accepted by Issing. A rather different attitude to these issues is expressed by Padoa-Schioppa (2000) who is equally a member of the Executive Board of the ECB.

15 See Issing (1999) or from a rather different viewpoint Padoa-Schioppa (2000).

16 In a broader perspective, it is also worthwhile mentioning the perspective of reembedding the logic of short-run finance and central banks into other forms of social logics, e.g. via the creation of competing institutions with different areas of competence gradually to be extended to encompass monetary and financial issues. Among other things, such a development would obviously require important changes at the level of the production of social sense. These issues are presently pursued in a paper in preparation but shall not be elaborated any further here.

References

Akerlof, G., W. Dickens and G. Perry (1996): The Macroeconomics of Low Inflation, *Brookings Papers on Economic Activity*, no. 1.

Bassoni, Marc and A. Cartapanis (1995): Autonomie des banques centrales et performances macro-économiques. Un réexamen, *Revue Economique*, vol. 46, no. 2, March, pp. 415-432.

Bowles, Paul and G. White (1994): Central Bank Independence: A Political Economy Approach, *Journal of Development Studies*, vol. 31, no. 2, December, pp. 235-264.

Buiter, Willem (1999): Alice in Euroland, *Journal of Common Market Studies*, vol. 37, no. 2, June, pp. 181-209.

Commissariat Général du Plan (1999): *Le gouvernement économique de la zone euro*, Rapport du groupe présidé par Robert Boyer, Paris: La Documentation Française.

Cross, Rod and D. Strachan (1999): 'Soros on 'Free Market' Equilibria', in M. Setterfield (ed.): *Growth, Employment and Inflation. Essays in Honour of John Cornwall*, London: Macmillan, pp. 27-40.

Dyson, Kenneth and K. Featherstone (1999): *The Road to Maastricht. Negotiating Economic and Monetary Union*, Oxford: Oxford University Press.

De Grauwe, Paul (2000): *Economics of Monetary Union*, Oxford: Oxford University Press, (Fourth Edition).

Forder, James (1999): 'Central bank independence – reassessing the measures', *Journal of Economic Issues*, vol. 33, pp. 23-40.
Gowan, Peter (1999): *The Global Gamble*, London: Verso.
Hall, Peter A. and R. J. Jr. Franzese (1998): 'Mixed Signals: Central Bank Independence, Coordinated Wage Bargaining, and European Monetary Union', *International Organization*, vol. 52, no. 3, Summer, pp. 505-535.
Helleiner, Eric (1994): *States and the Reemergence of Global Finance*, Ithaca, New York: Cornell University Press.
Hirschman, Albert O. (1970): *Exit, Voice and Loyalty. Responses to Decline in Firms, Organisations and States*, Cambridge, Mass.: Harvard University Press.
Issing, Otmar (1999): 'The Eurosystem: Transparent and Accountable or 'Willem in Euroland'', *Journal of Common Market Studies*, vol. 37, no. 3, September, pp. 503-519.
Iversen, Torben (1998): 'Wage Bargaining, Central Bank Independence, and the Real Effects of Money', *International Organization*, vol. 52, no. 3, Summer, pp. 469-504.
Kelstrup, Morten (2002), this volume.
Luttwak, Edward (1997): 'Central Bankism', in P. Gowan and P. Anderson (eds): *The Question of Europe*, London: Verso.
Madsen, Poul Thøis and H. Plaschke (1998): *Den forbudte debat om ØMU'en*, Århus: Rådet for Europæisk Politik & Systime.
Madsen, Poul Thøis and H. Plaschke (1999): 'Hvad vil de europæiske socialdemokrater med Europas økonomi', *Politiken*, January 11.
Marcussen, Martin (2000): *Ideas and Elites. The Social Construction of Economic and Monetary Union*, Aalborg: Aalborg University Press.
Moatti, Gérard (2000): 'Après l'Union Monétaire: L'euro sans maître', *Le Monde*, February 22.
Moravcsik, Andrew (1994): *Why the European Community Strengthens the State: Domestic Politics and International Cooperation*, WP. no. 52, Cambridge, MA: Center for European Studies, Harvard University.
OECD (1999): *Estimating Prudent Budgetary Margins for 11 EU Countries*, Economics Dept., WP. no. 216, ECO/WKP(99)8.
Padoa-Schioppa, Tommaso (2000): 'L'euro et le politique', *Le Monde*, September 6.
Pivetti, Massimo (1996): 'Maastricht and the Political Independence of Central Banks: Theory and Facts', *Contributions to Political Economy*, vol. 15, pp. 81-104.
Plaschke, Henrik (1998): 'Europæisering af pengepolitikken og den økonomiske politik', *GRUS*, no. 55, pp. 5-23.
Plaschke, Henrik and P. T. Madsen (2000): 'Den ufuldendte ØMU', *Samfundsfagnyt*, no. 133, September.
Regini, Marino (2000): 'Between Deregulation and Social Pacts. The Responses of European Economies to Globalization', *Politics & Society*, vol. 28, no. 1, March, pp. 5-33.
Ruggie, John Gerard (1982): 'International regimes, transactions and change: embedded liberalism in the postwar economic order', *International Organization*, vol. 36, no. 2, Spring, pp. 379-416.
Skott, Peter (1997): 'Stagflationary Consequences of Prudent Monetary Policy in A Unionized Economy', *Oxford Economic Papers*, vol. 49, no. 4, October, pp. 609-622.
Soros, George (1997): 'The capitalist threat', *The Atlantic Monthly*, February, pp. 45-58.
Soskice, David (1999): *The Political Economy of EMU*, DP FS I 99-303, WSZ, Berlin (see: www.wz-berlin.de/wb/pdf/i99_302.en.pdf).
Stiglitz, Joseph (1997): *Central Banking in a Democratic Society*, Tinbergen Lecture, Amsterdam (see: www.worldbank.org/html/extdr/extme/js-101097/tinbergen97.pdf).

Part IV

The Welfare State and the EMU

9 Money's not Everything – The EU and the Danish Welfare State*

PETER ABRAHAMSON AND ANETTE BORCHORST

Introduction

In the Danish EU debate the implications of EU for the welfare state have occupied a prominent place. As might be expected – one is tempted to say – widely differing conclusions have been drawn. EU opponents and sceptics have contended that the European integration process is heading to the harmonisation of social provisions and, in the long run, to the dismantling of the Danish welfare state. The 'Yes' side maintains for its part that social policy is a national prerogative and that the EU and, therefore, the EMU, represent an economic guarantee for future welfare. So there is firstly disagreement as to whether EU initiatives have had an impact on the Danish welfare state or not, and secondly whether the future effect will be of a primarily economic or political nature. The third point of contention is whether EU initiatives threaten or safeguard the Danish welfare state.

In what follows we analyse whether, and in which way, EU initiatives have impacted on welfare systems, and we discuss the effects of the EMU in connection with other initiatives. It is not our purpose to pass judgement on the possible positive or negative effects of these initiatives, nor, indeed, do we agree on that matter ourselves.

Section two presents the main conclusions of studies carried out on the welfare models applied at present in EU member states. The aim here is to illuminate the main differences between them. This will enable us to assess whether they are nearing each other, that is, converging, and in what way. The third section provides an empirical description of differences and similarities among the Western European welfare states. In section four we list the main features of EEC and EU regulations on social policy from the outset and up to the present. Section five discusses their impact on the Danish welfare state, including the implications of the EMU. In conclusion we discuss the paradoxes and dilemmas associated with the choice of retaining national sovereignty over welfare policy and attempts to strengthen EU's social policy image. This we do from the viewpoint of, *inter alia*, the question of democratic legitimacy.

Welfare State Models[1]

Since the 1960s there has been a debate in the social sciences concerning qualitatively different approaches to the organization of the welfare state. It has not really been about theorizing the modern welfare state's form and function, more an attempt to determine ideal-typically central and qualitative differences between various regimes. When we in what follows discuss different models, we do so within an idealized and abstract perspective. The American political scientist Harold Wilensky set the agenda for many years with his distinction between a residual welfare state and an institutional one (1958). As he saw it, the emergence and growth of the welfare state was a function of the processes of modernization and industrialization, and that less well-developed welfare states, the residual states, given time, would develop into institutional welfare states. The main criterion was the expansion of collective safety mechanisms empirically estimated in relation to the proportion of GNP allotted to spending on welfare. He saw, then, a clear connection between economic growth and the scope of the welfare state.

In 1971, Richard Titmuss in Great Britain widened this distinction, adding what he termed the performance achievement model. He launched at the same time a vital addition to Wilensky's view, i.e., that the models exist side by side temporally and spatially (1971). The decisive criterion as far as the British sociologist was concerned was the principle that was applied in the allocation of benefits. Gøsta Esping-Andersen (1990) extended this approach in 1990 with the addition of a typology of three welfare models. Political ideology is key here; Esping-Andersen connected the residual model to liberalism, the institutional to a social democratic ideology and the performance model to a conservative ideology. A more historically inclined section of the social sciences looked for distinctions in state constitutions and geography in the early 1900s. This resulted in a distinction between constitutional-dualistic monarchies with either limited (Greece, for instance) or broad elective franchise (Germany, for instance); liberal democracies (Great Britain, for instance); and mass democracies (Scandinavia, for instance) (Flora & Alber, 1981). In these perspectives, democracy and political ideology determine the differences between welfare states.

Despite the robustness of this three-pronged idea it has nevertheless faced challenges from a number of social scientific quarters. Some critics would have liked to have seen some of the models subdivided, creating, for instance, a separate model for Southern Europe (Leibfried, 1992; Ferrera, 1996). Geographic location has represented the point of departure for some typologies which have discriminated between a *Nordic*, a *continental-European*, an *Anglo-Saxon* and a *Southern European* model. Other critics have condemned the fact that almost all typologies were initially based on income transfers such as pensions, sickness and unemployment benefits and child allowance and that typologies over the different ways of organizing *services* were added on almost as a postscript (Antonnen & Sipilä, 1996). The services in question are nursing homes, hospitals, domiciliary help, childcare facilities and so on. Services are place-dependent, while income transfers are almost as mobile as the recipients. Many researchers in the field of women's studies have argued that the typologies ignore differences in the position of women in society and the significance of the family. In extension of this, typologies have been constructed to balance the *male breadwinner aspects* found in the models (Lewis & Ostner 1994; Sainsbury 1996).

The most widespread distinction, however, relates to the allocation criteria that are applied. A distinction can be made between whether access to welfare is based on *needs*, i.e. means-tested; whether it is tied to previous contributions and therefore *insurance-based*; or whether it is considered a civic right, determined by citizenship or legal residence in a country. It is also possible to identify a pre-modern though still important access criterion, i.e., *kinship*. In like manner a distinction can be made between the different types of social institutions that resource and organize the welfare systems. In this perspective, the fundamental distinction is that between state, market and civil society, including the family. From a slightly different viewpoint, a distinction is made between the public and private sector, the family, voluntary organizations or informal social networks. Finally, there is the vital role played by the funding aspect. Here we can differentiate between various approaches to the organization of welfare states, i.e. through systems of *social insurance*, *user payment*, *taxation* or whichever combination of these mechanisms is most representative.

In the following we define more closely the ideal-typical model approach.

The Insurance Model

The key factor in this model is the establishment of social insurance schemes based on the performance principle. This principle centers on contributions, and provisions are a reflection of them. For instance, the amount paid out in the form of a pension depends on the length of time the recipient has been active in the labor market and the amount he or she has earned while doing so. The administration and financing of the systems is the responsibility of the social partners and it is done on the basis of a fund principle, whereby every risk has its fund (for example the unemployment insurance fund, sickness insurance fund, funeral insurance fund). The stress is on the insured workers' right to transfers which, in certain circumstances, can be used to purchase services in the market such as treatment, therapy, etc. Citizens who are excluded from the labor market become dependent on their family, generally a spouse or parent, the local authorities or voluntary organizations, often ecclesiastical in nature. In short, the labor market does business with the 'normal' people – that is, wager workers – while deviants are left to the Church or municipality and housewives to their men's handouts. This model ascribes a key role to the family in the commission of social undertakings, including the provision of care, an area which, in contrast, is not particularly well developed at the level of the state. This performance-orientated model creates innumerable tiers of provision.

The Residual Model

The key assumption here is that citizens should as far as possible manage on their own through market or family mechanisms. In cases where this proves impossible, the state steps in with a universal, through restricted, range of provisions which are released only after careful consideration of the extent and severity of the need. The services of the welfare state are thus targeted at and restricted to the most impoverished section of the populace. Historically, '[s]ervices for the poor tend to be poor services' (Titmuss 1987). What we have here are publicly financed and produced services, but limited in quantity and quality. The stigmatization that adheres to the recipience of benefits is considerable in this system, and many with legitimate rights to benefits refrain from applying for them, creating the so-called 'low take-up' phenomenon. People with the means augment or replace public benefits with market-based solutions, just as voluntary, informal help also plays a major part. The public services provided in this model are limited, especially in the area of child care and care of the elderly.

The Universal Model

The basic assumption in this model, as in the liberal model, is that all citizens have a number of social rights by virtue of their citizenship or residence (legal residence). Also in line with the liberal model, the prevailing method of financing is through taxation. Where they diverge is in the universal model's relatively high provision levels and the high degree of inclusiveness. Welfare provisions are in principle available to all citizens, not only to those who have made contributions or are in need them. To take an example: in Denmark the elderly have a right to a state pension even though they might not have made any contributions by paying tax, or do not need a state pension because either their own or their spouse's income is sufficient. The emphasis lies on publicly regulated and produced services rather than transfers. A high level of care is extended to children and senior citizens at the same time as an ideal of equality prevails across social classes, groups and gender. This is a decentralized model in that counties and local authorities employ most of the people who work in the education, health and social sectors. The welfare state is also a major employer.

In Figure 9.1, we summarize the main differences between the three models.

	The Insurance Model	The Residual Model	The Universal Model
Criteria for entitlement	Contribution	Need	Citizenship
Political ideology	Conservative	Liberal	Social Democratic
Central institution	Voluntary organizations/ family	Market	State
Extent	Comprehensive	Limited	Comprehensive
Financing	Social partners via contributions	The state via taxes	The state via taxes
Demarcation of collectivity	Labor market affiliation	Citizenship	Citizenship
Effects on social stratification	Status preserving	Poverty regulating	Redistributing

Figure 9.1 Three ideal typical welfare models

The models differ then on points of principle, on main stakeholders and on financing arrangements as ways of organizing the welfare state. This has consequences on their impact. We illustrate this empirically in the next section.

The Danish Welfare State in Europe

In this section we compare the Danish welfare state with that of other European countries. The comparison has been performed on the basis of Eurostat's social statistics, but we would like to point out already at this stage that labor market conditions are an extremely important aspect of welfare states. The labor market statistics show that the Scandinavian countries differ in having the largest proportion of their populations in the labor market, and that the differences between EU countries are seen in particular in the frequency of women's involvement in paid work. On the other hand, the Scandinavian countries no longer have full employment, which distinguished them from other EU countries previously. They do, however, fare better in terms of youth employment and long-term unemployment than at least the countries of Southern Europe (European Commission, 1999).

A common way of assessing the scope of the welfare state is by looking into the percentage of the total economy that is administered by the welfare systems, that is, by comparing total spending on social measures with BNP. In this perspective, as Table A1.1 in the Appendix shows, spending grew relatively in EU countries as a whole in the 1990s from over 25 per cent to just under 28 per cent. We also see that the Nordic countries position themselves at the high end of the scale. Denmark and Sweden are the countries that relatively speaking spend most on welfare, to wit, a third. When Norway and Iceland are included, the whole scale is represented since Iceland spends only 18 per cent of its BNP on welfare, while Norway, with its 28 per cent, is spot on the EU average. The Scandinavian model is an expensive one then, though it compares with the other Northern European welfare states such as Germany, France and Holland, for which spending in 1998 ranged from 27 to 33 per cent of BNP. As one would expect, the Southern European nations channel fewer resources into collective institutional welfare arrangements, 22 to 25 per cent. The same goes for Great Britain, which represents a residual model: spending here is 27 per cent, just under the EU average.

There is one drawback to this relativizing perspective: nations are affected by changes in both numerators and denominators so that when BNP drops dramatically values can become very high indeed. It is therefore expedient to assess spending developments in absolute figures (Appendix, Tables A1.2 and A1.3). If we look first at the 1990s, we see that spending rose by 22 per cent in Denmark and in Finland and Norway by 19 and 20 per cent respectively; spending has not risen very much in Sweden and Holland (10 and 3 per cent respectively). There has been a steep rise in Great Britain, all of 35 per cent. In Germany, the rise was more moderate, stopping at 14 per cent. Portugal and Ireland, where spending is least, have seen the greatest increment, 89 and 44 per cent, respectively. There is evidence then of a certain amount of convergence taking place on this point since the countries that spend the most are growing slowly or moderately fast, while the countries that spend the least are the fastest-growing.

If we convert social spending per capita into purchasing power parity (PPP) and then make a comparison, Luxembourg comes way out on top as the country using most resources per capita on welfare, 9,258 PPP. Denmark, Germany, France, Sweden, Austria, Norway and Holland spend between 6,400 and 7,100 PPP, and Great Britain and Finland over 5,000 PPP, which is just below the EU average of 5,500 PPP per capita. In Portugal, Greece and Ireland two-thirds or less than the average goes to welfare policy. If we use this measure as an expression of a welfare state's 'generosity' to its citizens, we find that the four Nordic countries straddle the EU average. It is not the case, however, that Scandinavia differs from the Western European countries, which indeed are bunched around the average (cf. Appendix, Table A1.3).

The biggest share by far of social spending goes to the elderly and to the various areas of the public health sector. Table A1.4 shows that that these two areas together made up 80 per cent of total EU spending in 1998. The areas of unemployment and families and children stand for 7-8 per cent each of total spending, which leaves 3-4 per cent for help to the poor. Most spending in the European welfare state goes thus above all to care of the elderly and public health. There is nonetheless considerable diversity among the countries. The Nordic countries, with figures between 32 and 39 per cent, all lie below the average for spending on elderly and pensions, while the continental European countries are lumped together around the 46 per cent mean. The Southern European countries, like Italy for instance, have values far above the average. Spending on unemployment goes some way to illustrate the extent of the problem, and also to show the generosity of individual systems. The overall effect of these two factors is very disparate indeed. While Italy channels less than 3 per cent of its social spending on unemployment, 12 per cent is the figure for Denmark and Finland; the same is roughly true of Holland and Sweden. In the area of family policy, too, the Nordic countries do significantly better than the European mean.

Section 2 above would probably lead the reader to expect that the method of financing preferred by the Scandinavian countries would be primarily through taxation, and the reader would be right in this assumption. As Appendix, Table A1.5 shows, 67 per cent of spending in Denmark is funded in this way; for Ireland and Norway the figure is 60 per cent. Finland and Sweden score 45 per cent; but Iceland with its 53 per cent and Great Britain with its 48 per cent belong in this group as well. These levels should be seen in relation to an EU average of only 35 per cent, which is representative of many of the continental European countries. Holland and Belgium with 16 and 24 per cent of their welfare systems publicly financed make up the tail end of the list. The EU average of employers' share of social expenses is 38 per cent, while in Denmark we see only 9 per cent. In the other Nordic countries, employers contribute a far greater amount. Sweden and Finland lie slightly under the average of 38 per cent, Iceland slightly over with 39 per cent. In the EU as a whole, almost 25 per cent of total funding comes from insured individuals; in the Nordic countries, this share ranges from 8 to 18 per cent. It is clear, therefore, that in its financing of its welfare budget Denmark is the Scandinavian country that comes closest to the ideal-typical model. Over time, the public domination in welfare funding in Denmark has declined. In 1990 the percentage was 80, in 1998 it had dropped to 67. During the same period the share from the insured rose from

5 to 18 per cent. We see then that Denmark is nearing the dominant pattern in the EU (Amerini, 2000).

The overall effect of the labor market and the welfare state in EU member countries is illustrated in Table A1.6 where the variables are set out. We see from the first column that the differences in the scope of the welfare states are only partly explainable on the basis of the countries' general economic growth, since the difference in GNP per capita is far less than the difference in the magnitude of the resources expended by the various member states on collective social ends. Only in Greece, Spain and Portugal is it possible to see a connection of this type. The Nordic countries are distributed across either side of the EU mean of 19,000 euro, with Finland and Sweden slightly below and Denmark, Norway and Sweden slightly over. With almost 32,000 euro per capita, Luxembourg is in a class of its own.

The effect of the redistribution performed by the welfare state through social policy and taxation can be estimated by calculating the number of people in the low income bracket in each country before and after transfers. The difference in values in columns two and three show the extent of redistribution. Here we see how the Danish poverty rate drops from 29 to 11 per cent and in Finland, according to these data, from 34 to only 3 per cent. Conversely we see that taxation and transfers have practically no effect on redistribution in Italy and Greece, where the poverty rate falls only one to two percentage points. This is also the case for Iceland, unexpectedly perhaps. In Great Britain, Ireland and Holland, we see a moderate effect achieved with a reduction of about 13 percentage points. The continental European and Southern European type of welfare state does not redistribute resources to any great extent, in line with expectations. The poor here are defined as people whose income is less than half the average income. There is therefore a connection between the poverty rate and the income inequality measure, the Gini-coefficient, which is given in Table A1.6 too. It is a measure of the total income which would have to be relocated from the wealthiest half of the population to the poorest half to achieve complete distributional equality. So the lower the Gini-coefficient, the greater the equality. We see that the Scandinavian countries distinguish themselves with coefficients around 0.25 while the continental European countries on average score around 0.35. We can also see that Great Britain is higher than the average, as one would expect of a residual welfare state.

As a final measure of the differences between EU countries, we shall look at growth in services in relation to income transfers. Table A1.7 shows that services play a substantial role in the Scandinavian countries, where they make up about a third of all social spending, while they make up 8 per cent in the continental European countries. As expected, services are somewhat more extensive in the residual welfare countries. There is a connection between these differences and levels of women's labor market participation in member countries.

In summary, we can conclude that Denmark and the other Scandinavian countries are not particularly expensive welfare states, and it is clear that the scope of the welfare state is not directly proportional to economic prosperity, as Wilensky believed. It is also clear that it is in the area of financing that Denmark mostly clearly stands out from the other EU countries. Finally, we see that the Scandinavian countries, as an overall effect of taxation and welfare policies, are substantially less unequal with regard to income distribution, than is the case elsewhere. This is true of both classes (or social groups) and gender.

If we were to illustrate this point in relation to particular groups of the population, single parents would be a good critical case. Their situation mirrors both redistribution across genders and between social groups, when we look at the most disadvantaged members of the group. A range of studies have shown that the risk of poverty facing single parents is lowest in the Scandinavian countries, while it is far higher in countries like Great Britain, Ireland, Germany and the Southern European countries (Lewis, 1997).

We would finally like to point out that welfare states are dynamic by nature, and, moreover, that it has been possible to identify a wide array of changes and adjustments in recent years. Of the most substantial, we would mention the growth in labor market pensions throughout the 1990s and the concurrent growth in private health insurance schemes. We also see a tendency to invite private involvement in services for the elderly that once were exclusively the responsibility of the public (local authority) domain. These factors are tell-tale signs that the Danish state is edging towards the residual model and greater reliance on private insurance schemes.

EEC/EU Social Policy Initiatives Prior to the EMU[2]

Social policy has been a so-called 'low politics' area. For the first three decades it had no central place in EU cooperation. EU's social dimension, which consists of labor market and social policies, has comprised in particular community initiatives in the former area. The 1957 Treaty of Rome contained general provisions on the elimination of obstacles hindering the free movement of persons and labor (Articles 3 c and 49) and Article 117 dealt with the necessity of improving workers' living and working conditions and expressed hopes for the future harmonization of social systems. However, the legal verdict is that this Article was primarily programmatic (Nielsen & Szyszczak, 1997: 18 ff). According to Article 51, the Council could, following a proposal by the Commission, unanimously adopt social security measures deemed necessary to realize the free movement of labor. The Article referred vaguely to two principles, codified and specified in a Regulation[3] of 1971 (1408/71) on the social security of migrant workers. The first was the *principle of aggregation*, which means that periods of contribution, which confer a right to social benefits, can be aggregated. The second was the *principle of exportability*, which maintains that workers and their families shall be entitled to social benefits irrespective of the country in which they are residing. It was also decided that only one country's legislation could be applied, to avoid benefits being paid twice over. In a regulation from 1968 (1612/68), it is stated that all workers, irrespective of nationality, shall be treated equally with regard to social and tax-related advantages. Differential treatment of workers from other EEC states was quite simply forbidden. Regulation 1408 spelt out, however, that what was intended was not the harmonization of social insurance schemes but a *coordination* of them,[4] and that it is 'necessary to respect the special characteristics of national security legislations'. The aspirations expressed with respect to harmonization in Article 117 of the Treaty of Rome were soon to be dashed. At the end of the 1950s a decision was passed pointing out that harmonization was unnecessary and that EU institutions lacked the formal authority to pursue it (Berghmann, 1997).

The adoption of the Single Market in 1986 established through numerous directives the free movement not only of labor but of goods, services and capital. The decision was motivated by a desire to enhance EU's competitiveness *vis-à-vis* the USA and Far East, and this market logic underlay the ensuing directives. The 'EU package', as it was termed in Denmark, did not contain any new social policy statements, apart from a few expansive formulations in Article 130A on the strengthening of economic and social solidarity, words which in 1988 were followed up with the channeling of increased resources to the Structural Funds. This had a particular impact on the Southern European countries. Moreover, an opening was made for qualified majority voting on working environment issues.

So the fuel stoking early EU social policy regulations was first and foremost the wish to promote labor mobility, and the legal authority to do so lay primarily in regulations on migrant workers' social rights. The main emphasis was on negative integration arrangements with the elimination of barriers to the movement of labor.

In the latter half of the 1980s, the Delors Commission started work to create a social superstructure for the market project, spurred by fears of social dumping and social tourism (Abrahamson & Borchorst, 1996). By adopting a solemn declaration in the form of the Charter of Fundamental Social Rights of Workers it was successful in speeding up the process. There was some prior opposition, mainly articulated by Great Britain, but also by Southern European states. The latter voted in favor of the Charter, however, after allocations to the Structural Funds were doubled. The Charter set out a number of labor market and social rights, subsequently to be incorporated in the Maastricht Treaty in 1992. But the whole process was nearly derailed thanks to the blanket resistance being mustered by Great Britain to this devious way of smuggling socialism in through the back door, as Margaret Thatcher put it. In addition, the extent of qualified majority voting was a controversial point with the Southern European States (Christoffersen, 1992). The Solomonic solution was to append a protocol, which all member countries apart from Great Britain acceded to. According to the protocol, the eleven could use EEC/EU institutions to implement what, to all intents and purposes, was identical to the social charter. Anything remotely to do with social policy in a strict sense was to be regulated by unanimous vote while labor market policy would be determined by qualified majority voting.

In developing social policy, the Commission had availed itself of soft control mechanisms, i.e., the imposition of sanctions was not a response to lack of compliance. But the moral pressures brought to bear on member countries are considerable since they indicate a political obligation. At the same time, they often function as forerunners of subsequent initiatives. Examples are resolutions (Council Resolution of 6 December 1994 on certain aspects for a European Union social policy: a contribution to economic and social convergence in the Union 1994), communications (for instance the Council recommendation of July 27, 1992 on the convergence of social protection objectives and policies 1992), solemn declarations (for instance the Charter of the fundamental social rights of workers of 1989), and recommendations (for instance the Recommendation on Convergence of Social Protection of 1992).

In 1998, the protocol on the labor market and social policy was incorporated in the Treaty of Amsterdam, since the Blair Government in Great Britain was now prepared to accede to it. Few changes in labor market and social policy emerged, apart from the fact that parliament obtained greater influence over Article 42, which lay in extension of Regulation 1408 on migrant workers social rights. Decisions concerning workers' safety and social protection were to still subject to unanimous voting (Art. 137 (3)). The Amsterdam Treaty contained in addition a chapter on employment, which set the stage for a coordinated employment strategy (Art. 125–130).

The Treaty of Nice, which has to be ratified by all EU member states, does not involve any great changes in the area of social policy. At the December 2000 summit, it proved impossible to reach agreement on a transition to qualified majority voting, as proposed by the Commission, but it was decided that the Council unanimously may decide to use qualified-majority voting in certain areas.

In recent years social policy aims such as those that address unemployment and social exclusion, which are seen in connection with macro economic aims, have attracted greater notice. The chapter on employment has been followed up with discussions at the summits. The summit in Lisbon in March 2000 set out an ambition to become 'the most competitive and dynamic knowledge-based economy in the world'. Furthermore, government heads coupled economic liberalization with targets for employment and the development of an active and dynamic welfare state with a view to redressing social exclusion and poverty (European Council, 2000).

EU on numerous occasions has given greater definition to the regulations on migrant workers' social rights via a sequence of preliminary rulings by the European Court intended to be incorporated in member states' legislation (Lyon-Caen, 1995; Leibfried & Pierson, 1995a; Nielsen & Szyszczak, 1997). Court rulings have led to amendments to Regulation 1408, which has been amended over thirty times (1995a: 64).

Leibfried and Pierson summarize the principles codified in regulations and Court rulings as follows (1995a: 64):

1. A member state may no longer limit social benefits to its citizens. [...] Benefits must be granted to all or withheld from all.
2. A member state may no longer insist that its benefits apply only within its territory. [T]oday's member state can exercise its power to determine the territory of consumption only to a limited extent – basically when providing in-kind or means-tested benefits.
3. A member state [may not] prevent other social policy regimes from directly competing with the regime it has built on its own territory.
4. Member states do not have an exclusive right to implement claims to welfare benefits. Rather, the authorities of other nations may also have a decisive say in adjudicating benefit status in individual cases.

The security provisions covered by the regulations on migrant workers embrace benefits for sickness and motherhood, invalidity, old age and death, work-related accidents and occupational diseases, unemployment and family allowances. In 1981 the list of eligible persons was expanded with the addition of the self-employed (1390/81) and, in 1999, of students (307/1999).

In extension of the Regulation and the internal market's rules on the free movement of social provisions (Article 49), the Court ruled that member states may not decide who produces services for their nationals. In the so-called Decker and Kohll cases of 1995 and 1996 rulings were made that national sickness insurance schemes shall provide allowances for the purchase of health services (glasses and special dental treatment) in member states. The premises of the ruling contained a number of general considerations which opened up for reflections on legislative amendments in all member states (Embedsmandsgruppen, 1999).

While the Commission has given clear voice to aspirations to establish a common supranational social policy and, in the white paper on European social policy, for instance, has advocated a European welfare model (European Commission, 1994), member governments have not been convinced. Maintaining unanimity in the area of social security needs to be considered in connection with their stance on welfare policy as a national concern. Several countries have challenged the Court's rulings on Regulation 1408 (Leibfried & Pierson, 1995a; Nielsen & Szyszczak, 1997), and some countries, like France, have refused to comply with them (Lyon-Caen, 1995).

Social researchers disagree on whether the development of EEC/EU's social policy has resulted in a curtailment of national sovereignty, and, if it has, on how much, and, thirdly on what is propelling the process forward. Leibfried and Pierson found in 1995 that there was still some distance to go before a genuine European welfare state was in place. It is certainly true that the EEC/EU has pursued a distribution policy via its agricultural policy, but the EU does not collect taxes or tender actual social services. Leibfried and Pierson conclude, however, that the principle of member-state sovereignty over social policy has suffered at least partial erosion (1995a: 44). They advanced three explanations for this state of affairs. First, qualified majority decisions on labor market policy issues have driven the process forward; second, the EU Commission exerts considerable influence, both in its ability to shape the political agenda and as the body in charge of the process. In addition, the European Court plays a frequently overlooked but nevertheless vital role via its preliminary rulings. And third, decisions made in one area often reverberate on other decisions and become elements in negotiation arsenals. Thus governments, having once opposed decisions, sometimes find themselves agreeing to them (1995a, b).

A number of empirical analyses of social dimension developments confirm the crucial role played by the Commission and, to a degree, the Court, in them (cf. Abrahamson & Borchorst, 1996: chapter 5). Ross' participative observations of the Commission in 1991 reflect that its actions were partly intended and partly political spillover effects in which the one step led to the next (1995). Cram concludes that the Commission's desire to consolidate its own power has led it to conduct a bureaucratic politics to press the process onwards towards supranational social policy. Soft mechanisms were employed to achieve this end (1993).

Streeck agrees that the role played by EU's social policy is vital to the development of the process of integration, but he predicts that it will always take place in an interplay between the national and the supranational levels. He characterizes the process as a neo-voluntarist process which it has been in the interest of member governments, social partners and the Commission to pursue. Streeck does not see a contradiction between the retention of national sovereignty and the implementation of social policy initiatives at the European level (1995).

There are then widely disparate interpretations among researchers, both with regard to the nature of the development of the process and in identifying the most crucial factors and players.

To summarize the concrete developments, the significance of social policy to the integration process has grown. In the form of legally binding measures in treaty provisions and regulations, this has generally come about against the background of migrant workers' rights. Progress has been steady, and the legal foundation has been built around the preliminary rulings of the Court in particular. The emphasis has been on negative integration measures. With Maastricht came a genuine social superstructure. But it did not result in substantial changes in social policy because social security issues still had to be decided by unanimous vote, and the Nice agreement envisages only minor changes in this area.

EU and the Danish Welfare State

In Denmark, the question of EU's influence over social policy has become a key topic in debates on the EU. The Government and the 'Yes' parties invoke a declaration on social and labor market policy made at the Edinburgh summit in 1992, according to which the Maastricht Treaties 'permit each Member State to pursue its own policy with regard to distribution of income and maintain or improve social welfare benefits' (Annex 2 (2)). Importance has also be attached to the formulation in the protocol to the Maastricht Treaty on social and labor market policy which states that the article 'shall not prevent any Member State from maintaining more stringent protection measures compatible with this Treaty' (Article 137 (5)). The opposing side has argued that signals emanating from the EU on increased regulation of social policy have caused a retrenchment of Danish social policy and that aspects peculiar to the Danish welfare model are under threat. Contention has often centered on the harmonization of social services, while the implications of the coordination of migrant workers' social rights to the end of the 1990s went almost unnoticed. The Court has thus far not initiated legal proceedings against Denmark in connection with Regulation 1408, but Denmark has had an obligation to comply with its preliminary rulings, as have other countries.

There has been a tendency on the part of the Danish Government to downplay the impact of the EU initiatives on political decision-making, given the broad popular displeasure over what is perceived as interference in social policy. It is therefore difficult to pinpoint exactly which policy amendments have been directly motivated by EU regulations, in contrast to countries like France and Italy for instance, where unpopular measures on several occasions have been legitimated with reference to EU decisions, a tactic which has tended to give them greater significance than they probably would otherwise have had.

There are not many instances of important changes being made to Danish social policy as a direct result of a need to adapt to EU regulations. We believe that the following two examples are the most important.

The decision on contributions to the Early Retirement Scheme, which was passed in connection with the compromise reached on the Finance Act in December 1998, and the waiving of the scheme's residence clause in March 2000 is the first example. On 25 September 1998, the Commission sent a letter to the Danish Government which took as it point of departure complaints from foreign workers who had been denied a retirement pension. The Commission pointed out that contributions made to insurance schemes in other countries had not been included in the application for membership of the unemployment fund (*A-kasse*), and that Danish rules were based on a residence requirement. The Commission argued that Danish practice had violated the prohibition against differential treatment set out in Regulation 1612/68 and the treaty's Article 48 (European Commission, 1998). The Danish Government sought to avoid having to amend the early retirement pension by claiming that what was at issue here was a labor market measure and not a social security one. The Commission maintained, however, that the Regulation's wording on social security advantages should not be understood in a strict sense. The Early Retirement Scheme was based initially on a modified insurance principle since it was linked to membership of the unemployment fund, but it did not presuppose payment of contributions. The introduction of the subscription contributions and the link between premium and disbursement strengthened the insurance principle.

Another adjustment to EU regulations happened with the amendment of the Public Health Insurance Act in April 2000 in response to the Decker and Kohll rulings. An opening was created to provide allowances for medical and dental services, physiotherapy, etc., given on a profit-making basis. Publicly produced health services are not affected by this amendment. The Act authorized the minister to set out regulations for the purchase of health services and goods in other EU states, *inter alia*, because clarity had yet to be achieved on the implications of the Court's ruling and possible amendments to legislation to be put in place by the other member states.

As mentioned above, it is impossible to make any more precise assessment of the extent to which adjustments to the Danish welfare state can be traced back to the initiatives coming for the EU. There is, however, a tendency for EU opponents and sceptics alike to attribute cut-backs in the Danish welfare state to EU regulations. The tendency to either play down or exaggerate the effects of EU regulations reflects the degree to which the issue has become politicized in the Danish EU debate.

It is also impossible to isolate the effects of the Single Market from the various phases of the EMU, but in what follows we give an assessment of future trends in social policy development and consider the possible implications of EMU should Denmark decide to join its third phase.

If the economy as a whole is widely affected by Danish accession to the EMU's third phase, it will naturally have implications for welfare services too. Since considerable disagreement on this question has reigned among Danish economists (cf. Ministry of Finance & Ministry of Economic Affairs, 2000; The Economic Council, 2000), we will not discuss this aspect further. EMU's convergence requirements regarding inflation limits and national budget deficits are healthy economic principles of importance to ensure funding of welfare services. In periods of economic contraction, when pressures on welfare services tend to grow considerably, the reduced room for economic maneuver may impinge on distribution policy priorities as a consequence of the clear priority given to price stability in the convergence requirements.

With regard to the political repercussions, a report from the Institute of Foreign Policy, which is affiliated to the Ministry of Foreign Affairs, concluded that no one, or very few, wanted a European central state, and that the outcome would depend on how the political contest between national constellations of interested parties developed in the coming years (2000: 85ff). The relative strength of the national players will, of course, be decisive, but the outcome will also depend on the relative strength of and interplay between national and supranational institutions, a crucial factor in EU's management of social policy up to now. There has been a tendency for periods of progress in the social area to bear the imprint of initiatives from the Commission, while member governments, on the other hand, have tended to play a more conspicuous role in periods of integrational stagnation. This was the case after the adoption of the Maastricht Treaty, for instance, when the breaks were put on in the area of social policy. At the same time, it is clear that the European Council, via its choice of Commission chairman, exerts influence on whether integration is promoted or slowed down. The appointment of Delors and Prodi signaled a wish on the part of the Council to boost the integration process, though the election of Santer marked a desire for a slower tempo.

Two further factors that will have a major influence on EMU's political implications is that it has been built as a superstructure over the Single Market, and that it is closely intertwined with the latter's modus operandi. In a communication from 1999 on a concerted strategy for the modernization of social protection the Commission said the following:

> Given the greater degree of inter-dependence between Member States' economies brought about by EMU, social protection becomes more and more a matter of common concern among Member States. Reforms in the social protection systems of one Member State are of interest to, and can potentially impact on, others. EMU does not of itself call into question the long recognised primary responsibility of each Member State for the organisation and financing of its own system. However, side by side with the need to create coherent, mutually reinforcing economic policies among Member States, the case for a concerted approach to the modernisation of social protection is reinforced by EMU. Member States have a shared interest in developing such an approach.

In conformity with this understanding, the Commission is of the opinion today that the Single Market, and the addition of as many as twenty-eight new member states, would 'bring out and accentuate the remaining imperfections of the Single Market, notably in the areas of social policy and taxation', and that this, seen in connection with the EMU, would intensify the need for a more determined coordination of economic and structural policies, including economic and social policy (European Commission, 2000). We can conclude, then, that the mounting interdependence of member states has created a need for expanded social policy cooperation.

Independent of proposals from the Commission, member governments have altered their approach to social policy cooperation. They are more minded now to develop EU's social dimension. This needs to be seen in connection with the strengthened economic harmonization that government heads want to coordinate with social policy. It is significant here, that, at present, the number of social democratic government heads is far higher than before. At the summit in Lisbon in March 2000, 'benchmarking', or the method of open coordination was adopted in the shape of quantitative and qualitative indices for general targets. It implied the expression of common targets for employment for the year 2010, and ascribing a stronger guiding and coordinating role to the European Council. A decision was also made to give priority to cooperation on the long-term development of social protection and tenability of the pension schemes in the years up to 2020. On the rhetorical level, the change in member states' stance is mirrored in the references by government heads to a European social model and the development of a single, active and dynamic welfare state (European Council, 2000). At the Nice summit, these decisions were confirmed and strengthened.

Broadened political cooperation on social policy has thus been placed as a key issue on the EU agenda. It is discussed at intergovernmental conferences too. To round off, we want to discuss what in our view may be the future impact of the EU on the Danish welfare system on the basis of the dimensions we presented in Figure 9.1.

Allocation criterion: We anticipate that the universal schemes will come under pressure and it is likely that insurance-based services will become more widespread in consequence of the mounting coordination on social policy within the EU. This process will be stronger the more inclusive the groups that are given the right to transnational services, but it will apply in particular to those services that are not territorially anchored, that is, the income transfers. As long as the production of Danish services remains predominantly a public task, we do not expect them to be affected by regulations for service mobility. The impact of income transfers will depend on the extent of actual mobility, which, up to now, has been limited. We should keep in mind, however, that insurance payments are affected by Regulation 1408 thanks to the rules on aggregation of insurance periods. On the other hand, means-tested provisions fall beyond the scope of these regulations.

Central institution: Over the past years there has been a movement towards a mixture of welfare components in all countries, balancing the parts played by state, market, family and voluntary organizations. This process towards genuine convergence has been supported by the EU, but, in our opinion, it has been stimulated by a number of other factors too.

Extent: We do not anticipate a fall in the overall level of social provisions as a consequence of increased harmonization. As we touched on above, inter-country convergence in this area has been a topic of discussion.

Financing: As considered in section 3, it is in this area that Denmark differs the most. We expect pressures to mount on the taxation-funded schemes if revenue drops as a result of harmonization of taxes and duties. While a harmonization of income tax is not on the cards, it is a distinct possibility for indirect taxes, especially if the voting rules are amended. The abolition of the twenty-four-hour rule for border trade will also shrink the revenue base. Financing by taxes will also come under pressure if expenditure rises, for instance if the right to social services across borders is widened and if mobility increases too. It is, however, not totally the case that the EU is going in the direction of increased financing by contribution. In France, for example, the level of tax financing has risen. If the integration of women in the labour market causes non-Scandinavian countries to increase publicly funded child care facilities, financing by taxation will increase there too.

Effects: If we are right in our supposition that insurance-based schemes will expand, it will probably put pressure on benefits with redistributive effects and stimulate growth in benefits that preserve the status quo.

Overall we anticipate that the specific properties of the Danish model in the form of taxation-based universal schemes will face increasing pressure, but that, in some areas, countries will tend to converge on one another. In relation to the public services, we will possibly witness a movement towards the Danish (and Swedish) solutions.

Conclusion and Perspectives

In this article we have concluded that the various models at work in EU's member states, despite a certain degree of convergence, continue differ quite fundamentally in their approaches to allocation, financing and effects in relation to conserving or redressing social divisions. The Danish welfare model stands out with the highest rate of financing through taxation, and, along with the other Nordic models, it is the most service-inclined and redistributive.

In the first thirty years of the EEC very few efforts were made to harmonize social systems because social policy had not yet become one of the central pillars of the European integration process. There has nevertheless been a gradual movement towards closer coordination of migrant workers' social rights, particularly in response to rulings from the European Court.

But the implementation of the Single Market over the past ten to fifteen years has increased pressure on reaching a harmonization of taxation, labor market and social policies, for both economic and social policy reasons. This pressure will grow with the EMU and EU's eastwards expansion. Cooperation on social policy will intensify because government leaders at the last summits have decided to strengthen social policy cooperation in connection with their general economic targets. Working groups have been appointed at departmental level to prepare the ground.

Our conclusion is that any further harmonization of welfare policies will put pressure on universal schemes, but that the level of pressure will depend on the extent of mobility. A shrinking revenue base in the form of falling earnings will bring even more pressure to bear on the tax-based schemes. Insurance schemes will multiply and the involvement of the private sector and user payment will grow. And we should note that moves in this direction are already under way in Denmark, although it is impossible to ascribe them directly to the workings of EU initiatives. But neither can we discount an indirect influence. We also need bear in mind that some of the other countries will increase the level of tax-funding, which will mean convergence in taxation between the countries. At the same time, the integration of women in the labor force throughout Europe sets the need for a strategy for non-familial child care and care of the elderly on the agenda. In this context the Danish approach is highlighted as a model.

With regard to the points of contention listed at the beginning of the chapter, we have concluded that a gradual evolution towards social policy coordination within the EU has in fact taken place. We have not made any judgements concerning the overall economic implications of a possible Danish accession to the EMU's third phase, but we feel that, at the present time, there are strong indications that the political process towards European cooperation is gaining in momentum. If we turn to the implications for the Danish welfare state, we anticipate, given present trend levels, a fall in taxed-based financing and a proliferation of insurance schemes. Whether this is considered a threat to the Danish welfare state depends on one's subjective stance, but it will also be affected by further harmonization.

In conclusion we want to point out a number of paradoxes and dilemmas in the Danish EU position, as viewed through welfare state glasses. The economic harmonization of EU's member states has put the need for greater social policy coordination in the EU on the agenda, and it is becoming increasingly difficult – especially for social democratic governments – to resist an EU-level effort in this area. The social challenges in both existing and future member states are pretty much the same and will be even more so with closer economic cooperation.

The slowly advancing integration process based on migrant workers' social rights has increasingly highlighted the ambiguity of the signals in the legal foundation and statements coming out of the Commission and the European Council. Words continue to be spoken about the need to respect national differences in the social security systems, but the same differences are portrayed more and more as a problem for the Single Market and the EMU project.

Finally we would like to elaborate on the democratic dilemmas at the present stage of European cooperation, where expansion is happening both vertically and horizontally at the same time. Ensuring democratic support and the development of the welfare state are closely interlocked issues because welfare policy requires a clear legitimate basis. Social rights must of necessity build on and find their justification in a sense of solidarity with others. This is probably even more the case for the collective solidarity on which the taxation-based systems have to rely. In general, welfare systems in all their various forms enjoy substantial popular support in the respective member states.

The culture of democracy in Denmark contains a powerful norm concerning public debate, due, among other things, to the relatively wide influence wielded by popular associations and movements. It is reflected in a belief that vital decisions should be discussed in public. This applies in particular when the decisions have to do with established welfare services and provisions. The widespread reactions to the introduction of contributions to the early retirement pension scheme illustrates the problems that can flare up when decisions are passed with no advance public discussion. If national decision-making authority is curtailed, by, for instance, qualified majority decisions in the social security area, the opportunity to engage in popular debates on distributive politics will also suffer. From a democracy point of view, it is also intriguing that there exists in the Danish (and Swedish) population a far higher sense of confidence in one's ability to influence national decisions than EU decisions. On the other hand, the space for national decision-making, which is absolutely vital to the welfare state's *raison d'être*, has shrunk noticeably over the past decade.

It is well and good that the impact of the EU on the Danish welfare state is a central topic of discussion, but it is our opinion that these democratic dilemmas will continue to feature in the EU project for many years to come – not least in the Danish debate.

Notes

* Translated by Christopher Henry Saunders.
1 This section is partly based on Abrahamson (1999) and Abrahamson & Borchorst (1996).
2 For a more detailed examination of EF/EU's social policy initiatives, see Abrahamson & Borchorst (1996).
3 On adoption, Regulations become statutory in all member countries.
4 However, specifications as to how any possible coordination is to be defined have never been forthcoming (Nielsen & Szyszczak, 1997: 127).

References

Abrahamson, P. (1999): 'The Welfare Modelling Business', *Social Policy and Administration*, vol. 33, no. 4.
Abrahamson, P. & A. Borchorst (1996): 'EU og socialpolitik, Copenhagen, *Rådet for Europæisk Politiks*, Skrift nr. 13.
Amerini, G. (2000): 'Social protection in the European Union, Iceland and Norway', *Statistics in Focus. Population and social conditions*, Theme 3 - 15/2000, Luxembourg: Eurostat.
Anttonen, A. & J. Sipilä (1996): 'European Social Care Services: Is it possible to identify models?', *Journal of European Social Policy*, vol. 6, no. 2.
Belorgey, J. M. (1997): 'How can the union support and enrich the activities of its member states in the field of social security?', *Bulletin Luxembourgeois Des Question Sociales*. vol. 4: 143-50.
Berghman, J. (1997): 'Can the idea of benchmarking be applied to social protection?', *Bulletin Luxembourgeois des Questions Sociales*, vol. 4.
Castel, R. (1995): *Les Métamorphoses de la question sociale: cronique du salariat*, Paris: Fayard.
Christoffersen, P. S. (1992): *Traktaten om den Europæiske Union*, Charlottenlund: Jurist- og Økonomforbundets Forlag.
Clasen, J. (2000): 'Motives, means and opportunities: Reforming unemployment compensation in the 1990s', *West European Politics* vol. 23, no. 2, pp. 89-112.
Commission of the European Communities (2000): *Communication from the Commission. Supplementary contribution to the Intergovernmental Conference on institutional reforms*, Brussels: COM 114 final.
Council of Ministers (1989): *Charter of the fundamental social rights of workers*. Brussels: DG V.
Council of Ministers (1992a): 'Council recommendation of June 24, 1992 on common criteria concerning sufficient resources and social assistance in social protection systems', *Bulletin of the European Communities* no. L 245, 1992, pp. 46-48.
Council of Ministers (1992b): 'Council recommendation of July 27, 1992 on the convergence of social protection objectives and policies', *Bulletin of the European Communities* no. L 245, 1992, pp. 49-52.
Council of Ministers (1994): 'Council Resolution of 6 December 1994 on certain aspects for a European Union social policy: a contribution to economic and social convergence in the Union', *Official Journal of the European Communities*, no. C 368, 1994.
Council of Ministers (1997): *Council Resolution of December 15 1997 on The 1998 Employment Guidelines*, Brussels: DG V.

Cram, L. (1993): 'Calling the tune without paying the piper? Social policy regulation: the role of the Commission in the European Community social policy', *Policy and Politics*, vol. 21, no. 2.
DUPI (2000): *Udviklingen i EU siden 1992 på de områder, der er omfattet af de danske forbehold*, Copenhagen.
Eardley, T., J. Bradshaw, J. Ditch, I. Gough & P. Whiteford (1996): *Social Assistance in OECD-Countries: Synthesis Report*. Department of Social Security Research Report no. 46, London: HMSO.
Embedsmandsgruppen (1999): *Redegørelse fra Embedsmandsgruppen til vurdering af konsekvenserne af EF-domstolens afgørelser i Decker/Kohll-sagerne*, Copenhagen.
Ersbøll, N. (1998): *Referat af mødet i Rådet for Europæisk Politik d. 19. januar*. Copenhagen: Ministry of Foreign Affairs.
Esping-Andersen, G. (1990): *The Three Worlds of Welfare Capitalism*, Cambridge: Polity Press.
Esping-Andersen, G. (1997): 'Do the spending and finance structures matter?' in W. Beck, L. van der Maesen, A. Walker (eds.): *The Social Quality of Europe*, Amsterdam: Kluwer Law International, pp. 121-125.
Esping-Andersen, G. (1999): *Social Foundations of Post-Industrial Economies*, Oxford: Oxford University Press.
Esping-Andersen, G. (2000): 'Challenge to the welfare state in the 21st century. Report to the Portuguese Presidency of the European Union', Barcelona: Universitat Pompeu Fabra.
European Commission (1993a): *The Future of Social Policy: Options for the Union. A Green Paper*, Brussels: DG V.
European Commission (1993b, 1995a, 1998c): *Social Protection in Europe*, Brussels: GD V.
European Commission (1993c): *Proposal for a Council decision establishing a medium-term action programme to combat exclusion*, COM (93) 435.
European Commission (1994): *A White Paper – European social Policy – A way forward for the Union*, Brussels: GD V.
European Commission (1997a): *Modernising and improving social protection in the European Union*, Communication from the Commission, COM (97) 102. Brussels: DG V.
European Commission (1997b, 1999c): *Employment in Europe*, Brussels: DG V.
European Commission (1998): *Brev til den danske regering v. Poul Skytte Christoffersen [Letter to the Danish Government by Poul Skytte Christoffersen]*, 25.9, Brussels.
European Commission (1998a): *Social Action Programme 1998-2000*, COM (1998) 259 final, Brussels: DG V.
European Commission (1998b): *From guidelines to action: the national action plans for employment*, Brussels: DG V.
European Commission (1999): *Eurostat Yearbook. Edition 1998/99. A Statistical Eye on Europe. Data 1987-1997*, Brussels: European Commission.
European Commission (1999a): *Employment in Europe 1999*, DG V, Brussels.
European Commission (1999b): *A coordinated strategy for modernising social protection*, Communication from the European Commission COM (1999) 347 fin, Brussels.
European Commission (2000a): *Social Trends: prospects and challenges*, Communication from the Commission. Brussels: DG V.
European Commission (2000b): *The Lisbon European Council – an Agenda of Economic and Social Renewal of Europe. Contribution of the European Commission to the Special European Council in Lisbon, 23 to 24th March 2000*, Brussels.

European Council (2000): *Presidency Conclusions: Lisbon European Council 23 and 24 March*.
Eurostat (1999a): 'Social benefits and their redistributional effects in the EU', *Statistics in focus: Population and Economic Conditions*, Luxembourg: Eurostat.
Eurostat (1999b): *Eurostat Yearbook 98/99*, Luxembourg: Eurostat.
Evers, A. (1990): 'Shifts in the welfare mix: Introducing a new approach for the study of transformations in welfare and social policy', in A. Evers and H. Wintersberger: *Shifts in the welfare Mix*. Frankfurt: Campus Verlag, pp. 7-30.
Falkner, G. (2000): 'The treaty on European Union and its revision: Sea change or empty shell for European social policies', in S. Kuhnle (ed.): *Survival of the European Welfare State*, London and New York: Routledge, pp. 185-201.
Ferrera, M. (1993): *EC Citizens and social protection*, Pavia: University of Pavia.
Ferrera, Maurizio (1996): 'The 'southern model' of welfare in social Europe', *Journal of European Social Policy*, vol. 6, no. 1.
Ferrera, M. & M. Rhodes (2000): 'Recasting European Welfare States: An Introduction', *West European Politics* vol. 23, no. 2, pp. 1-10.
Ferrera, M. & M. Rhodes (2000): 'Building a Sustainable Welfare State', *West European Politics* vol. 23, no. 2, pp. 257-82.
Flora, P. & J. Alber (1981): 'Modernization, Democratization and the Development of Welfare States in Western Europe', in P. Flora & A. Heidenheimer (eds.): *The Development of Welfare States in Europe and America*, New Brunswick: Transaction Books.
Gustafsson, B. & P. J. Pedersen (eds.) (2000): *Poverty and low income in the Nordic countries*, Aldershot: Ashgate.
Hirst, P. & G. Thompson (1995): 'Globalization and the future of the welfare state', *Economy & Society* vol. 24, no. 3, pp. 408-442.
Jespersen, J. (1998): Personal correspondence.
Kuhnle, S. (2000): 'European welfare lessons of the 1990s', in S. Kuhnle (ed.): *Survival of the European Welfare State*, London and New York: Routledge, pp. 234-7.
Kuhnle, S. & M. Alestalo (2000): 'Introduction: Growth, adjustments and survival of European welfare states', in S. Kuhnle (ed.): *Survival of the European Welfare State*. London and New York: Routledge, pp. 3-18.
Leibfried, S. (1992): 'Towards an European Welfare State?', in Z. Ferge & J. E. Kolberg (eds.): *Social Policy in a Changing Europe*, Frankfurt am Main: Campus Verlag.
Leibfried, S. & P. Pierson (1995a): 'Semisovereign Welfare States: Social Policy in a Multitiered Europe', in S. Leibfried & P. Pierson: *European Social Policy. Between Fragmentation and Integration*, Washington: The Brookings Institution.
Leibfried, S. & P. Pierson (1995b): 'The Dynamics of Social Policy Integration', in S. Leibfried & P. Pierson: *European Social Policy. Between Fragmentation and Integration*, Washington: The Brookings Institution.
Lewis, J. (ed.) (1997): *Lone Mothers in European Welfare Regimes. Shifting Policy Logics*, London: Jessica Kingsley Publishers.
Lewis, J. & I. Ostner (1994): *Gender and the Evolution of European Social Policies*, Zes-Arbeitspapier nr 4, Bremen: Universität Bremen.
Lyon-Caen, A (1995): 'Social security and the principle of equal treatment in the Treaty and Regulation no. 1408/71', *Social Security in Europe: Equality between Nationals and Non-Nationals*, Lissabon: Departamento de Relações Internacionais e Convenções de Segurança Social.

Ministry of Finance & Ministry of Economic Affairs (2000): *Danmark og euroen. Konsekvenser ved forskellig tilknytning til eurosamarbejdet*, Copenhagen.
Ministry of State (2000): *Regeringskonferencen 2000. Forhandlingsgrundlag*, Copenhagen.
Nielsen, R. & E. Szyszczak (1997): *The Social Dimension of the European Union*, Copenhagen: Handelshøjskolens Forlag.
OECD (1981): *Welfare States in Crisis*, Paris: OECD.
OECD (1994): New Orientations for Social Policy, *Social Policy Studies* no. 12, Paris: OECD.
Ramprakash, D. (1997): 'Income distribution and poverty in EU-12 1993', *Statistics in focus. Population and social conditions* no. 7/1997, Luxembourg: Eurostat.
Ross, G. (1995): *Jacques Delors and European Integration*, Cornwall: Polity Press.
Sainsbury, D. (1996): *Gender Equality and Welfare States*, Cambridge.
Streeck, W. (1995): 'From Market Making to State Building? Reflections on the Political economy of European Social Policy', in S. Leibfried & P. Pierson: *European Social Policy. Between Fragmentation and Integration*, Washington: The Brookings Institution.
The Economic Council (2000): *Dansk Økonomi forår 2000*, Copenhagen.
Titmuss, R. (1971[1987]): 'Developing social policy in conditions of rapid change: the role of social welfare', in S. M. Miller (ed.): *The Philosophy of Welfare. Selected Writing*, London: Allen & Unwin.
Touraine, A. (1991): 'Face à l'exclusion', *Esprit* no. 141, pp. 7-13.
Townsend, P. (1995): 'Working Paper for a UN Committee. New York: United Nations', *Treaty of Amsterdam* (1998), Copenhagen: EU-information of the Danish Parliament.
United Nations (1989): *Social Policy in Transition: Adjusting to the need of the 1990s*, New York: United Nations.
United Nations (1993): *Final Report. Conference of European Ministers Responsible for Social Affairs – United Nations European Region*, Vienna: European Centre.
van Kersbergen, K. (2000): 'The declining resistance of welfare states to change?', in S. Kuhnle (ed.): *Survival of the European Welfare State*, London and New York: Routledge, pp. 19-36.
Vobruba, G. (1997): 'Social policy for Europe', in W. Beck, L. van der Maesen & A. Walker (eds.): *The Social Quality of Europe*, Amsterdam: Kluwer Law International.
Wilensky, H. & C. Lebaux (1958): *Industrial Society and Social Welfare*, New York: Russel Sage Foundation.

10 EMU – A Defense Mechanism for the Nordic Welfare State
WOLFGANG ZANK

Introduction: Markets Against Social Justice?

Many participants in the Danish debate, both inside and outside academia, have voiced the position that joining EMU would imply the destruction or at least a substantial reduction of the Danish welfare state. In this chapter, the main arguments in this context will be scrutinized. According to the present author, these arguments do not seem to be compelling. In his view, the EMU can basically be regarded as neutral in relation to the structure or the level of welfare state arrangements. The EMU works, however, as a barrier against grave policy mistakes which otherwise might indeed endanger a Nordic welfare state – and which in the past actually have brought the Danish one 'to the brink of the abyss'. For instance Hardy Hansen, the former chairman of *Specialarbejderforbundet i Danmark*, a union which organizes unskilled and semi-skilled workers, was quoted as having said that EMU gives priority to market forces, at the expense of social justice for ordinary Danish citizens. The result would be the extension of user payments, privatization and reductions of social transfer payments.[1] Arguments of his kind have been forwarded in many versions. The Danish EMU-critics have in particular pointed at the following elements in the construction of the European currency:

- price stability as the overarching guideline for monetary policy;
- the restrictions on fiscal policy which the convergence criteria and the Stability and Growth Pact imply;
- the loss of the possibility to devalue the Danish crown, and last but not least;
- free capital movements across the national borders.

I refer to these points as the 'critical points' of the EMU. Some Danish authors have expressed their concern that 'uncontrolled' market forces, in particular free capital movements, might start a process which undermines welfare capitalism by eroding its tax basis.[2] These concerns are part of a global debate, given the point that free capital movements are perhaps the most controversial aspects of globalization.

These four 'critical points' are directly related to the construction of the EMU. Other authors see the Danish welfare state threatened by European integration in general. In case taxation becomes an EU issue and a process of tax harmonization starts, Denmark might be forced to reduce her high tax levels. Not the least the VAT, currently at 25 per cent, would come under downward pressure if harmonization means convergence to the EU average.

Other authors see an increase in cross-border mobility as a potential threat to the Danish model. In this line of argumentation, high mobility is more compatible with individualized payments and individual rights which can be taken along when moving, as opposed to the universalistic features of the Danish system. For instance, the so-called national pension scheme which gives equal coverage to all residents who have been in the country for at least 40 years is one of these features. In this volume, Peter Abrahamson and Anette Borchorst argue that increased mobility in connection with the EU legislation and decisions of the European Court of Justice presumably will build up a growing pressure on Denmark towards more individualized social security systems. In the controversies prior to the Danish EMU referendum in September 2000 these arguments gained great prominence when the tabloid *Ekstra Bladet* could correctly report that an aide to cabinet minister Henrik Dam Christensen, in a letter to a concerned citizen, had confirmed this line of reasoning. *'National Pension Scheme in Danger'*, the headline wrote. This was highly embarrassing for the 'yes'-campaign, given the point that Mr. Christensen was the coordinator of the Social Democrat pro-euro campaign, and that the Social Democrat leadership had repeatedly rejected the idea of a connection between People's Pension and the euro.

Finally, according to other reasoning, the EMU must be supplemented with a system of fiscal transfers across national borders; otherwise it cannot be stable. David McKay has presumably presented the most elaborate academic version of this reasoning so far. On the basis of much empirical evidence and sophisticated reasoning, McKay concludes: 'Ultimately, it will be the willingness of some states and regions to subsidise others and/or the extent to which mass publics will tolerate centrally induced welfare state retrenchments that will determine whether the union stands or falls'.[3] In this volume, Professor Sverker Gustavsson, of Stockholm University, argues in this line. Given the point that Denmark's GDP is relatively high, it would be a net-contributor to such a system of cross-border subsidies.

This in turn would burden the financial basis for Denmark's welfare state. Prior to the Danish EMU-referendum, a journalistic short-hand of this reasoning entered the quality paper *Berlingske Tidende* in the form that within a few years the Danes could expect an EU tax corresponding to 20 per cent of GDP.[4] Obviously, this would put the Danish welfare state under enormous financial strain.

In contrast to these positions, the present author is of the opinion that the Economic and Monetary Union is compatible with a Nordic welfare state model. If it is going to have an effect at all, it will be a supporting one. In this contribution, the present author tries to explore the effects of the EMU, both the 'critical aspects' of its construction and the more general problems, upon a Nordic welfare state. And given the point that EMU hardly is a static construction, some potential future developments will also be considered.

I define a 'Nordic welfare state' as follows: a welfare state which is primarily based upon tax contributions and which redistributes considerable parts of the GDP via general transfers such as a national pension or child maintenance allowances to all citizens; it also secures a decent minimum standard of living for everyone through social security. Insurance-based systems or private savings supplement the public transfers. To a Nordic welfare state belongs a well-equipped public sector which provides free general services to all citizens in the fields of health care, education, child care and care for senior citizens. A well-developed system of active labor market policy is in place to combat unemployment and social marginalization. A high level of employment figures prominently on the list of political priorities. If the construction of the EMU implied higher unemployment, it should be regarded as weakening the Nordic model. This would also be the case if EMU produced rising inequality.

The Nordic economies have been open mixed economies with large public sectors and with strong private business sectors. In contrast to, for example, Great Britain or Italy, the nationalization of industry or commerce has never been on the agenda of the Nordic governments, except for temporary emergency situations (Swedish shipyards in the 1970s, Swedish and Finnish banks in the beginnings of the nineties). The welfare states were set in place in order to domesticate capitalism, not to abolish it.

There are differences among the Nordic countries, and the Nordic welfare states have changed over time. In Denmark, for instance, labor-market related and private pension schemes have become more important, and some public services were put out to tender or were privatized. These changes were the result of the Danish political process and were not caused by EU directives.

The present author is a sympathizer of the Nordic model. If he does not regard the EMU as a threat to this model, then this is based to a high extent on the Danish experiences of the last 20 years. A retrospective might be useful.

'Euro Politics' in Practice

After a series of restrictive measures in fiscal policy in the years 1979-82, the Danish economic policy was placed on a new basis in 1982. The government declared that it would follow a course of a 'stable crown'; devaluations would not be applied anymore. Inflation should be significantly lowered, the budget brought into balance, and the capital movements across the borders be liberalized. These measures formed a consistent package. For instance, the restrictions on capital movements were lifted in order to attract foreign capital, which in turn should bring interest rates down. This move was successful; the interest rates fell from 20 per cent to 12 per cent within a year. But it was a necessary condition for this success that investors could be rather confident that the crown would not be devalued; otherwise their investment would be devalued too. But devaluation could only be avoided if inflation fell substantially; otherwise rising costs would drive Danish exporters out of their markets, which in turn would create a strong pressure to devalue again, in order to restore competitiveness. And inflation could only be brought down with restrictive fiscal and income policies.

In our context, the decisive point is that at that time Denmark *de facto* introduced 'euro policies'. The above-mentioned 'critical points' of the EMU construction (price stability, a rather restrictive fiscal policy, stable exchange rate and free capital movements) have all been in place since the middle of the 1980s. In 1982, the euro was not on the agenda, and nobody talked about convergence criteria. But already the governments under Prime Minister Poul Schlüter (Conservative) made Denmark comply with those criteria. We also notice that the change of policy in 1982 was a result of the internal Danish political process, without any pressure from the EC whatsoever.

A similar change took place in several other European countries at about the same time, for instance in France. Still, in 1981 the newly-elected socialist government inaugurated a huge expansive program, but the result was not growing employment, but growing budget and balance of payment deficits, rising inflation and devaluation of the franc. In February 1982, President Francois Mitterand engineered a *tournant* and announced that the budget deficit should be of a magnitude of at most three per cent of the GDP. This figure became later, on French initiative, incorporated into the Maastricht Treaty, and so were the other convergence criteria.[5] After the *tournant* a whole series of restrictive measures followed. In December 1984 the socialist government decided to liberalize the French capital market, including movements across the national borders.[6] The French franc stepwise became *franc fort* with a stable exchange rate to the D-Mark. This means that French socialists and Danish conservatives followed more or less the same program.

From January 1987, after some years with minor adjustments, Denmark has kept a stable exchange rate to the D-Mark. In January 1999, this policy became extended to the euro.[7] In 1993, the Social Democrats gained control of the government, but this did not imply a change as to the 'critical points', apart from a minor fiscal expansion (see below). In the last few years the social democratic governments have practiced a fiscal policy which has been more restrictive than that of the Schlüter governments in the 1980s.

The 'euro policy' was highly controversial in the first years of the Schlüter governments. Today, there is a kind of consensus almost throughout the political spectrum. For instance, Jes Lunde, by then the chairman of the parliamentary group of the Socialist Peoples' Party (to the left of the Social Democrats), wrote in April 2000: 'During the last many years the economic development has been of a kind that the policy of a stable exchange rate has proven to be prudent and producing good results. We have no plans to alter this for the foreseeable future'.[8] And about the EMU convergence criteria he wrote: 'They impose limits on inflation, interest rates, public debt and public sector deficits. All of them very reasonable rules'.[9]

The consensus in parliament as to the guiding principles of economic policy is strongly established. Therefore, in the foreseeable future Denmark will continue her 'euro policy', regardless of the results of general elections and possible new EU referenda.

If the 'critical points' which lie at the bottom of the EMU had an undermining effect on the welfare state then, this effect should be visible in Denmark, given the point that Denmark has been following this policy for almost 20 years. Table 10.1 shows three indicators which illustrate the general development of the Danish welfare state.

Table 10.1 The Danish public sector during the years of 'euro policy', general indicators

Year	Public sector employment in 1,000	Taxes, rates and dues as % of GDP	Public expenditure as % of GDP
1980	693	44.2	55.7
1990	771	46.8	56.8
1997	800	49.4	56.9
2000	813	48.2	52.4

Source: Finansministeriet, *Finansredegørelse 98/99*, København, February 1999: 73; OECD, *Economic Survey Denmark*, Paris 1999: 143; Finansministeriet, *Finansredegørelse 2001*, København, May 2001, statistical annex.

As we see, the Danish welfare state has not become demolished. On the contrary, measured by the number of public-sector employees, it experienced a strong expansion when the conservative Poul Schlüter was Prime Minister. In the 1990s, the expansion continued, albeit at a more moderate speed. The GDP share of public expenditure rose slightly in the 1980s and has been more or less stable in the 1990s, falling slightly during the last years. But this was only a relative decline due to a continuous GDP growth. In absolute figures the expansion continued:

Table 10.2 The development of the Danish welfare state, selective indicators

Year	Social expenditure in 1997 prices, million DKK	No. of children in public child care institutions in 1,000	No. of physicians in general public-sector hospitals, converted to full-time jobs	Nurses (full-time jobs)
1987	240,709	290	9,189	20,483
1997	330,126	481	8,915	25,020

Source: Danmarks Statistik, Statistisk Tiårsoversigt, København, 1999: 56 and 59.

In the 1980s, Poul Schlüter was repeatedly criticized for being a 'Robin-Hood-turned-upside-down'; i.e. someone who takes from the poor and gives to the rich. The statistical material does not confirm this picture. From 1983 to 1996, the Gini-coefficient fell from 24 down to 22.[10]

The level of employment (see Table 10.3) did indeed fall until 1994, in particular after the so-called 'potato cure' in 1986, a restrictive taxation package targeted against excessive private consumption lending. So, the 'euro policy' has had negative employment consequences. But these were temporary. This was the price to be paid in order to correct the unsustainable policy of the previous years (see below).

After 1994, the picture changed dramatically, unemployment fell from above 11 down to about 5 per cent. In the Danish press, which tries its best to be critical, this remarkable improvement has often been depicted as being the result of statistical cosmetics; allegedly, the number of registered unemployed people fell only because more people were placed in labor-market and vacation schemes. There was indeed a (rather small) effect of this kind in the middle of the 1990s. But in 2000, the number of people registered in these vacation schemes was considerably lower than in 1995. As Table 10.3 shows, the level of actual employment has risen notably:

Table 10.3 Danish employment and unemployment in absolute figures

Year	Persons employed in 1,000	Unemployed in 1,000
1989	2,626	265
1993	2,531	349
2000	2,687	150

Source: Finansredegørelse 2001, statistical appendix.

Currently (2001), after about eight years of constant improvement of the labor-market situation, all prognoses point at a continuation of this positive development.

All in all, the Danish experiences seem to indicate that the 'euro policy' has been beneficial to the development of the welfare state and employment. This is perhaps the reason behind the above-mentioned consensus among the Danish politicians as to the continuation of this policy. But some participants in the debate seem to be of the opinion that the positive development has occurred, not because of the Danish policy, but in spite of it. I therefore scrutinize the components of the 'euro policy' in more detail.

Price Stability and Employment

The point that the Maastricht Treaty stipulated that price stability is to be the major aim of the monetary policy, has been repeatedly and massively criticized. According to these critics, employment should be the main target, or at least of equal importance.

In certain situations the goals of combating inflation and of promoting employment can indeed be mutually exclusive. For instance, in principle it is possible to stimulate investment and thus employment by means of a reduction of the interest rates. But if at the same time a high risk of inflation does not permit lower interest rates, then politicians and central bankers are facing a dilemma. Seen this way the aims of combating inflation and promoting employment are conflicting.

In the economic literature, the negative correlation between inflation and employment has usually been presented under the heading of 'Phillips-curve', after an Australian economist who explored this connection statistically. Until the 1970s, the Phillips-curve was part of economic orthodoxy. The German Chancellor Helmut Schmidt, himself an economist, expressed it in the 1970s as follows: 'Rather five per cent inflation than five per cent unemployment'.

But as the experiences of the 1970s have shown, after some time the unemployment figures began gliding upwards once higher inflation was tolerated. Higher inflation has been implying higher interest rates and higher wages, and both have had adverse effects on employment. It did not take a long time before Helmut Schmidt faced both five per cent inflation and five per cent unemployment. Politicians all over the Western world made similar experiences. One of them was the then Dutch minister of finance Willem Duisenberg, currently the president of the European Central Bank (ECB). Also the Danish experiments illustrate this mechanism in a very graphic way:

Table 10.4 Inflation and unemployment in Denmark, 1960-82

Year	Unemployment (as % of labour force)	Inflation (changes in %, GDP deflator)
1960	1.8	1.8
1970	1.3	8.3
1975	5.3	12.4
1980	7.0	8.2
1982	9.8	10.6

Source: OECD National Accounts of the OECD countries and OECD, Economic Outlook, as quoted in Hansen, E., Jensen, S.E.H., Kjærsgård, K and Rosted, J., *Dansk økonomisk politik. Teorier og erfaringer*, Aarhus, 3. Edition, 1996: 291.

As we see, at the beginning of the 1970s the Danish government and National Bank could keep unemployment down by being tolerant as to inflation. But then the Phillips-curve began gliding upwards. In 1982, Denmark had to register inflation and unemployment figures at around 10 per cent. In practically all Western countries theoretical arguments and empirical evidence point in one direction: combating inflation and promoting employment are contradictory aims only in the short term. In the longer term, a monetary policy which supports employment best is the one which aims at a stable inflation rate at low levels. The long-term interest rates will fall only if inflation is at low and calculable levels. And it is in particular the long-term interest rate, which is determined at the financial markets and which the central banks cannot steer administratively, which has the greatest impact on employment.

With rising inflation interest rates also rise, but not only 'correspondingly', so that the real interest rate (nominal rate minus inflation) remains the same as before. The rising inflation also creates more uncertainty; investors will not place their assets in an uncertain country, unless compensated for by a real-interest supplement which covers the risk. Conversely, if inflation comes under control, the interest rates (bonds) can fall dramatically, as the Danish, and not only the Danish, experiences have shown:

Table 10.5 Interest rates and inflation in Denmark, 1988-98

Year	Inflation (consumer price index)	Interest rate (bonds)	Interest rate minus inflation
1988	4.4	9.9	5.5
1991	2.4	9.3	6.9
1994	2.0	7.8	5.8
1997	2.2	6.3	4.1
1998	1.8	5.0	3.2

Source: Finansredegørelse 98/99: 306f.

The significant decrease in the Danish interest rates has been one of the most important factors behind Denmark's positive development. Usually, economic textbooks stress the importance of the impact of real interest rates on investment and employment. In 1998, it was down to 3.2 per cent, as compared to 10 per cent in 1982. Furthermore, newer research has shown that in some cases the nominal rates are of greatest relevance.[11] And the nominal rates fell from above 20 per cent in 1982 to 10 per cent in 1988 and 5 per cent in 1998.

A policy which aims at stable and low inflation rates is therefore the policy which has the most beneficial effects on the long-term interest rates, nominal and real. But we also notice that a policy which brings inflation down involves costs. As Table 10.5 shows, the lowering of the inflation during the 'potato cure' (1988-1991) had only a moderate effect on the long-term interest rate. This implied that the real interest rate actually rose – a development which was reflected in rising unemployment (Table 10.3). But these costs were temporary. After 1993, employment rose again, and perhaps more important, these employment gains have proven to be sustainable.

Some of the critics of the Maastricht construction object that they do not want higher inflation at all; they just want to see employment higher on the priority list of the ECB. But this kind of argumentation circumvents the real problem. According to the EMU construction, the ECB steers the monetary policy, i.e. mainly the short-term interests, in a way that in a medium-term perspective prices rise in an interval between 0.5 and 2 per cent. In concordance with this aim, the ECB brings the short-term interest so much down until they reach a point where a further reduction would imply rising inflation. And until now (2001), the interest rates have been at a rather low level. Under these conditions, how could a monetary policy that 'also takes employment into consideration' look like? The critics are hardly of the opinion that interest rates should be raised. This leaves only the way downward. But this means by implication an inflation risk.

In the Danish debate, Madsen and Plaschke have rejected the idea that a further interest rate reduction automatically leads to rising inflation: there are many possibilities to prevent this through a strict income and fiscal policy.[12] Certainly, they are right that higher inflation can be avoided this way. This is exactly what e.g. Wim Duisenberg, or the former Bundesbank president Hans Tietmeyer, or Poul Schlüter or the Danish social democrat minister of finance Mogens Lykketoft have said for many years. And this is exactly what has happened in Denmark. But it also means that if the governments *are not restrictive* as regards fiscal policy and wages, then there is no room for further interest rate cuts. And the provision of the Stability and Growth Pact that public sector deficits ought not to exceed 3 per cent of GDP was exactly put in place in order to keep interest rates as low as possible. A member state ought not to, by following an overly loose fiscal policy, reduce the ECB's room for maneuver in this respect.

Of course, it is possible that the ECB misjudges the inflation risks. But the experiences of the last decades have shown that the US, the Dutch, or the German central banks have hit the target interval quite accurately. The uncertainty as to the effects of the instruments of monetary policy has obviously not been so great as often depicted. Currently (June 2001) in the Euro-zone, the inflation rate is at about 3 per cent, i.e. higher than targeted. But core inflation, excluding food and energy, is only at 2.1 per cent, and likely to fall.[13] Until now, at least, the ECB has been capable of keeping inflation (and interest rates) at low levels. And this is the criterion for judging whether the euro is a success or not. The point that the media have often focussed on the exchange rate to the US-dollar and concluded that the euro is a 'fiasco' is rather absurd, given the point that the dollar rate is not an ECB-policy target. Previously, also the D-Mark had shown huge fluctuations in this respect. In the 1980s, the dollar exchange rate jumped from 1.80 D-Mark per dollar up to 3.50 and back to 1.80 within a few years. No one talked about a 'weak' D-Mark at that time. Furthermore, in the 1980s and 1990s the fluctuations in the dollar exchange rate drove the European currencies away from each other because they varied as to their exposure to the dollar. Dollar fluctuations therefore implied European monetary instability. This is not the case any more, the transition to the euro solved a substantial problem – another substantial success.

As long as there is political consensus about a target interval between 0.5 and 2 per cent inflation is reasonable (and the vast majorities in all parliaments in the EU member countries think it is), then it is necessary, already out of pragmatic reasons, to delegate the implementation of such a target to a specialized institution, the ECB. The ECB is an example of a specialized institution, like schools or air traffic control, whose guiding goals were defined in a democratic and parliamentary process, but which is entitled to handle the technical aspects of its work in relative autonomy. The present author cannot see serious democratic problems in this construction. Serious democratic problems would, however, arise if parliaments and governments defined an inflation interval as policy target and thereafter the ECB would tolerate substantially higher inflation. For a slightly divergent view, see Henrik Plaschke's contribution in this volume.

Inflation and Public Sector Deficits: On 'Robin-Hoods-Turned-Upside-Down'

The critics of the EMU construction have been remarkably silent as regards the distributional effects of inflation. Inflation, in particular *unexpected* inflation, redistributes fortunes on a large scale and among many groups. The aggregate picture is complex but the main direction is clear. From wage earners to asset owners, from low to high, from poor to rich. A policy, which accepts high inflation rates, is a clear 'Robin-Hood-turned-upside-down' policy.

For this reason Gösta Rehn, in the 1950s and 1960s an influential economist working for the Swedish trade unions, coined the motto: '*At hata inflationen! – to hate inflation!*' Repeatedly, Swedish economists who worked for the trade unions criticized the social democratic government if an overly lax fiscal policy created overheating phenomena. These produced bottleneck problems on the labor market and wage drift, which in turn undermined the solidaristic wage policy ('equal wage for equal work'). Unemployment should not be combated by pushing demand up artificially, but rather by an active labor market policy. Together with Rudolf Meidner, Rehn elaborated the theoretical basis for such a policy.[14] Sweden became the international pioneer of an active labor market policy. Today, also Denmark is a country with a set of sophisticated and innovative policy instruments in this field.

Also the provisions of the Maastricht Treaty concerning public debt and public-sector deficits have been subject to severe criticism. According to the treaty, the public debt ought not to exceed a sum corresponding to 60 per cent of GDP. But a country with a higher debt could qualify for participation in the EMU in case the debt was approaching the threshold. As concerns Denmark, these provisions are not relevant any more. A solid public-sector sector surplus made the accumulated debt shrink rather quickly. In 1997, the figure was still at 61 per cent, but in 1999 it was already down to 52.5 per cent.[15] In a few years, it will presumably be down to zero.

According to the Stability and Growth Pact, the public-sector deficits normally ought not to exceed a sum corresponding to 3 per cent of GDP. Some participants in the Danish debate argued that this provision implied a dangerous restriction on Denmark's options on the field of fiscal policy. There is presumably consensus that in a time of recession it makes sense to rise public expenditure in order to stabilize demand. This idea became translated in practical politics, for instance when the newly-formed Social Democrat government under Prime Minister Poul Nyrup Rasmussen in May 1993 constructed a tax reform in a way that taxes in some fields were lowered first, whereas compensating 'green' tax rises became implemented with a delay of up to several years. In 1993 this meant a fiscal expansion, and it contributed to bringing unemployment down. But when the program started, according to official estimates the public-sector deficit was already at a level of about 3 per cent GDP.[16] According to a detailed study published by the Danish trade union central (LO), Denmark might have risked paying a minor fine to Brussels if the Stability and Growth Pact had been in place by that time. This fine would, however, been much smaller than the loss of interest income which Denmark incurs by holding a large liquid reserve of foreign currency.[17]

In the new millennium, Denmark does not incur any risk of this kind any more. In 2000 the public sector *surplus* was of a magnitude corresponding to 2.4 of GDP; in 2001 the figure is presumably even at 2.8 per cent.[18] This means that there was a distance of almost 6 per cent to the limit. A program like the one of 1993 would not even imply a budget deficit. It would take a very severe recession to bring the budgetary balance again near the minus-three per cent limit. But in this case the Stability and Growth Pact explicitly allows for larger deficits. If GDP shrinks by more than 2 per cent, the limit is automatically cancelled, and in case of a minor recession (GDP shrinks by 0.75 per cent) the country in question can ask the other member states for being exempted from the 3 per cent threshold. But as regards Denmark (and the UK), these problems are not relevant because the distance to the minus-3 per cent limit is so large.

According to the EMU construction, careful stabilization policy, which accepts temporary deficits in order to buttress demand, is not forbidden. But inhibited is the previous irresponsible practice, shown by many European governments, of habitually running huge deficits year after year.

No member state has an interest in impeding a neighbor country to combat a recession. On the contrary, it is part of the EMU construction that the member countries use their budgets to balance business cycles or external shocks. But all countries have an interest in that a neighbor does not habitually accumulate huge deficits. Such a practice means by implication an upward pressure on the interest rate, and in an EMU rising interests hit all. This is not a problem which EMU created, or rather, prior to the EMU, all Western European countries were hostages to German interest rates. This problem was particularly severe in the beginning of the 1990s. The German budget near-collapsed because the Kohl governments, for reasons of election tactics, did not finance unification properly, and this pushed German inflation up. In 1993 the *Bundesbank* raised interest rates in order to bring inflation under control again. Germany's neighbors were forced to raise their interest rates likewise. For Denmark whose economy was stagnating at this time, this was a substantial burden. But currently, in 2001, Denmark and Germany's other neighbors are protected against this kind of surprises because the Stability and Growth Pact forbids a repetition of Kohl's policy.

It is surprising that many observers who have placed themselves on the political left seem to have rejected the idea that budgets should be balanced over the business cycle. Habitual deficits produce a rising debt burden, and the debt must be paid back with interest and compound interest payments. Still in 1998 9.2 per cent of the Danish public sector expenses, or 5.1 per cent of GDP, were interest payments. The figures corresponded rather accurately to the expenses for the public health service.[19] This means Denmark could have financed a health service of double the actual size, if it was not for the previous debt accumulation. In 1986 even 16 per cent of the public expenses were interest payments. Is it a left-wing policy to tax wage earners and then transfer the money to some capitalists as interest payments?[20]

It is therefore not easy to understand why the EMU demands as to the limits of public deficits have been criticized in sections of the Danish trade unions. This is, at least partly, based on the simple misunderstanding that the EMU provisions restrict the *size* of the public sector.[21] In reality they do not say anything about the size; they exclusively demand that it is financed in an orderly way. Denmark has been doing so for many years by now.

Why Have Socialists Liberalized Capital Movements?

Free capital movements across national borders have been a controversial subject. They are an essential element of the EMU construction, and at the same time of globalization. The problems which free capital movements create are the same, irrespective of whether a country is part of the EMU or not. In spite of the public controversies, vast parliamentary majorities in all highly developed countries are united by a consensus to maintain this freedom of movement.

Again a retrospective is useful. Until the 1960s the capital movements were strictly regulated. Governments and government-controlled national banks could raise or lower interest rates or push inflation up, without that this generated capital flight. The capital was locked inside the borders. But in the 1960s and 1970s those regulations turned increasingly problematic. Firstly, the regulations burdened real transactions. Just to give a small example: In 1961 the founder of LEGO, Godtfred Kirk Christiansen, was doing business in Chicago. His American partners demanded 25,000 dollars cash, which he did not have. To borrow the money in an American bank was forbidden, and when he phoned to his own bank in Denmark the director informed him that he needed a special permission from the national bank; this would take at least three weeks.[22]

Furthermore, it became increasingly difficult to implement the restrictions in practice. They created many bureaucratic burdens, but proved increasingly ineffective.[23] Also the great imbalances in the international trade patters created a powerful motive for liberalization. For instance the multiplying of the oil price generated huge dollar flows to the oil-exporting countries. The consequences for the Western economies were much less severe than originally anticipated because the assets were re-invested in the West. The financial markets could broker the transfers rather smoothly. In general capital markets proved to be an efficient instrument to finance deficits on the balance of payments.[24]

Restrictions have a deterrent effect on investors because they place a high value on the possibility of taking their assets out again quickly. If this possibility does not exist, they make the investment only if rewarded by a risk supplement on the expected return. When capital movements are free, investors can diversify their investment and thereby spread the risk, and companies can find many more ways to find capital sources. Restrictions protected domestic banks and investors against external competition which implied higher interests. By contrast, liberalization builds up a downward pressure on the interest rate, with positive effects on employment. To formulate things only slightly simplified: It is in the interest of the working class if there is more competition among the capitalists.

On the other hand, free capital movements mean a higher risk of speculative 'bubbles'. But speculative movements become huge and successful only when severe political mistakes have created the necessary conditions. It is for example an outright classical mistake to declare a stable exchange rate and then not to combat inflation accordingly. Under this constellation the currency becomes overvalued and the massive loss of export earnings undermines the credibility of the stable exchange rate. This was the case as to many European currencies in 1992 and 1993, and in Southeast Asia in 1997. But conversely, under the conditions of prudent policies the danger for these kind of speculative waves is rather small.

Against this background it hardly can come as a surprise that no relevant political force in the highly developed countries demands the reintroduction of restrictions. It is true, among the public at large there are sympathizers of the so-called Tobin tax. Nobel-price winner James Tobin proposed to impose a small tax of (0.25 per cent) on financial cross-border transactions, in order to slow down the at times frantic movements forwards and backwards. But this tax would burden also the real transactions. And if not implemented all over the globe, which is highly unlikely, it would imply higher interest rates for those countries which introduce it. It is therefore uncertain whether the tax would produce positive net results. And at any rate, the Tobin tax is no instrument to restrict capital movements in principle, for this purpose the tax would be too small. It is meant as an instrument, in a world of free capital movements, to reduce excessive fluctuations. It therefore does not alter the principle problems which are associated with free capital movements.

The EU member countries have liberalized capital flows to a very high extent even before the Internal Market and the EMU came on the agenda. The liberalization program could be implemented rather smoothly because the governments in question, Swedish Social Democrats, Dutch Christian Democrats, or French and Spanish Socialists, had reached the same conclusion beforehand.

To summarize these points: the EMU does not imply that market forces have become more important than social justice. On the contrary, the EMU constitutes a frame inside which the market forces can develop in a more civilized way than before. Nothing in its construction undermines a Nordic welfare state (or any other type of welfare state). But it impedes the grave policy mistakes which were committed in the 1970s, and which had extremely negative consequences from a social point of view. These indeed endangered the Danish welfare state. 'We are standing at the brink of the abyss', the Social Democrat Finance Minister Knud Heinesen said in 1982. The EMU prevents Denmark (or other member countries) embarking again on a course which brings them back to the brink.

The EMU – Inherently Unstable?

In the debate about the EMU many positions were voiced according to which the EMU either had to be altered rather profoundly, or it would disintegrate. As already mentioned, David McKay had presented a rather elaborate version of this reasoning; according to him, the EMU would not be stable in the long run unless it will be supplemented by a corresponding set of fiscal institutions which centrally at EU level collect and redistribute taxes (which, of course would imply a burden for the Danish welfare state).[25]

The idea of an inherently unstable EMU poses perplexing questions as to the quality of modern governance. Again a retrospective can be relevant. At the Hanover Summit in 1988 the heads of states asked the presidents of the central banks of the EC countries to elaborate a draft which should specify the necessary conditions under which a common currency would be stable. This draft became the basis for the EMU. Obviously, none of the central bankers were aware of the 'necessity' of a centralized fiscal policy. Nor were the actors at the Intergovernmental Conference which negotiated the Maastricht Treaty. Although many participants, e.g. the German delegation, had wished for more substantial political European integration than actually could be reached, they worked under the clear guideline to construct a 'technically viable and durable EMU'.[26] It must have been a case of remarkable collective myopia that neither central bankers nor top officials from the finance ministries could see the necessity of EU-wide transfers.

In academia and the media, various lines of argumentation have been forwarded to support the idea that EU-wide transfers are necessary. One focuses on so-called external shocks.[27] A member country could become subject to an adverse economic shock, e.g. drastically falling demand for its export products. Given the point that countries cannot devalue their currency any more, given also that monetary policy is centralized at ECB-level and fiscal policy bound by the restrictions of the Stability and Growth

Pact, and given finally the point that labor mobility across the border is low, the country in question is practically helpless in front of this shock. To cope with the shock the country has either to secede from the EMU, or the EU must provide for substantial fiscal transfers to help this country, in a similar way as the US government does to a crisis-hidden state. A similar argument addresses the uneven effects of monetary policy. For instance a rent rise might be justified for the EMU zone as a whole, but produce strongly negative effects in some member states. If the EU wants to avoid strong tensions which threaten its existence, the negatively hit countries must receive compensating transfer.

According to a group of euro-sceptic German economists,[28] within EMU the weaker regions are exposed to harder competition and will experience rising unemployment. Also this allegedly makes more transfers necessary. Finally, in a more culturally-minded line of argumentation, the common currency makes income disparities more visible. High disparities are – allegedly – not compatible with a European identity. If the EU wants to keep its cultural, and hence political, cohesion intact, it must practice more solidarity with its poorer regions.

It is indeed quite *possible* that the member states will increase the size of the EU budget; one reason could be the Common Foreign and Security Policy. Common defense expenses would, however, replace national expenses and therefore not lead to a higher tax burden. It is also possible – though not likely – that the regional policy will be more generously funded in the future. But the argumentation which state that there is a *necessity* to increase the EU budget, which by implication means a pressure on the national welfare states, are unfounded.

To begin with, the argumentation of the 'asymmetric shocks', which is based on models of Optimal Currency Areas, has been highly abstract so far. None of its proponents have ever substantiated a shock that asymmetrically would hit, say Denmark, but not its neighbors. Of course various shocks can be imagined, but in the context of this argumentation they should be of a character *that would motivate a devaluation.* Certainly, Danish bacon exports to the UK might be hit by the outbreak of a Mad Pig Virus. But no Danish government would ever contemplate a devaluation in such a case. It would – overnight – destroy the fruits of 20 years of stabilization policy. Investors would loose confidence in the stability of the crown, with the consequence of massive interest rate hikes which strangle a substantial part of her economy. Many of the other EU member states have also gone through long phases of stabilization policy; for many of them, in particular in the South, the road has been much tougher than in Denmark. None of these governments, regardless of their ideological stance, will put the achievements at risk by a devaluation, being EMU members or not.

Besides, as already discussed above, the Stability and Growth Pact does not impede a Keynesian policy of deficit spending in times of an economic setback. Given the remarkable improvements which all EU members could register as to their budget situation, there is, albeit to a different degree, space for substantial fiscal expansion in all member countries. And in a case of a severe setback, this limit will be automatically lifted. So 'asymmetric shocks' (presumably imaginary anyhow) do not create a necessity for an EU fiscal policy.

Nor do the asymmetric effects of monetary policy. Measures taken by the ECB have indeed a different impact on the countries in question, and some can be negative. But this provides these countries neither with juridical nor with political arguments for demanding compensation. The idea that they might secede from EMU if they do not receive payments, misses the point completely. For most countries, and in particular for the peripheral and Mediterranean countries (which are the most likely candidates for being adversely affected) the transition to the EMU has meant a dramatic improvement of their monetary conditions, as shown by strongly falling long-term interest rates:

Table 10.6 Nominal and real long-term interest rates for Mediterranean countries and Ireland

	1994	1999
Nominal long-term interest		
Italy	10.5	4.7
Ireland	8.0	4.8
Portugal	10.4	4.8
Spain	10.0	4.7
Real long-term interest		
Italy	7.0	3.2
Ireland	6.3	0.8
Portugal	4.1	2.2
Spain	6.0	1.6

Source: OECD, *Economic Outlook*, no. 67, Paris, June 2000: 279. Real interest rate: Nominal interest rate minus GDP deflator (ibid.: 258).

Against this background, the possible adverse effects of a rise of the short-term interests of the ECB are almost trivial. And certainly no government would ever contemplate putting the achievements and advantages of the EMU for their countries at risk by forwarding threats of secession.

As to the development of regional disparities, so far European integration has not led to a rising polarization. Rather on the contrary, Robert Barro and Xavier Sala-i-Martin have shown in a very detailed study on seven European countries that for the period 1950 to 1985 as whole, regional disparities have become markedly reduced.[29] This is not the case for every year, and a few regions fell actually back *relative* to the national average, but the main tendency has been convergence. And most important: No one became poorer in absolute terms. There is simply no empirical basis for the claim that the regional development under EMU conditions *necessitates* higher payments to economically weaker regions.

And finally, the arguments that EU-wide transfers are necessary because the income disparities will become more manifest, which in turn should undermine a European identity, is based on a misunderstanding of the character of European integration. It has progressed because and when all actors saw that further integration gave them advantages. Rising transfers to some regions just because they are poor will in itself not be in the interest of the richer regions, and therefore it will hardly happen, except in a package deal. Rising cross-border transfers would even substantially weaken the EU, given the point that opinion polls in all countries consistently have shown that the vast majority of the citizens have more a national than a European identity. Rising transfers presumably would provoke populist revolts, similar to the *Lega Nord* in Italy. Being poor has in itself not been a sufficient argument for asking the other member states for money.

To sum this point up, it is perfectly possible that the EU budget will increase in size, but the arguments that the EU *has to* establish a system of substantial EU-wide transfers do not survive closer scrutiny.

On Future Developments

Many of participants in the debate who have seen the EMU as a danger for the Danish Welfare State have pointed to future developments. Discussions about the future are unavoidably speculative to a high extent, so there can be no certainty. But there are, as far as the present author can see, no strong arguments to support the view that the future development of the EMU will endanger the Danish welfare state.

The argument that rising cross-border mobility will build up a pressure to change the Danish system in the direction of a greater weight of individualized contributions and rights, as opposed to the general traits of the Nordic Model, is plausible at first sight. And it is also true that within the EU the removal of barriers to mobility have been prominently on the agenda. The European Court of Justice has been active in this field on many occasions (see the Abrahamson and Borchorst contribution in this volume). But all this does not alter the basic fact that cross-border mobility is very low. And it is not likely to increase substantially. The main source of long-distance mobility in Europe has been the abject poverty and hopeless job conditions in previously economically backward rural regions such as Sicily, Andalucia, or Anatolya. Within the EU the former emigration countries, mainly the Mediterranean countries and Ireland, have become immigration countries; and since 1973 Turkish emigrants are not allowed into the EU member countries any more. The Eastern enlargement might produce some migration movements, but all studies indicate that this will be a limited phenomenon. So all in all, substantial increases in cross-border migration are not likely, and the actual level is by far too small to propel significant changes in the structure of the welfare states. Besides, as we have discussed above, the *low* level of mobility was one of the arguments which EMU-skeptic economists have forwarded as an indication that the EU was not an 'optimal currency area'.

This does not imply that countries such as Denmark will not move towards more individual contributions and rights. There has already been a tendency that private and labor-market pension schemes have become more important in relative terms, at the expense of the Peoples' Pension. Also private or labor-market health insurances have gained in importance, the (until now few) private hospitals are booming. But all this has nothing to do with the EMU, it is the result of internal pressures, e.g. lower tolerance towards waiting lists in the public health service.

The EMU construction is *not optimal,* but the divergences from the theoretical optimum are not of such a character that they would render the project inherently unstable. One obvious problem is the insufficient coordination of the fiscal policies of the member countries. The aggregated fiscal effect of the state budgets is in part a casual outcome, whereas in the theoretical optimum monetary and fiscal policy would be closely tuned in relation to each other at every point in time.

But this lack of coordination is not a new problem. In many EU member countries the fiscal policy has been highly 'sub-optimal' for many years when high deficits were the product, not of careful stabilization policy, but of highly insufficient political processes. By comparison, the aggregate fiscal policy of the Euro-zone is much closer to the optimum than in, say 1980. Furthermore, countries such as Germany have been structurally incapable of following an 'optimal' fiscal policy: the *Länder* and the local authorities together have been moving much larger sums than the federal budget, and their policy has often been 'pro-cyclical' (much spending in good times, restricted spending in bad times), i.e. very 'unoptimal'. But Germany did not disintegrate for this reason.

It would, of course, be progress if the member countries could coordinate their policies better. Would this undermine the Danish welfare state? On the contrary, this would have no implication for the size of the welfare state, but it would smooth the business cycle and thereby reduce unemployment.

A better coordination of tax policy would also be advisable. Currently, the market forces put some forms of taxation under pressure. These problems are part of globalization and exist independently of the EMU. Some countries, Denmark among them, have worked for common minimum standards in taxation. Would they endanger the welfare state? On the contrary. Harmonization does not mean downward harmonization, but common minimum standards. All in all, if one discusses future developments not in general terms, but more in concrete measures which are already on the agenda, or which are likely to come on the agenda, then there is nothing which points at the weakening of the Danish welfare state. If the EMU will have an effect, then it is a positive one.

In parts of the Danish political left there seems to exist a deeply-rooted fear that more economic integration and more market forces necessarily undermines a welfare state. Behind this lies a perception that capital flows thereto were every thing is cheapest. But this idea is erroneous. Capital flows to places where the return is highest, and this is something completely different. For instance, low wages and low taxes are, from a capitalist point of view, of no use if the work force is not properly educated. And a welfare state produces goods, which are indispensable for a capitalist economy. In 1998 the *Economist* conducted an opinion poll among investors on where there was the best business climate.[30] The Netherlands were on place number one, i.e. a highly developed welfare state where the public expenses corresponded to 50 per cent of GDP. And in practically all Western countries, rhetoric not withstanding, the GDP share of public expenditure is higher than 20 years ago. Economic integration and welfare states are not enemies.

And finally, in the Danish debate prior to the referendum in September 2000 the controversies among the experts seem to have followed a rather clear line of demarcation. Many, perhaps the majority of the academic economists expressed a negative attitude to the EMU. On the other hand, practically all experts who work with practical matters, whether it be at the national bank, bigger companies and banks, the trade unions or the Confederation of Danish industry, have been in favor of the EMU. These experts compared the EMU with the actually existing situation and concluded that Denmark's participation would imply an improvement. By contrast, many academic experts compared the EMU with theoretical optimum models (e.g. 'Optimal Currency Area'). And because the EMU did not fulfil the conditions for optimality they concluded that the project was of no use.

Notes

1 Dagbladet *Arbejderen*, May 1st 2000: 1.
2 See for instance Madsen and Plaschke (1998: 60).
3 McKay, David, *Federalism and European Union. A Political Economy Perspective*, Oxford University Press, 1999: 173.
4 *Berlingske Tidende*, 13th July 2000: 7.
5 'The specification of the convergence criteria was decisive for the French ... Clear and tough criteria were a demonstration of commitment to be alongside the 'stability-oriented' states. From this perspective, the idea of weak, imprecise criteria was anathema to the French ... The final outcome, with its specific reference values and scope for discretionary judgement, was in this respect a resounding success for the French.' Dyson, Kenneth and Featherstone, Kevin, *The Road to Maastricht. Negotiating Economic and Monetary Union*, Oxford, 1999: 140f.
6 Dyson and Featherstone, p. 150.
7 Denmark participated in the EMS cooperation which implied that exchange rates were to fluctuate by at most 2.25 per cent. The exchange rates could, however, after a mutual agreement among the governments involved, be adjusted. In relation to the ECU, the accounting unit of the EMS, the crown became revalued four times (March 1983, July 1985, April 1986, and September 1992). But in 1983 and 1986 the D-Mark became revalued even more, and it became revalued again in 1987; this implied a slight devaluation of the crown in relation to the D-Mark. After January 1987, the exchange rate of the crown was stable towards the German currency. See table 7.2, Tsoukalis, Loukas, *The New European Economy Revisited*, Oxford University Press, 1997: 147.
8 'I de sidste mange år har den økonomiske udvikling været sådan, at fastkurspolitiken har været både klog og gavnlig. Det har vi ingen planer om at ændre på i overskuelig fremtid.' *Nordjyske Stiftstidende*, 20th April 2000: 7.
9 'Der sættes grænser for inflation, rente, den offentlige gæld og underskuddet på de offentlige finanser. Alt sammen meget snusfornuftige regler.' Ibid.
10 Finansredegørelse 98/99: 84.
11 Danmarks Nationalbank, *Pengepolitik i Danmark*, Copenhagen, 1999: 95.
12 Madsen and Plaschke, 1998: 53.
13 *The Economist*, 23rd June 2001: 11.
14 See e.g. Rudolf Meidner, *I arbetets tjänst*, Stockholm, 1984, in particular chapter II, 5, 'Aktiv arbetsmarknadspolitik och målkonflikten mellan prisstabilitet och fyll sysselsätning', pp. 287-318.
15 Danmarks Statistik, Statistical ten-year review 2000, Copenhagen, 2000: 147.
16 Landsorganisation i Danmark, *Beskæftigelse og fælles mønt*, København, 1999: 43.
17 Ibid., p. 44.
18 Finansministeriet, *Finansredegørelse 2001*, Copenhagen, May 2001, statistical appendix.
19 *Samfundsstatistik 1999:* 76 and 79.

20 The deeply unsocial character of this policy becomes, of course, mitigated by the fact that part of the interest flows are paid to pension funds and similar savings collectors, which implies that wage earners get part of these payments back again.
21 In a Danish left-wing paper (*Dagbladet Arbejderen* 1.5.00: 1) Eva Persson, the trade union representative of the wage earners employed by the city of Copenhagen, was quoted this way.
22 Cortzen, Jan, *LEGO-Manden – historien om Godtfred Kirk Christiansen*, Copenhagen, 1996: 188.
23 As to the French experiences, see Dyson and Featherstone, 1999: 150.
24 James, Harold, *Rambouillet, 15. November 1975. Die Globalisierung der Wirtschaft*, München, 1997: 165.
25 The present author has dealt with this problem more extensively: Wolfgang Zank, 'The Mythology of EU-wide Transfers – A Critique of David McKay and other 'fiscal federalists'', European Research Unit, *European Studies – Series of Occasional Papers* 29, Aalborg University, 2000.
26 Dyson and Featherstone, 1999: 424.
27 McKay, 1999: 142-6.
28 As quoted by McKay, 1999: 149.
29 Barro, Robert and Sala-i-Martin, Xavier 'Convergence across States and Regions', *Brookings Papers on Economic Activity*, 1/1991: 102-182.
30 *The Economist*, 7-13 March 1998.

References

Barro, Robert and Sala-i-Martin, Xavier (1991): 'Convergence across States and Regions', *Brookings Papers on Economic Activity*, 1/1991, pp. 102-182.
Cortzen, Jan (1996): *LEGO-Manden – historien om Godtfred Kirk Christiansen*, Copenhagen: Børsens Forlag.
Danmarks Nationalbank (1999): *Pengepolitik i Danmark*, Copenhagen.
Danmarks Statistik (1999): *Statistisk Tiårsoversigt* 1999, Copenhagen.
Danmarks Statistik (2000): *Statistical ten-year review* 2000, Copenhagen, 2000.
Dyson, Kenneth and K. Featherstone (1999): *The Road to Maastricht. Negotiating Economic and Monetary Union*, Oxford: Oxford University Press.
Finansministeriet (1999): *Finansredegørelse 98/99*, Copenhagen, February 1999.
Finansministeriet (2001): *Finansredegørelse 2001*, Copenhagen, May 2001.
Hansen, E., Jensen, S.E.H., Kjærsgård, K and J. Rosted (1996): *Dansk økonomisk politik. Teorier og erfaringer*, Aarhus: Handelshøjskolens Forlag, 3. Edition.
James, Harold (1997): *Rambouillet, 15. November 1975. Die Globalisierung der Wirtschaft*, Munich: dtv.
Landsorganisation i Danmark (1999): *Beskæftigelse og fælles mønt*, Copenhagen: LO.
Madsen, Poul Thøis and H. Plasche (1998): *Den forbudte debat om ØMU'en*, Rådet for Europæisk Politik no. 2, Aarhus: Systime.
McKay, David (1999): *Federalism and European Union. A Political Economy Perspective*, Oxford: Oxford University Press.
Meidner, Rudolf (1984): *I arbetets tjänst*, Stockholm: Tidens Förlag.
OECD (1999): *Economic Survey Denmark*, Paris.
OECD (2000): *Economic Outlook*, no. 67, Paris, June.
Tsoukalis, Loukas (1997): *The New European Economy Revisited*, Oxford: Oxford University Press.

Zank, Wolfgang (2000): 'The Mythology of EU-wide Transfers – A Critique of David McKay and other 'fiscal federalists'', European Research Unit, *European Studies – Series of Occasional Papers 29*, Aalborg: Aalborg University.

Part V

The EMU – A Political Construction

11 Political Implications of the Economic and Monetary Union

SØREN DOSENRODE

In the previous ten chapters it has been stressed over and over again, that the EMU is a highly political construction, although one often gets the opposite impression when looking through the northern European press-coverage of the EMU which tends to treat the ECB as a purely economic/technocratic institution.

In this chapter, I attempt to pull together the findings of the previous analyses along the lines of the structure of the book; i.e. the role of the EMU in the EU-integration-process, the EMU and the democratic aspects of the EU, and then the question of the influence of the EMU on primarily the Nordic welfare state model. At the end of this chapter follows an analysis of the state of the European Union.

The EMU and the European Integration Process

An important question is what role the EMU has in connection to the overall European integration process. Does it strengthen it, weaken it or is it basically neutral?

The EMU and the Integration Process: a Motor of Integration?

There is agreement concerning the importance of the EMU for the whole EU-project (e.g. Tsoukalis (chapter 4), Gustavsson (chapter 5) and Kelstrup (chapter 6)). Tsoukalis states that the EMU is one, if not the most important event in the history of European integration and that its economic and political consequences will be far-reaching if (!) it succeeds. The reason for the addition of this important 'if' is Tsoukalis' observation, that the architects of the EMU have created an unsustainable construction:

a centralized monetary policy, based on a decentralized fiscal system and an even more decentralized political system. Hoffmeyer strikes the same cord when remarking that the EMU-construction is sustainable as long as the political will is there. This analysis runs parallel to Gustavsson's in chapter 5, who also expresses his doubts:

> The asymmetry of the European Union's present system raises serious questions over its long-term sustainability.

What are the possible consequences of this situation? Inspired by McKay, Gustavsson develops his analysis, and sets up four scenarios: 1) Complete success (the asymmetrical set-up works); 2) Fiscal federalism (the Stability and Growth Pact fails, and the member states are forced into a fiscal union); 3) Authoritarianism (common currency unpaired with a fiscal union, no democracy); and 4) Complete failure (member states abandon both stability pact and democracy). The latter two possibilities are, hopefully, only theoretically possible, thus we will concentrate on the first and second scenarios.[1]

In case of 'complete success' there need not be any constitutional changes in the EU; the Stability and Growth Pact succeeds in making the common currency work without a fiscal union, as was the original design of the politicians designing the EMU. But as stated above, this possibility seems rather unlikely.

In causa fiscal federalism Gustavsson foresees that the decision-makers in the member states cannot withstand the strain on the Stability and Growth Pact, and that they are, at the same time, obliged to democracy. Thus the 'only' solution is to create a full-fledged, democratic state. For some the optimal solutions, for others *faute de mieux*. Thus the unsustainable construction would further the integration.

Schmitter expresses his doubts about any kind of automatic neo-functionalist spill-over in chapter 7. The reasons for this doubt is that the citizens have become aware of the political implications of further integration. Instead the EMU:

> [is] more likely to generate diffuse reactions within a large clusters of public opinion that focus on responses by circumscribed groups of beneficiaries and victims.

In their analysis of the welfare states, Abrahamson and Borchorst conclude, that the EMU and the Single European Act create a pressure for further harmonization and integration.

Thus my tentative conclusion of the above discussion is, that the EMU bears in it the (strong) seeds for further integration, but that it will not happen automatically. The asymmetrical construction of the EMU is fairly unstable, e.g. the Stability and Growth Pact is not equipped to solve larger tensions caused by different developments in the various regions. This may press for further (eventually fiscal) integration. On the other hand, the EMU is strongly segmented *and* further integration can hardly be sold to the electorate as 'technical'. It would be the highest of high politics, and the public support would be uncertain. Thus, the EMU creates a pressure for further integration, but there is no automatic spill-over. The EMU may thus be seen as an important stone in the building of the European state, the one preparing for the next important integrational steps, of which one is either a tax harmonization or a tax union. A tax union would be the preferable solution, according to the 'logic of integration' but the way to it may very well pass over a phase of tax harmonization.

This conclusion once more reminds us that integration is created by human beings and can be stopped by them. Integration has to be nursed like a plant to survive, there are no automatics involved. Nearly as important is it to remember, that the European integration during its more that fifty years of history never stopped; sometimes it went fast ahead, at other times it barely moved, but it never stopped. There has always been a political will in a majority of the EC/EU member states to let the process proceed.

An important characteristic of the European integration process is, that it has deepened (more policy areas are placed under in the supranational 'pillar I') as well as widened (new policy areas constitute a part of the cooperation in the EU, and nearly all policy areas in a state are influenced by EU-rules),[2] but at the same time the process has been fairly open-ended; 'an ever closer union'. This lack of a common or codified concrete vision of what the EU should end up being has been a useful – although dangerous – instrument for promoting the integration. By not sticking to one single solution – e.g. a European federation as the American one – it has been possible to go on deepening and widening the integration, as all involved parties could choose interpretations of the development in accordance with a vision suitable for their particular electorate.

The dangerous point of this tactic arrives when the integration process passes the point the politician told the electorate it would never reach, as it has happened in Denmark several times.[3] It creates mistrust between larger parts of the population and their political leaders.[4]

The EMU and the Question of Democracy and Legitimacy

In the EMU, the monetary policy-making power has been transferred from the 12 EMU-member states to the E(S)CB. A power transfer has taken place and has contributed to establishing a strong monetary power at a global level. Buiter (1999: 198) expresses this forcefully:

> Monetary union involves a transfer of national sovereignty to the central or federal level. Unless this transfer of power is perceived as legitimate by Euroland residents, the authority of the institutions of the ECB and the ESCB will be challenged by those who perceive themselves adversely affected by it.

Thus it is relevant to approach the consequences of this power transfer from a democratic side.[5]

The question of the EMU and democracy was approached in three different, but supplementary ways in this book. Kelstrup (chapter 6) took a broad approach, addressing the general question of democracy in the EU and on that background discussed the democratic aspects of the Euro-cooperation including the question of how the EMU may influence democracy in the EU. Schmitter (chapter 7) also took a broad approach, asking whether the EMU will make it easier or more difficult to make the EU *an sich* more democratic, before he starts out sketching a way of democratizing the EU. And Plaschke (chapter 8) sets out to analyze the principles for steering the economic policy in the EMU.

Developing the model of Beetham and Lord, Kelstrup sets up a model with five dimensions of democratic legitimacy: 1) the legality of the decision, 2) criteria for participation, 3) the structure for representation, responsibility and control, 4) decision and outcome, and 5) support to the system. After a general discussion of the democratic situation of the EU, Kelstrup turns to the EMU which he considers a part of the EU-system.

After a discussion of the democratic legitimacy, structured along the lines of the mentioned model, Kelstrup concludes that it is too early to give any final result concerning the democratic legitimacy of the EMU. But two elements will be decisive for the EMU to win legitimacy: First, will the euro become an accepted, stable and fairly strong currency? And second, it will be important that the EU-economy will be able to prevent a too asymmetrical growth among the EMU-member states, as that might cause withdrawal of support in states and regions.

Addressing the democratic consequences of the EMU on the national democracies, Kelstrup states, that, on the one hand, the EMU is most likely to stabilize economic matters, but also on the other hand, that the EMU most likely will weaken the national democracies, as the participants lose a policy-instrument – the ability to follow a monetary policy of their own. But this 'loss' is perhaps only theoretical, as the alternatives were either to participate in the turmoil of the market or tying one's currency to a strong one – in the old days, the *D-Mark*.

Kelstrup *inter alia* concludes:

> It has been pointed out that important uncertainties exist as to whether the EMU will contribute to increasing stability in Europe or not. The expectations are that large political problems will arise when the EMU is developed further, and that these will result in increased politicization of EU- and EMU-questions, It is very important whether EU's overall political system is responsive to these problems. In this sense democracy in all of the EU is challenged.

Schmitter's starting point is that time is neither ripe for a full democratization of the EU, nor for a full scale constitutionalization yet. But it is timely to begin working on a democratization of the union: 1) because rules and practices at the level of national democracies are no longer blindly accepted by the citizens, and 2) because the European citizens are becoming aware of how much the EU legislation is affecting them, but also that these decisions are taken far away from them. Thus we are in a situation where the legitimacy of the member state and of the EU is in danger of suffering with the consequences which Kelstrup reminds us of.[6] At least the last development, the growing awareness of the citizens, is considered a positive development by Schmitter, namely as a starting point for a process leading to a democratic EU. But he warns us that the process will give trouble:

> Euro-democratization, especially under such unprecedented circumstances and for such a large-scale polity, is bound to activate unexpected linkages, to involve less predicable publics and to generate less limited expectations.

Democratization has to be looked upon as a process, not as a concrete event, and it has to happen piecemeal:

> Only by deliberately politicizing the issues involved at the level of Europe as a whole and by gradually building up expectations concerning a more definitive set of rules with regard to citizenship, representation and decision-making can one imagine a successful constitutionalization of the EU.

Is the EMU such an issue, which can be used as a lever for the democratization process? Schmitter is pessimistic, but:

> Fortunately, however, monetary unification is not the only new policy area on the horizon of the European Union. It is only when one combines the uneven effects its decisions are bound to have upon member states with different endowments and social groups with different capacities to respond to the opportunities and threats of globalization/Europeanization with other issues

such as enlargement to include the countries of Central and Eastern Europe, enhanced cooperation in internal security affairs and the formation of a common external security policy that the prospect for Euro-democratization begins to look more promising – and imperative.

Plaschke's opening statement says:

> [economic] policies have played an important role in the formation of an economic foundation of societal democracy. Therefore the formation of economic policy is a matter of politics rather than a matter of techniques. In the domain of politics *choice* exists and economic policies reflect among other things political priorities and power interests. As economic policies constitute a crucial element of economic steering they tend to be contested and to be an arena for political and ideological interests.

But the construction of the EMU has made it hard to make compromises between economic and the political power, as monetary policy has been technified, and globalization is much less regulated than the national economies.

A central point for Plaschke, and indeed all of us is:

> Political choices to be made regarding the role and position of the EMU will exercise an important influence on the future of European societies in crucial fields. Who is to make these choices, in which fora, according to which criteria and with what sort of interest representation are these choices to be made?

The preliminary answer is that the national governments have been rather passive towards the ECB, which has strengthened the bank: 1) the TEU specifies the main target of the ECB to secure price stability (the governments have not tried to specify this further); 2) the TEU is rather vague on the secondary aims of the ECB, the ECB has defined these aims itself; and 3) the governments have *grosso modo* refrained from discussing the policy of the ECB, whereas the ECB has felt no inhibitions advising the ECOFIN. All together, the ECB has been able to strengthen its powers, especially as the Euro-12-group has not been able to agree on a common economic policy strategy (cf. Dosenrode, chapter 3).

Plaschke then, as Kelstrup and Schmitter,[7] reminds us that there may be advantages or at least traditions for institutions, which are independent from other parts of the political system; i.e. the courts, the military. Based on an analysis of the mentioned institutions Plaschke discusses five questions: First, he asks whether there is some kind of 'checks and balances' in the EU system towards the ECB, and he replies that it is weak. Secondly he asks which form of political or democratic legitimacy the

ECB has, and reaches the conclusion that the political legitimacy is clearly rooted in the treaties, whereas the democratic legitimacy is less clear. The third question is, whether the independent institution has to make technical or political decisions, and Plaschke replies – not surprisingly – that it is a mix, and that some of the political decisions are highly political. The fourth question was: Is the independent institution neutral towards social and political interests? And Plaschke states that national banks traditionally have been closely related to the rest of the financial sector. The last question was whether there is a clear division of labor between the independent institution and the rest of the political system. As mentioned by other contributors too, Plaschke mentions the interplay between a centralized monetary policy and a decentralized fiscal policy which creates grey zones of unclear competencies. His conclusion is important:

> An asymmetry follows: on the one hand the ECB with a very clear-cut understanding of economic policy issues - based on its financially orientated political interests - and on the other hand a series of governments *choosing* a policy of passivity regarding important issues in economic policies formation. [...] In other words: to a considerable extent governments seem tacitly to accept that the ECB dominates the grey zone.

From these five points of discussion Plaschke arrives at the result that the location of the ECB within the politico-economic system of the Union adds to the already existing democratic deficit. But the responsibility for this lies with the political systems, and especially the governments of the member states.

Plaschke concludes that:

> [the] establishment of the EMU in its current shape institutionalizes a constraint on the democratic steering of economic policies. The EMU, however, at least potentially also constitutes an instrument for reinforcing the political regulation and steering of the global economy.

And he adds, that there are no reasons for claiming that the EMU does not aggravate the democratic problems of the EU further.

The three contributions show that there is no clear-cut answers concerning the democratic legitimacy of the EMU. On the one hand, there seems to be an agreement, that the EMU in its present form does impair the democracy both on the national and the supranational level, at least theoretically. At the national level, the transfer of the monetary policy to the supranational ESCB has implied a loss of sovereignty, and at the supranational level, the independence of the ECB is so strong, that it is impossible to control it (the parallel to the member states has been mentioned several times). Only by changing the treaty by an intergovernmental conference is that possible. On the other hand, both Kelstrup and Plaschke mention the potential of the EMU as an instrument for countering the negative effects of globalization, thus adding an element of legitimation by delivering a stable economic environment, prosperity etc. thus giving the *constructum* some kind of legitimacy.

Before ending the discussion of the legitimacy of the ESCB, one has to remember that the part of legitimacy stemming from control, information and participation could be developed further, if only the Member States governments would use the tools laid down in the TEU and the Statute of the ECB. Thus a part of the 'sub-optimal' democratic legitimacy of the ECB is due to the political will or rather lack of political will of the EMU-Member States governments, not to the construction itself.

The Nordic Welfare State and the EMU

Three authors, in two contributions (Abrahamson & Borchorst in chapter 9 and Zank in chapter 10) discuss one of the most contested topics in the Danish referendum campaign: the influence of the EMU on the Nordic (primarily Danish) welfare state. Still, the discussion is not only of 'Nordic interest', as both contributions, but especially the first (Abrahamson & Borchorst) have a comparative approach to the topic, looking at European welfare state models. The two contributions contrast on many points, e.g. as their starting point Abrahamson and Borchorst take a comparative politics approach whereas Zank's point of departure is primarily an economic one.

All three authors share an overall agreement on the definition of the Nordic welfare state model as one which, to use Zank's words:

> is primarily based upon tax contributions and which redistributes considerable parts of the GDP via general transfers such as a People's Pension or child maintenance allowances to all citizens; it also secures a decent minimum standard of living for everyone through social security. Insurance-based systems or private savings supplement the public transfers.

Abrahamson and Borchorst start out with a comparative analysis of the various welfare state models, which prevails in Europe i.e. the insurance model, the residual model and the universal model (the latter is the Nordic version). Following this analysis, the authors compare the Danish welfare state with that of the other EU states on the basis of social statistics. The Danish welfare state model seems to come close to the ideal universal-type welfare state. It is concluded that it is in the area of financing that Denmark most clearly stands out from the other EU states (67 per cent of the spending is funded via taxation).

Following the analysis of welfare states, Abrahamson and Borchorst scrutinize the social policy initiatives of the EEC/EU and relate the development to Denmark. They conclude that the importance of social policy to the integration process has grown, and with Maastricht the Union got a genuine supranational social structure. The authors recognizes that it is methodologically difficult to isolate the effects of the Internal Market from those of the EMU should Denmark join the EMU. By referring to the Commissions and the European Councils statements they are able to conclude, that there is a need for expanded social policy cooperation (created by the EMU and the Internal Market), and that this has been recognized by the member states (one talks rhetorically about a European welfare state). A further harmonization, which can be expected, will put a pressure on the universal welfare state model as we know it.

Zank analyzes the economic foundation of the welfare state, and the conditions under which it is more likely to succeed and develop. His starting point is an analysis of the Danish economic experience over the last 20 years, on the background of which he argues that; 1) Denmark has conducted a policy very much like the one laid down in the Maastricht treaty and the Stability and Growth Pact the 1980s. All criteria have been met, and Denmark still does so. And 2) keeping this policy has been a good way of securing the Danish welfare state, with a low rate of unemployment and a low inflation rate.[8] After a discussion of what Zank has termed 'the critical points' which the opponents of the Danish EMU-membership launched during the campaign,[9] his main conclusion is that:

> The EMU does not imply that market forces have become more important than social justice. On the contrary, the EMU constitutes a frame inside which the market forces can develop in a more civilized way than before. Nothing in its constitution undermines a Nordic welfare state (or any other type of welfare state).

Thus we stand with two contributions with fairly different conclusions: Abrahamson and Borchorst conclude that the Nordic welfare state model is under pressure following the pressure for harmonization due to the EMU and SEA whereas Zank's conclusion is the opposite, that nothing undermines the Nordic welfare state model. We will leave it at this point, letting the reader draw his or her own conclusions.

The Present State of the European Union

In the first part of this chapter, the findings of the book were summarized. What is missing now is an analysis of the EU to indicate what it is the EMU is a part of and a contribution to. The political importance of the EMU becomes clear, when looking at the EU from a state-building perspective. Thus the starting point of the following part is that of state theory, attempting to compare the EU to a 'normal state', to create an impression of the present statehood of the EU.

According to Schwartzmantel (1994: 208): *'The modern state claims a monopoly of power over a unified national territory, and seeks to gain legitimation for this power'*. It is a basic definition of what a state does, founded upon the classical Westphalian Model, but modernized in-so-far as 'legitimation' is included. It can be used as a starting point but cannot stand alone. Dunleavy and O'Leary have tried to distill five characteristics of a modern state which can easily be operationalized:

1) The state is a recognisably separate institution or set of institutions, so differentiated from the rest of its society as to create identifiable public and private spheres.

2) The state is sovereign, or the supreme power, within its territory, and by definition the ultimate authority for all law, i.e. binding rules supported by coercive sanctions. Public law is made by state officials and backed by a formal monopoly of force.

3) The state's sovereignty extends to all the individuals within a given territory, and applies equally, even to those in formal positions of government or rule-making. Thus sovereignty is distinct from the personnel who at any given time occupy a particular role within the state.

4) The modern state's personnel are mostly recruited and trained for management in a bureaucratic manner.

5) The state has the capacity to extract monetary revenues (taxation) to finance its activities from its subject population. (1987: 2).

What Dunleavy and O'Leary and Schwartzmantel – and most other state scholars lack – is to include the international system as a variable in the state-foundation and development process. The state and its organization is also, but not only, an answer to its surrounding environment, and the challenges it poses. Thus a sixth point must be added to the model:

6) It is the state – represented by its government – that conducts foreign

Political Implications of the Economic and Monetary Union 257

policy and is the central actor in international relations.

The forms which states can vary greatly, and are products of the state's history and culture. Examples are the centralized unitary states like Denmark and France, decentralized unitary states like Spain, centralized federations like Austria and decentralized federations like Germany and so forth. But the central point is that states and their forms are not final, they develop over time. As scholars we must keep this in mind, and not close our eyes to forms of states not looking exactly like what we are used to.

Turning to the EU, the discussion of 'what it is' has often been concluded by stating, that the EU is more than an international organization but less than a state.[10] After the development beginning with the European Single Act in 1987, followed by Maastricht (1992), Amsterdam (1996), Pötsach (1998), Helsinki (1999) and Nice (2000), the EU has changed not only quantitatively but also qualitatively.

Applying Dunleavy and O'Leary's model[11] to the EU gives us the following tentative result:

A state has to be a recognizable, separate institution, so differentiated from the rest of its society as to create identifiable public and private spheres. To cut a long argument short, it should be enough to look at the public attributes which the EU possesses: the large number of institutions - the European Parliament, Council of Ministers, Commission, Court of Justice etc, the Union has abolished its internal borders with Schengen, it has a citizenship, its own flag, a national anthem, its own (embryonic) armed forces, and its own money. The Union clearly fulfils this first criterion.

The second criterion states that the state has to be sovereign, or the supreme power, within its territory, and is by definition the ultimate authority for all law, i.e. binding rules supported by coercive sanctions. Public law is made by parliaments and backed by a formal monopoly of force. It is equally essential that states do not legislate or otherwise interfere in other states' 'internal affairs'. The EU passes legislation binding on the population of its 15 member states. If an inhabitant does not follow the legislation (s)he risks to be send to court; equally if not more important in this case: if a citizen feels his rights, as granted by EU-legislation, are violated by his state, he or she can sue this state before the EU Court of Justice; something running against the tradition of public international law, where it is the states, not the citizens, which are the subjects.[12] It has been estimated that between 70 per cent and 80 per cent of Danish legislation is initiated in Brussels,[13] and for EMU member states this figure could easily be higher. Thus it is not exaggerated to accept, that the EU today has the right to pass legislation.[14] The rest is left to the member states, quite like in a federalist state model.

The third and fourth criterions for a modern state were: that the state's sovereignty extends to all the individuals within a given territory, and applies equally, even to those in formal positions of government or rule-making. And that the state's personnel are mostly recruited and trained for management in a bureaucratic manner. Both of these criteria are fully adhered to; EU law must be obeyed by those it addresses and civil servants are chosen by the so-called *concours*, who make sure that they are adequately trained.

The fifth criterion said that the state should have the capacity to extract taxes to finance its activities from its subject population. This is a clearly underdeveloped ability if one looks at the EU today. Today, the EU has four main sources for its income: customs duty, levies a part of the VAT and the gross national product tax.[15] The question is of course whether this model will last. This is not the place to try to look into the crystal ball, but there are forces pressing to get a genuine EU-tax introduced,[16] In this volume, Schmitter argues that the EMU will lead to discussions of taxation questions, and Gustavsson, in chapter 5, goes further, arguing that a monetary union without a fiscal union i.e. tax-union will not be sustainable, unless a number of measures are taken. Gustavsson then argues that it will be very hard to transfer the power of taxation to the Union. Dyson, too, indicates, that the transfer of this power of taxation would require the Union to either create a *gouvernement économique* (the old French idea, to which Germany is opposed), or give the European Parliament further powers, what France is opposed to, but Germany likes. Tsoukalis argues, that the tax-question (in one form or the other) is sneaking on to the political agenda. Thus there is agreement, that the tax-question will be on the political agenda, due to the EMU (as was the case in Nice 2000). Zank, too, finds it *'perfectly possible'* that the EU budget question will rise, but disagrees, that it has to do so (chapter 10).

I will briefly mention two other factors increasing the pressure for an EU-tax: 1) To secure the social cohesion of the Union, i.e. to avoid too large differences between regions, and 2) the ideological factor.

1) It is unlikely that the Union, as a growing point of political gravitation in Europe, will be able to withstand too large internal disparities within the Union, in spite of the Stability and Growth Pact, if the integration project itself is not going to fall apart, as a consequence of disappointed citizens. Concretely, one can imagine two forms of disparity: a) there will be regions which will not be able to benefit from the Internal Market and the EMU, either due to structural problems of a more permanent character, or due to the transfer of capital to other, more profitable regions, and b) the transparity, due to the euro, will make it

Political Implications of the Economic and Monetary Union 259

clear that there are fairly large differences in salary and standard of living throughout the Union (differences which will become larger, as the EU expands over the next years). *If* the European citizens, over the years are supposed to transfer parts of their loyalty to the EU, the Union will have to deliver the welfare and security where the member states did before, and in order to do so the Union needs money.[17] But that the EU needs money does not necessarily imply that it needs a tax union; the member states could decide to give the money to the Union e.g. by raising their 'membership fees'. But whereas this would suit the northern EU-sceptical countries well, it does not really go with the EU-credo.[18]

2) There is an ideological argument, too. Fazal quotes Wheare for saying (1997: 75):

The federal principle requires that the general and regional governments of a country shall be independent each of the other within its sphere, shall not subordinate one to another but co-ordinate with each other. Now, if this principle is to operate not merely as a matter of strict law but in practice it follows that both general and regional governments must each have under its own independent control financial resources sufficient to perform its exclusive functions.

Thus the fifth criterion is hardly fulfilled. But as the discussion above shows the EMU does create pressure for placing the question of a tax union on the EU agenda. Its shape is of course uncertain. In my opinion – which of course can be contested – it would properly be of a federal character to strengthen the Union's statehood, but I would like to stress that there is nothing automatic in such a process.

The last of the criteria was that of a state as foreign political actor. As argued elsewhere (Dosenrode & Stubkjær, 2002) today's EU possesses its own foreign-political actor capability. An actor capability which by far exceeds many if not all of the individual EU-member states. Especially on the economic level, the EMU has strengthened this development, by establishing a strong economic entity which cements the EU as a global economic power. One of its tasks is to create a safeguard against the negative aspects of globalization.

The EU's actor capability is 'mixed'. One, supranational, part is exercised by the EU-Commission, and the other, quasi-intergovernmental[19] part by the Council of Ministers, which also has appointed a so-called High Representative. In addition to this, the member states have kept a part of the actor capability for themselves. Thus, the EU has an actor capability, but it is shared, and it is the member states which have the last word.[20]

The previous discussion of Dunleavy and O'Leary's criteria has shown that the EU fulfils five of them and one only very rudimentarily. In my opinion 'statehood' must be looked at as a quality an entity can possess to a smaller or larger extent, analogous to Sjöstedt's seminar analysis of the EC's foreign policy actorness (1977).[21] In general the conclusion must be that:

1) the EU today possesses a high degree of statehood, but it is not yet fully developed to a 'super state';
2) the EMU has been a very important contribution to the creation of the Union's statehood;
3) the EMU is likely to be a step in the direction of fiscal union; and
4) the EMU itself raises important questions concerning the democratic order of the EU, but that the EMU does not add to the democratic deficit *per se*.

It is hard to play down, or even deny, the statehood of the EU, but there is – political – room to discuss what kind of state the EU is, and especially in which direction it would be preferable that it developed. The EMU is a huge element of real and symbolic importance for this project.

Notes

1 The combination of a democratic tradition in Western Europe and the amount of political prestige invested in the EMU makes these two scenarios fairly unlikely.
2 Dosenrode in Hanf & Soetendorf 1999.
3 Danish prime minister Schlüter told the electorate in 1986 that if they voted 'yes' to the European Single Act, 'the Union will be stone dead', and surprisingly prime minister Rasmussen used nearly the same words when the Danish electorate had to vote on the Amsterdam-treaty in 1997.
4 One may argue, that this is a question mainly for the 'new-comers' Denmark, Great Britain, Ireland, Sweden and perhaps Austria. The old states know what they embarked upon fifty years ago and the present candidate countries do so, too.
5 This question has caused some discussion in the academic world e.g. Buiter (1999), Issing (1999), de Haan & Eijffinger (2000), Madsen & Plaschke (1998).
6 See Kelstrup in this book.
7 Cf. also de Haan & Eijffinger (2000).
8 Zank remarks that an often overseen point in the Danish public debate, has been what he considers the very negative effects of inflation which redistribute wealth from the 'poor' and give to the 'rich'.
9 See Zank in this book.
10 Caporaso (1996) gives an account.
11 The question of democratic legitimization is not a part of this model, we return to it later.

12 An exception is the right of European (!) citizens to complain to the European Commission of Human Rights for violations of human rights; but that is still an exception.
13 Kelstrup in Dosenrode (2000: 158).
14 One can discuss the nature of the Union's legislation (cf. Joseph Weiler's oeuvres). My argument is that the supranational legislation resembles federal legislation more than international public law, as legislation invoked by qualified majority voting (QMV) is also binding on member states which voted against it, as it is in a federation.
15 Nedergaard, P. (2000: 192).
16 Cf. Romano Prodi's speech in the European Parliament September 12th, 2000.
17 The so-called Lisbon process is an intergovernmental attempt to tackle the problems through harmonizations; the problem remains that less rich countries do not have as many resources to 'harmonize with' as richer countries. Cf. Schmitter, chapter 7.
18 Zank (chapter 10) argues against this reasoning.
19 'Quasi-intergovernmental', because the Common Foreign and Security Policy consists of a tightly woven net of rules and procedures, as well as a few supranational elements.
20 Shared policy competencies is a fairly common phenomenon in federations. One finds them in e.g. Austria, Belgium, Germany, and Switzerland.
21 The various stages of the EU's statehood have been analyzed by e.g.: Dosenrode & Dosenrode: The EU possessing statehood (2001), Majone: Conceptualising the EU as a regulatory state (1994), and Caporaso: EU as an international state (1996).

References

Buiter, Willen H. (1999): Alice in Euroland, *Journal of Common Market Studies*, vol. 37, no. 2, June.
Caporaso, James (1996): 'The European Union and Forms of State: Westphalian, Regulatory or Post-Modern?', *Journal of Common Market Studies*, vol. 34, no. 1, March, pp. 29-52.
de Haan, Jakob & Sylvester C. W. Eijffinger (2000): The Democratic Accountability of the European Central Bank, *Journal of Common Market Studies*, vol. 38, no. 3. September.
Dosenrode, Søren & Andrea Dosenrode (2001): Den Europæiske Stat – Nogle refleksioner, *Økonomi & Politik*, vol. 74, nr. 2, Juni.
Dunleavy, Patrick & Brenda O'Leary (1987): *Theories of the State*, Macmillan Press, London.
Hanf, Kenneth & Ben Soetendorp (ed.) (1998): *Adapting to European Integration – Small States and the European Union*, Longman, London.
Issing, Otmar (1999): 'The Eurosystem: Transparant and Accountable or 'Willem in Euroland?', *Journal of Common Market Studies*, vol. 37, no. 3, September.
Madsen, Poul Thøis & Henrik Plaschke (1998): *Den Forbudte debat om ØMU'en*, Rådet for Europæisk Politik no 2, 1998, Systime.
Majone, Giandomenico (1994): 'The European Community: an independent fourth branch of government?' in G. Bruggemeier (ed.), Verfassung für ein Civiles Europa, Baden Baden: Nomos Vorlag, pp. 23-42.
Schwartzmantel, John (1994): *The State in Contemporary Society, an Introduction*, New York: Harvester & Wheatsheaf.

Appendix

Appendix

Table A1.1 Total social expenditure 1990-98

	1990	1993	1996	1998
Belgium	26.4	29.5	28.8	27.5
Denmark	28.7	31.9	31.4	30.0
Germany	25.4	28.4	30.0	29.3
Greece	23.2	22.3	23.1	24.5
Spain	20.5	24.7	22.5	21.6
France	27.6	30.9	31.0	30.5
Ireland	18.7	20.5	18.5	17.2
Iceland	17.1	18.9	18.7	18.3
Italy	24.3	26.2	25.2	25.2
Luxembourg	22.6	24.5	25.2	24.1
Netherlands	32.4	33.5	30.1	28.5
Norway	26.4	28.8	26.2	27.9
Austria	26.7	28.9	29.6	28.4
Portugal	15.8	21.3	22.0	23.4
Finland	25.1	34.6	31.6	27.2
Sweden	33.1	38.6	34.5	33.3
United Kingdom	22.9	29.1	28.0	26.8
EU	25.4	28.9	28.6	27.7

Source: Amerini, 2000.

Table A1.2 Total social expenditure at fixed prices 1990-98, index 1990 = 100

	1990	1993	1996	1997	1998
Belgium	100	115	177	118	119
Denmark	100	113	122	121	122
Germany	100	104	114	112	114
Greece	100	96	104	111	120
Spain	100	124	120	121	124
France	100	111	117	118	120
Ireland	100	119	133	139	144
Iceland	100	104	113	118	127
Italy	100	109	113	118	118
Luxembourg	100	120	134	138	150
Netherlands	100	104	102	103	103
Norway	100	113	119	122	127
Austria	100	110	118	118	120
Portugal	100	144	163	174	189
Finland	100	116	122	120	120
Sweden	100	108	106	106	109
United Kingdom	100	130	135	135	135
EU	100	113	119	120	122

Source: Amerini, 2000.

Table A1.3 Total social expenditure at fixed prices 1998 in PPP

Belgium	6131
Denmark	7098
Germany	6459
Greece	3139
Spain	3224
France	6418
Ireland	3372
Iceland	4043
Italy	5292
Luxembourg	9258
Netherlands	6703
Norway	6547
Austria	6297
Portugal	3110
Finland	5171
Sweden	6515
United Kingdom	5306
EU	5532

Source: Amerini, 2000.

Table A1.4 Functional distribution of total social expenditure in per cent 1998

	Old age & survivors	Sickness/ health care & disability	Unemployment	Family & children	Housing & social exclusion
Belgium	42.8	33.3	12.7	8.5	2.7
Denmark	38.3	30.8	11.7	13.0	6.2
Germany	42.3	36.1	8.7	10.1	2.8
Greece	52.6	30.4	4.8	8.1	4.2
Spain	46.1	37.3	13.5	2.1	1.0
France	44.0	34.1	7.6	9.8	4.5
Ireland	24.9	41.4	15.5	12.7	5.5
Iceland	31.7	50.1	2.6	12.6	2.9
Italy	64.0	29.5	2.7	3.6	0.1
Luxembourg	44.2	36.7	3.5	14.1	1.5
Netherlands	41.1	40.3	7.3	4.5	6.8
Norway	32.6	47.9	2.9	13.3	3.3
Austria	48.2	34.9	5.5	10.0	1.4
Portugal	42.7	45.9	4.7	5.3	1.5
Finland	34.5	37.1	12.0	12.8	3.6
Sweden	39.4	35.0	9.3	10.8	5.5
United Kingdom	43.9	36.9	3.6	8.6	7.1
EU	45.7	35.1	7.2	8.3	3.7

Source: Amerini, 2000.

Table A1.5 Financing of total social expenditure 1998

	The public	Employer	Insured	Other
Belgium	24.4	50.6	22.4	2.6
Denmark	67.2	8.7	17.9	6.3
Germany	30.9	37.4	28.7	3.0
Greece	29.2	37.6	24.1	9.1
Spain	27.2	52.2	17.5	3.1
France	30.7	46.5	19.9	2.9
Ireland	61.3	23.9	13.6	1.2
Iceland	52.9	38.9	8.2	0.0
Italy	38.3	44.7	14.8	2.2
Luxembourg	46.3	25.0	24.2	4.4
Netherlands	15.7	30.1	34.3	19.9
Norway	60.7	24.0	14.3	1.0
Austria	34.5	37.5	27.1	0.9
Portugal	42.6	29.5	17.8	10.0
Finland	43.1	36.2	13.8	6.8
Sweden	45.8	39.1	9.3	5.9
United Kingdom	47.9	27.0	24.4	0.7
EU	35.4	38.2	22.7	3.7

Source: Amerini, 2000.

Table A1.6 **Wealth, poverty, redistribution and inequality in Europe mid-1990s**

	GDP per capita 1997[a]	% poor before transfers 1994[b]	% poor after transfers 1994[b]	Gini-coefficient 1993
Belgium	21456	30	18	31
Denmark	21751	29	11	25
Germany	20865	24	18	30
Greece	13138	22	21	38
Spain	14758	27	19	35
France	19817	28	16	33
Ireland	18294	34	21	34
Iceland[c]	21294[c]	12	10	38
Italy	19239	21	19	37
Luxembourg	31531	26	14	32
Netherlands	19835	23	10	34
Norway[d]	22776[c]	..	6	24
Austria	21349	27	17	..
Portugal	13415	28	24	42
Finland[c]	18726	34	3	22
Sweden[d]	18672	..	6	22
United Kingdom	18929	34	20	37
EU	18979	26	18	35

[a] Calculated as EURO-Purchasing Power Standards; [b] Pensions omitted; [c] 1996; [d] Values for the other Nordic countries concerning poverty and inequality are not fully comparable with the values given by Eurostat for Denmark and the rest of the European countries, since they are based on two different data sets.

Source: Amerini, 1999; Eurostat, 1999a, 1999b; Gustafsson & Pedersen, 2000; Ramprakash, 1997.

Table A1.7 Ratio of services versus transfers in three welfare regimes

Universal welfare regimes	0.34
Continental welfare regimes	0.08
Residual welfare regimes	0.12

Source: Esping-Andersen, 1999: 166.

Index

abolition, democratic deficit 126
Abrahamson, Peter 195-220, 222, 248, 254-5
accountability 92, 98
acts of legitimation 128
administration levels 91-2
administration states 124
aggregation principle 205
allocation criteria, welfare state 197, 213
Amsterdam Treaty (1996/97) 30, 82, 151, 206, 216, 257
Andersen *see* Esping-Andersen
Anglo-Saxon model 197
asymmetry
 economic shocks 137, 140, 237-8
 European Monetary System 74
 present union 87-8
 pressures 159
 unification comparisons 111
au-dessus-de-la-melée strategy 153
authoritarianism 106-7
authority
 European Central Bank 148
 transfer 12

banks 172-4, 177-83
 see also European Central Bank
Barro, Robert 239
Beetham model 250
Belgium-Luxembourg Economic Union 159
benchmarking 36
benefit differentials 157
BNP 201
Borchorst, Anette 195-220, 222, 248, 254-5
Brandt/Pompidou initiative 11
Bretton Woods system 23, 73
Britain *see* United Kingdom

Broad Economic Policy Guidelines (Maastricht Treaty) 36
budgets
 consolidation 33
 transfers 78
Buiter, Willem 185-6, 250
Bundesbank 172-3

CAP *see* common agricultural policy
capital
 flight 166
 liberalized movements 76
 movements 171, 234-6
capitalism, national models 34
Cardiff process 28
Casini, C. 52, 60
cause-effect relationships 17, 18-19, 22
central institutions 213
centralization
 economic policies 169
 monetary unification 94-5
 taxation 93
 see also fiscal centralization
CFSP *see* common foreign and security policy
Charter of Fundamental Social Rights of Workers 206
children in care 226
Christian Democrats 109
collective agreements, social policy 158
Cologne European Council (1999) 30
Cologne process 59, 62
Commissariat Général du Plan (1999) 175
Commission, cooperation 151
Committee of Central Bank Governors 45
Committee of Permanent Representatives (COREPER) 64
common agricultural policy (CAP) 72, 88, 154

common exchange and interest rate
    policy 155
common foreign and security policy
    (CFSP) 71
comparative federalism 87
competencies distribution 181-3
competitive pressures 156
complete failure concept 107-8
complete success concept 99, 100-3
concours 258
constitution and law states 124
continental-European model 197
control structures 128, 137
cooperation, Commission 150-1
coordination, fiscal policies 82
COREPER *see* Committee of Permanent
    Representatives 183
costs and benefits, distribution 153
Council of Economic and Finance
    Ministers (ECOFIN) 41, 58-60
    Cardiff meeting (1998) 47
    EURO-12 Group interaction 58-60
    motive for urgency 154
    national policy coordination 82
credibility theory 32
cross-border mergers 82-3
currencies
    construction 221
    hard 158
    merging 148
    soft 158

de-democratization 131
de-legitimation 138
    see also democratic legitimacy
de-politicizing, exchange and interest
    rates 160
debt burden 233
decentralization, economic policies 169
decisions, legality 127
decisions and outcome dimensions 128
Decker case 208, 211
defense mechanisms 221-44
defensive governments, European
    Central Bank 173-4
delegation, sovereignties 113
Delors Commission 25, 132, 205-6
Delors Report (1989) 12, 35-6, 44-5, 132

democracy
    accountability 92
    chain of governance 124
    culture 123, 166
    democratic legitimacy 122-3
    Denmark 216
    dilemma 125-7, 143
    domestic 160
    double bind 149-50
    double perspective 138-41
    EMU 121-45, 249-54
    European Central Bank 165-91
    European Union 121-45
    institutionalization of EMU 134-6
    models 121
    points of view 129-32
    political systems 176-7
    societal 122, 166
    Stability Pact importance 99-108
    supranational 150
    suprastates 105
    theorists 162
    threat replacement 95-6
    understanding 122-3
    vitalized rather than apathized 115-16
democratic deficit
    abolition 126
    EU 125
    preservation 126
democratic legitimacy
    EMU 134-8
    European Union 122-3
    five dimensions 127-8, 129-30
    perspectives 136-8
democratization
    desirability 150
    Euro-polity 150
    European Union 124-32
    feasibility 150
    legitimacy 127-9
    points of view 129-32
demos concept 130, 152
Denmark
    BNP 201
    central welfare institution 213
    children in care 226
    democracy 216
    ECB discussions 135

employment 226, 227-31
EMU effects 26
EU debate 126, 195
EU welfare state 209-14
euro policy years 226
European welfare state 200-4
inflation 228-30
interest rates 229
Maastricht Treaty 45, 212, 255
nearness/subsidiarity 161
nurses 226
public expenditure 226
social expenditure 226
Stability and Growth Pact 230, 232, 255
taxation 226
trade unions 232
unemployment 227, 228
welfare state 195-220, 221-44
   allocation criterion 213
   future 239-42
   indicators 226
   see also Nordic welfare state
desirability, democratization 150
devaluation, France 10-11
developments 1989-2002 44-6
differential empowerment 160
differentials visibility 156-7
dilemmas, European Central Bank 183-7
disintegration, Soviet Union 75
distribution, social expenditure 268
domestic democracy, differential empowerment 160
domestic opinion management 21
Dosenrode, Søren 41-68, 247-61
double bind, future democracy 149-50
double perspective, democracy 138-41
Dunleavy, Patrick 256, 257, 259-60
Dyson, Kenneth 17-40, 116

'E' in EMU 46-8
Early Retirement Scheme 210
eastern enlargement 84
ECB see European Central Bank
ECJ see European Court of Justice
ECOFIN see Council of Economic and Finance Ministers
economic analysis, sufficiency 88-90
economic shocks 137, 140

Economic and Financial Committee 61-2
economic policies
   centralization 169
   characteristics 168
   decentralization 169
   European Central Bank 169-76
   monetary policy 166
   political framework 165-91
   principles 165-91
economics
   hard to soft policy coordination 35-7
   history 31-4
   policy coordination 35-7
   risk 81-4
EEC see European Economic Community
effective output 130
efficient solutions 131
elections, first order 98-9
embedded liberalism 167
EMCF see European Monetary Co-operation Fund
EMI see European Monetary Institute
employment
   Denmark 226, 227-31
   ECB numbers 57
   Treaty of Amsterdam 206
Employment Pact (1999) 47, 58
EMS see European Monetary System
EMU-cooperation 121
England see United Kingdom
enlightened understanding 109-10
ERM1 39
ERM2 26-7, 39
ERM, see also Exchange Rate Mechanism
ESCB see European System of Central Banks
Esping-Andersen, G. 196
ethnos concept 152
EU-cooperation 126
EU, see also European Union
euro policy years, Denmark 226
EURO-11 Group 48
EURO-12 Council 83
EURO-12 Group 58-60
   gouvernement économique 60
Euro-cooperation 121, 126, 135
Euro-democracy 147-64

contemplation 149-52
see also democracy; democratization
Euro-polity 150
Euro-Zone
  ECB-centricity 29
  establishment 26, 29
  from ERM2 move 26-7
  history 17-40
  paradigm shift 35-7
'Europe of 1000 Haiders' 141
European Central Bank (ECB)
  authority 148
  Bundesbank 173
  centralization/decentralization 169
  competencies distribution 181-3
  creation 9-16
  Danish discussions 135
  defensive governments 173-4
  democracy 165-91
    political systems 176-7
  economic policies
    centralization/decentralization 169
    fiscal policy autonomy 169-70
    new framework 169-76
    political framework 165-91
  employee numbers 57
  EMU dilemmas 183-7
  Euro-cooperation 135
  financial market agents 170-2
  fiscal policy autonomy 169-70
  independent institutions 176-7
  infallibility 182-3
  institutionalization 133
  legitimacy 178-9
  lender of last resort 186
  Maastricht Treaty 173-4
  member states 172
  organization 49, 53-7
    charts 54-6
  political counterpart 174-5
  political framework 165-91
  political neutrality 180-1
  political regulation 170-2
  political/technical decisions 179-80
  power balance 172
  price stability 158, 179
  question checks and balances 178
  Rules of Procedure 53
  social neutrality 180-1
  technical/political decisions 179-80
European Commission 151
European Convention for Protection of Human Rights and Fundamental Freedoms (1950) 106-7
European Council 57-8
  June 1988 meeting 41
  Lisbon 2000 32
European Court of Justice (ECJ) 160
European Economic Community (EEC) 72, 204-9
European integration process 247-9
European Monetary Co-operation Fund (EMCF) 45
European Monetary Institute (EMI) 45
European Monetary System (EMS) 24, 73
  asymmetry 74
  European Union 132
  formation 72
European Parliament 62-3
European Single Act (1987) 19, 41, 75, 257
European System of Central Banks (ESCB) 48-53
  institutions 51-3
  organization 49
  tasks 50-1
European Union (EU) 119, 132-4
  Commission 62
  Danish welfare state 209-14
  democracy 121-45
    dilemmas 125-7
    legitimacy 122-3
    points of view 129-32
  democratization 124-32, 147-64
  EMS 132
  institutional development 141-3
  monetary unification 147-64
  politicization 141-3
  present state 256-60
  social policy prior to EMU 204-9
  welfare state 204-9
exchange rate
  de-politicizing 160
  policy differential impact 155
  stability 73-4
Exchange-Rate Mechanism (ERM) 18, 27-8

experimentation, supra-national democracy 149-50
exportability principle 205

Fazal, 259
feasibility, democratization 150
federal fiscal policies *see* fiscal federalism
Feldstein, Martin 89-90
Finance Act (1998) 210
financial crisis (1998) 47
financial market agents, ECB 170-2
financing
　social expenditure 269
　welfare state 214
Finland 102
first order elections 98-9
fiscal centralization 96-8
fiscal federalism 103-6
fiscal policies
　autonomy 169-70
　coordination 82
fiscal union resistance 104
fixed exchange rate 171
fixed prices 267
flexibility, Stability Pact 157-8
Foreign Policy Institute 211
form identities, definitions 18
France
　devaluation 10-11
　German project 9-15
　hegemony 147
　success story 15-16
free-riders, Stability and Growth Pact 81

de Gaulle, General 102
GDP *see* Gross Domestic Product
Genscher initiative 24
German Constitutional Court 113, 115-16
Germany
　1989-90 unification 34
　French project 9-15
　hegemony 147
　success story 15-16
　unification comparisons 110-11
Gini-coefficient 203, 226, 270
Gisçard-Schmidt committee (1991) 15
Gisçard-Schmidt initiative 11

globalization 123-4, 166, 184
GNP *see* Gross National Product
Gold Standard 159
gouvernement économique 60
governance 88, 112, 124, 139
Governing Council
　ECB 53
　ESCB 51-2
Greece 26, 83
Gross Domestic Product (GDP) 270
　per capita 270
　shrinkage effect 233
Gross National Product (GNP) 95
Group of Seven meetings 83
Gustavsson, Sverker 87-118, 222, 248

Hague Summit (1969) 22-3
Hannover Summit (1988) 236
hard currencies 158
hard to soft economic policy coordination 35-7
harmonization, taxation 157
Heads of State and Government meeting (December 1969) 42
hegemony 147, 188
Helsinki Treaty (1999) 257
high politics 75-81
high-risk strategies 84
history 7-68
　ECB creation 9-16
　economics 31-4
　EMU effects 26-31
　EMU significance 22-6
　Euro-Zone 17-40
　integration dynamics 72-5
　markets 31-4
　negotiations 9-16
　politics 22-6, 31-4
Hobbesian culture 116
Hoffmeyer, Erik 9-16

identity criteria 127-8
IGC *see* Intergovernmental Conference
IMF *see* International Monetary Fund
income and price differentials 156-7
independent institutions
　banks 173-4, 177-83
　democratic political systems 176-7
　indirect political effects 159-61

inequality, by country 270
infallibility, European Central Bank 182-3
inflation
　credibility theory 32
　Denmark 228-30
　fiscal policies 104
　public sector deficits 231-4
Institute of Foreign Policy 211
institutional development 141-3
institutional framework 41-68
institutionalist concepts 101
institutionalization
　EMU democracy 134-6
　European Central Bank 133
　sound money and finance paradigm 38
institutions expressing disquiet 98-9
instruments behind EMU 43-4
insurance model 198
integration dynamics 69-118
　history 72-5
interest rates
　de-politicizing 160
　Denmark 229
　Ireland 238
　Mediterranean countries 238
　policy differential impact 155
Intergovernmental Conference (IGC) 13, 14, 15, 25
　1990-1 45, 76
　changes 142
intergovernmentalism 114-15
interlocked core executive governance 88
International Monetary Fund (IMF) 83
Ireland, interest rates 238
'iron' law 110, 111
isolation, UK 78
Issing, Otmar 43, 54

Jospin, Prime Minister 46-7
juridical imperialism 160

Kantian culture 116
Kelstrup, Morten 121-45, 250-1
Kerneuropa integration 142
Keynesianism 35, 72
Kohl, Helmut 77, 79, 110

Kohll case 208, 211

Lafontaine experience 30-1
law states 124
legality
　decisions 127
　EMU management 136
legitimacy
　dimensions 130
　EMU question 249-54
　European Central Bank 178-9
　sociology 108-9
legitimation 128
LEGO example 234
Leibfried, S. 207
lender of last resort 186
Lepsius, R. M. 100
Lincoln, Abraham 116
Lisbon European Council (2000) 114-15
Lisbon process (2000) 58
Lockean political culture 116
loose money 96-8
Lord model 250

Maastricht Treaty (1992) 257
　Broad Economic Policy Guidelines 36
　changes 185-6
　Denmark 45, 212, 255
　ECB primary goal 173
　ECB secondary goal 174
　enthusiasm 78
　historical perspective 18, 19
　mother of all spillovers 151
　sound money and finance paradigm 30
　sustainability 109
　see also Treaty of the European Union; Treaty on European Union
Macro-Economic Dialogue 30
McCormick, John 43
McKay, David 90-1, 94-9, 108-9, 222
Madsen, P. T. 230
male breadwinner aspects 197
management legality, EMU 136
market economy 187
markets
　history 31-4
　social justice 221-4

means-testing 197
Mediterranean interest rates 238
member states, power balance 172
membership criteria 128, 136
membership fees 88
mergers, cross-border 82-3
migrant workers 207, 216
Milward, Alan 90
Moatti, Gérard 174
models
   capitalism 34
   Optimal Currency Areas 237
   welfare state 196-200
modernization, social protection 212
monetary discipline 96-8
monetary integration *see* monetary
   unification
monetary policy
   economic policy 166
   making 249-50
   technicalization 166
monetary stability, EMS 74
monetary unification
   centralization 94-5
   direct effects 155-8
   enthusiasm 79
   EU democratization 147-64
   Euro-democracy 149-52
   indirect effects 159-61
   motive for urgency 154-5
   political centralization 94-5
   reaching a conclusion 161-3
   relaunching 76-7
   sustainability 88
   temptation avoidance 152-3
Monnet, Jean 41
Monnet Method 150
Moravcsik, Andrew 90
motherhood 207
motive for urgency 154-5
motor of integration 247-9
Mundell criteria 89, 90

nation states 124
national currency, merging 148
national democracies
   de-democratization 131
   double impact 139
   globalization 123-4

   vitalized rather than apathized 115-16
national interests, definitions 18
national models 34
national policy coordination 82
natural course of events 100-1
nearness/subsidiarity (Denmark) 161
needs, welfare state 197
negative EMU-scenarios 140-1
neo-liberal economics 33
neo-liberal Hobbesian culture 116
Neo-liberal/Ordo-liberal economic
   theory 20
new institution interaction 48
Nice Treaty (2000) 207, 257
'no taxation without representation'
   principle 21
no-demos thesis 130
Nordic welfare state 197, 221-44, 254-5
   definition 223
   euro policies 224-7
   future 239-42
   see also Denmark
North European views 175
nurses, Denmark 226

objectives behind EMU 43-4
OCA *see* Optimal Currency Areas
O'Leary, Brenda 256, 257, 259-60
'one-size-fits-all' policy 81
Optimal Currency Areas (OCA) 89, 237
Ordo-liberalism 19-20
organization charts, ECB 54-6
Ostpolitik policy 23

paradoxes, welfare state 215
parallel fiscal union
   administration levels 91-2
   democracy importance 99-108
   economic analysis sufficiency 88-90
   political visibility variation 92-3
   Stability Pact 96-8, 99-108
   success conditions 111-16
   sustainability 87-118
parallel political union 12
participation criteria 128
pension schemes 222
Phillips-curve 228
Pierson, P. 207
Plaschke, Henrik 165-91, 230, 252-4

polarization hypothesis 156
policy coordination 82
policy space 22
political centralization 94-5
political construction 245-61
political democracy 122
political frameworks 165-91
political implications 247-61
political institutions 177-83
political neutrality 180-1
political opportunity space 153
political regulation 170-2
political stakes 81-4
political v. technical decisions 179-80
political visibility variation 92-3
politicians, accountability 98
politico-cultural foundations 168
politization 141-3
Pompidou/Brandt initiative 11
popular support *see* public opinion
positive EMU-scenarios 140
Pötsach (1998) 257
poverty, by country 270
power balance, member states 172
PPP *see* purchasing power parity
prices
    differential visibility 156-7
    European Central Bank 158, 179
    fixed 267
    stability 158, 179, 227-31
printing money 101-2
Prodi, Romano 44
public expenditure, Denmark 226
public opinion 80, 104
public sector deficits 231-4
purchasing power parity (PPP) 201

redistribution
    by country 270
    welfare state 203
    see also distribution
Regini, Marino 184
Regulation 1408/71 (1971) 205, 210
Regulation 1612/68 (1968) 205, 210
representation structures 128, 130, 137
residual model 198-9
responsibility structures 128, 130, 137
revocability, sovereignties 113
Rhineland capitalism 29

right of the strong and mighty 129
Riker, William 91-2, 106
risk, economic 81-4
Robin-Hood's-turned-upside down concept 231-4
Ruggie, J. G. 171
Rules of Procedure, European Central Bank 53

Sala-i-Martin, Xavier 239
Santer Commission 129
Scandinavian model 201-3
    see also Denmark; Nordic model
Scandinavian Monetary Union 159
Scharpf, Fritz 113
Schmidt-Gisçard d'Estaing initiatives (1969/1978) 11
Schmitter, Philippe C. 147-64, 251-2
Schwartzmantel, John 256
security policy (CFSP) 74
self-constitutionalization 152
self-employed persons 207
services v. transfers 271
short-run capital taxation 185
sickness benefits 207
Single European Act (1987) 19, 41, 75, 257
Smaghi, L. 52, 60
social democracy 18-22
Social Democrats 109
social dimension development 208-9
social expenditure
    1990-98 265-6
    by country 265-7
    Denmark 226
    distribution 268
    financing 269
    fixed prices 267
    functional distribution 268
    see also welfare state
social insurance 197
social justice 221-4
social neutrality 180-1
social policy 158, 206
social protection 212
Social Rights of Workers Charter 206
socialism, capital movements 234-6
societal control 166
societal democracy 122, 166

sociology, legitimacy 108-9
soft currencies 158
soft economic policy coordination 35-7
Soskice, David 175
sound money and finance paradigm 30
  institutionalization 38
  political determination 33
South European views 175
Southern European model 197
sovereignty
  delegation 113
  pooling 101
  revocability 113
  transfer 14
Soviet Union 75, 95-6
spill-over effects 151, 159
stability of EMU 236-9
Stability and Growth Pact 18, 19, 46
  authoritarianism 106-7
  budget consolidation 33
  complete failure 107-8
  complete success 99, 100-3
  constraints 157
  democracy importance 99-108
  Denmark 230, 232, 255
  finance paradigm 30
  fiscal federalism 103-6
  flexibility 157-8
  free-riders 81
  interpretation 30
  outcomes 96-8
  sound money paradigm 30
statehood 260
Streeck, W. 209
strong men concept 183
Structural and Regional Funds 154
Structural Funds 205
structure of EMU 7-68
students 207
success conditions 111-16
  national democracies 115-16
  offensive intergovernmentalism 114-15
  suprastatism 112-13
  'vitalized rather than apathized' 115-16
supranational democracy 150
supranational politics 160
suprastatism 105, 112-13

sustainability
  Maastricht Treaty 109
  monetary union 88
  parallel fiscal union 87-118
Sweden 102
  EMU effects 26
  trade unions 231
systematic inequalities 187

taxation
  centralization 93
  cohesion 102
  Denmark 226
  EU factors 258-9
  harmonization 157
  policy coordination 241
  short-run capital 185
  states 124
  Tobin tax 235
technical v. political decisions 179-80
technicalization, monetary policy 166
technocratic conceptions 19
technocratic policy 50
temptation avoidance 152-3
terminology, Dyson 116
TEU *see* Treaty on European Union
theorists, democracy 162
Third Way (Blair) 21
threats, Soviet Union 95-6
Titmuss, Richard 196
Tobin, James 235
Tobin tax 185
trade unions 22, 232, 2321
trade-offs, Treaty of European Union 84
transfers v. services 271
transition to EMU 79
Treaty of Amsterdam 82
  employment 206
  results 151
  social policy 206
Treaty of Nice (2000) 84, 207
Treaty of Rome (1957) 9, 71
Treaty on The European Union, *see also* Maastricht Treaty (1992)
Treaty on The European Union (TEU) 45-6
  art.4 57
  art.99.4 58
  art.108 50

art.113 51
  effects 82
  EMU schedule 133
  trade-offs 84
Tsoukalis, Loukas 71-85, 247-8

UK *see* United Kingdom
unemployment 93, 107
  Denmark 227, 228
  fund 210
unification comparisons 110-11
United Kingdom (UK)
  ERM membership 27-8
  isolation 78
United States of America (USA) 82
  hegemony 188
universal model 199-200
USA *see* United States of America

Value Added Tax (VAT) 222
'vitalized rather than apathized' 115-16

wage differentials 157
wealth 270
welfare state 124, 193-244
  allocation criteria 197, 213
  central institution 213
  Denmark 195-220, 221-44
  dilemmas 215, 216
  EEC 204-9
  EU 204-9
  financing 214
  means-testing 197
  migrant workers 207
  models 196-200
  motherhood 207
  needs 197
  Nordic 221-44, 254-5
  paradoxes 215
  perspectives 214-16
  redistribution 203
  Scandinavian model 201-3
  sickness benefits 207
  social insurance 197
Werner Report (1970) 23, 42
Wilensky, Harold 196, 204
Workers
  Charter of Fundamental Social Rights 206
  see also migrant workers

Zank, Wolfgang 221-44, 254, 255